Values for a Changing America

*University of Pennsylvania
Schoolmen's Week*

*Schoolmen's Week Meeting
October 7–10, 1964*

Values for a Changing America

*Fifty–second
Schoolmen's Week Proceedings*

Edited by
HELEN HUUS

Philadelphia
UNIVERSITY OF PENNSYLVANIA PRESS

© 1966 by the Trustees of the University of Pennsylvania
Published in Great Britain, India, and Pakistan
by the Oxford University Press
London, Bombay, and Karachi

Library of Congress Catalogue Card Number: 61-311

7488
Printed in the United States of America

Editor's Preface

WHILE CONTEMPORARY American society has been characterized as "affluent," the government has pointed out the problems of poverty and cultural differences of a fifth of the nation and has marshalled support to alleviate, in part, the economic and educational deprivation. That this must be done is the conviction of most Americans, but solving the economic problem alone will not solve the subtle, intangible aspects of the educational problem.

Education is more than amassing information and skills, more than possessing a body of knowledge or the ability to use fine muscular skills. It is, in great part, the attitude or approach to new problems and the ability to utilize known methods or to derive unique means by which to solve these problems that characterizes an educated man. It is, in addition, the ability to recognize those problems which ought to be solved. And it is in the realm of "ought" that the values one holds come into play. When choices are faced, decisions are made not only according to facts and results but also according to one's value system. In reverse, values can be inferred by what one chooses.

At the national level, too, values can be inferred by the choices a nation makes. What values are important to Americans today in a changing society that is embroiled in bombings at home and abroad, in strikes and threats of automation in industry, in a population boom and a teacher shortage in the schools?

It was to focus on this problem that "Values for a Changing America" was chosen as the theme for the Fifty-second Schoolmen's Week at the University of Pennsylvania, which was held October 7-10, 1964. These *Proceedings* contain several of the significant papers presented at this annual conference, and the complete program is contained in the Appendix, a practice that was resumed in 1962. Unfortunately, some of the very inspiring programs do not lend themselves to printed reports, and some of the papers could not be included because of space limitations. Nevertheless, we are grateful to all those who participated in the meetings, whether or not their presentations are included herein.

This volume has been organized into six sections, three relating to general topics and the remainder dealing with problems at three educational levels.

Section I contains the two addresses on the conference theme that were presented at the general sessions, the first by Dr. Arthur Larson, director of the Rule of Law Research Center at Duke University, and the second by Dr. Ralph W. Tyler, director of the Center for Advanced Study in the Behavioral Sciences at Stanford, California. The former approaches the topic from a national and international point of view, while the latter emphasizes the development of values by the individual.

The second section, "Contemporary Approaches," includes four papers that discuss the development of values in the school and how institutions reflect the values of the society. One paper describes the school at Summerhill, which, by its own admission, approaches education from a radical point of view.

The continued interest being shown in basic subjects at the elementary level—reading, writing, and arithmetic—is reflected in the papers contained in Section III. These describe some areas of conflict but also present ways by which teachers can apply, in the classroom, new learnings from research. The fourth paper in this group presents an integrated, K-12 program in descriptive grammars.

The reports comprising Section IV depict only a few of the contemporary concerns at the secondary school level. The first in this group, while pointing out the problems of interpreting history, also makes a plea for teaching about the past so that it becomes understandable to students. The second paper emphasizes the importance of teaching economics in the high school and discusses five pertinent questions relating to the content of such a course. A detailed description of the economics of ancient Rome is contained in the third and should be of interest not only to Latin scholars and historians

Editor's Preface

but to the general reader as well. The last two papers in this section are of special interest to home economists, for the one deals with new programs in home economics education and the other with interesting facts from research on textiles.

The papers contained in Section V are two of those presented at an all-day invitational conference on "The Education of the Professor of Education," which was held during the first day of Schoolmen's Week. All four papers have already been issued in mimeographed form to members of the conference. The two papers included here describe in some detail the scholarly, professional, and practical preparation needed by a professor of education.

The last section, Section VI, extends to farther fields. One report included here describes the work of the International Society for Education through Art in promoting international art education, and the other shows the chronological development of the tremendous expansion of collegiate education in England during the last two decades.

As in other years, Schoolmen's Week 1964 was the product of the thought and energy of many individuals and groups. Those who participated as members of the General Advisory Committee or Planning Committee, as a Contributing Specialist, or as a representative of a co-operating organization are listed in the Appendix. Their unflagging interest and industry are heartily appreciated, for without their help, the program would lack the depth and scope it has been able to achieve.

Grateful acknowledgment should also be made to districts and organizations who contribute their financial support year after year. Their continued co-operation is indeed heartening. In addition, there are hidden costs absorbed by the University of Pennsylvania, Drexel Institute of Technology, and those institutions who have generously allowed off-campus programs to be held in their buildings. This year, such programs were held in schools of Upper Darby Township, Upper Merion Township, and Downingtown Jointure; at the Lankenau Hospital; and at the Philadelphia Museum of Art. Their gracious hospitality is recognized with thanks.

As in the past, several programs were held in the Commercial Museum, but this year, for the first time, some rooms in Convention

Hall were used. Through the courtesy of the City of Philadelphia and with the knowledgeable assistance of Mr. Harry K. Newborn of the Commercial Museum staff, the physical arrangements were accomplished with comparative ease.

The five who formed the core of the working cadre of Schoolmen's Week deserve the highest praise: the three program co-ordinators—Mr. Richard D. Buckley, instructor of education, who ably synthesized the many suggestions into a comprehensive program at the elementary school level; Miss Helen Burchell, lecturer on education, who combined the work of many into a forward looking program for secondary education; and Dr. William W. Brickman, professor of education, who capably planned and carried through the programs in higher education, including the all-day conference on the preparation of professors of education; the executive-secretary, Dr. Richard S. Heisler, assistant to the dean, Graduate School of Education, who was an unfailing source of information regarding the many administrative details attendant to the room arrangements and who assumed complete responsibility for the exhibits; and to Mrs. Alice M. Lavelle, administrative assistant, who maintained the records and attended to the myriad of details with accuracy, dispatch, and good humor.

And finally, my sincere gratitude to Mrs. Eleanor Bennett for her meticulous checking and careful typing of the final manuscript of these *Proceedings*.

Without the work of all of these, the program and this report would not have become a reality. Such devotion to duty is truly appreciated.

                    HELEN HUUS
                    Associate Professor of Education
                    General Chairman of Schoolmen's Week

University of Pennsylvania
February 15, 1965

Contents

Editor's Preface   5

I   Values for a Changing America
Arthur Larson   13
Ralph W. Tyler   28

II   Contemporary Approaches
Teaching Moral and Spiritual Values in the Public Schools: The Philosophical Issues—Robert E. Mason   45
Summerhill: A Radical Approach to Education—George von Hilsheimer   59
A Descriptive Analysis of Approaches to School Desegregation—Peter Binzen   76
Education for Socially Disadvantaged Youth—N. Neubert Jaffa   90

III   Elementary Education
The Methods Controversy in Reading—Leo Fay   101
Off the Beaten Path in Spelling—Mary Elisabeth Coleman   113
Children's Language, Literature, and Composition—Ruth G. Strickland   122
An Integrated Program of Instruction in Descriptive Grammars—V. Louise Higgins   133
Techniques of Evaluation in Arithmetic—Ben E. Sueltz   153

IV   Secondary Education
Major Concepts in History: Implications for the Secondary   165

Social Studies Program—Russell F. Weigley
Teaching Economics in High School—Helen Raffel 177
The Economic Background of the City of Rome—Helen J. Loane 198
Home Economics Education Faces Another Challenge—Clio S. Reinwald 212
Consumer Textile Problems Stimulate Research—Dorothy Seigert Lyle 221

V Teacher Education

The Education of a Professor of Education—John Walton 233
The Professional and Practical Preparation of the Professor of Education—James L. Grace, Jr. 241

VI International Education

Art Education: International Aspects—Arthur R. Young 255
The Explosion in Higher Education in Britain—Harry K. Hutton 263

Appendix—Schoolmen's Week Committees and Program, 1964   283

Index   323

I
Values for a Changing America

Values for a Changing America

ARTHUR LARSON [*]

As we approach a subject as broad as this, we need to start with this question, "Why are we asking ourselves about these values right now? Why is there so much concern in America about our objectives, about our values, about the things we are for?" The reasons may vary with different people. It may depend, in part, on the background you bring to it. From my own point of view, the subject presents itself naturally against the backdrop of service with the U. S. Information Agency, which was the agency of the United States government concerned with telling the whole world about the United States, what its values are, and what it is *for*.

The reason that we are so concerned about values nowadays is that, for the greatest part of our history, we never particularly thought about these questions. When I was growing up, it never occurred to me that there was anything to argue about. The system I knew, the economic system, the political system, the educational system, seemed to me just about optimum. So what was there to worry about? Now, of course, the picture looks entirely different. We are being challenged on all sides. We are being forced to do something we never had to do before in our history, which is to articulate clearly, concisely, and convincingly, not just for ourselves but for people all over the world, what our values in a changing world really are.

---

[*] Director, Rule of Law Research Center, Duke University, Durham, North Carolina.

The "Negative" Image

Why is it, as we travel around the world or as people come to our shores, we find ourselves hurt and puzzled and disenchanted by the wildly improbable and unrealistic ideas people have about us and about what our values are? The primary reason probably is that in those precious years following World War II, when the so-called struggle of ideas was taking shape, we consumed too much of our ideological ammunition on being "against." Oh, we knew what we were against; that was easy: We were against Communism, and so most of our best programs and efforts were justified, not only to the Congress but to the public, in negative terms. We must have an overseas information program. Why? To counter the Soviet propaganda defensive. We must have an overseas cultural program. Why? To counter the Soviet culture thrust. We must have an overseas economic program. Why? To counter the Soviet economic thrust, and so on. It is so easy to be against, to go on the defensive.

But the net impression left by all this is that the active, positive force for change in a changing world is international Communism, while we, by contrast, represent a sort of amorphous, ill-defined force for countering change. The trouble with this is that most people in the world want change. You cannot blame them. They are not satisfied with their life and their world; they want it improved. And so if we get maneuvered into the position of being anti-change while our opponents are pro-change, we enter any competition for the hearts and minds of men with an absolutely hopeless handicap.

The truth is that what we are for is, in fact, the active, positive force in the world. This country's pioneering success in practical political democracy and in rapid industrial progress has for years been an explosive force inspiring other countries and colonies around the world.

Why then should there be danger of appearing to yield this role of active force for progress to international Communism?

A frequently heard explanation is this: The Communists have an advantage in that they have a single panacea in a simple, shining package. Its formulas—however unsound in fact—are easily under-

Values for a Changing America

stood and are guaranteed to cure all ills from poverty and hunger to oppression and war.

By contrast—so our excuse runs—what we stand for is so diverse that we cannot wrap it up and hold it forth as an affirmative ideology. What *do* we stand for? "Capitalism," says the businessman. "Rule of law," says the lawyer. "Representative democratic government," says the political scientist. "Primacy of the individual," says the philosopher. "Religion," says the preacher.

And some writers, like Walter Lippmann in *The Good Society*,[1] in their zeal to contrast our system with the planned societies of the dictators, conclude that our ultimate direction and goal can never be stated, since they are only a by-product of the decisions of millions of free persons within a framework of law.

I am going to venture a "switch" on this question of ideological disadvantage. If by ideology is meant a set of values and principles which have some claim to originality and some reasonable relation to reality, then the ideological advantage is all with us. We have an ideology of values which we have not articulated. The Communists have articulated an ideology which does not exist, in fact, anywhere in the world.

THE ECONOMIC ADVANTAGE

To develop this thesis, I shall use primarily one proving ground—economics, the relation of government to people, to business, and to labor in developing society. This is only one of the aspects that could be chosen; there are many others. One could talk, for example, about the religious, the philosophical, the sociological, the legal, the political, and others. But the economic has been chosen because it is this area that is going to count more than all the others so far as our relations with the newly developing countries of the world are concerned. The decision on their part whether to associate themselves with our values or with those of Communism is going to depend more upon what the aspiring country believes about the

---

[1] Walter Lippman, *The Good Society* (New York: Grosset & Dunlap, Inc., 1956).

relative ability of these systems to solve their economic and development problems than upon any other factor.

Accustomed as we are to the age of science, the age of the atom, even the age of space, we sometimes are inclined to overlook the fact that about two-thirds of the people of the world, even now, are living under conditions that are not essentially different from what they were 5,000 years ago. The authority for this statement is none other than Arnold Toynbee.[2]

When you check the per capita income, for example, of South Asia, the Middle East, or Southeast Asia, it still averages around a dime or a quarter a day. But now this 5,000-year sleep has been broken. These people, through education, through travel, and through communications, are beginning to find out what they have been missing, and they are determined to do something about it.

Recognizing all this, the Soviets make this kind of appeal: They say to these countries, "Look at us. A decade ago we were an agrarian nation like you. Now we are an industrial and scientific giant. True, the United States is an industrial and scientific giant too, but they have had over a hundred years to do it. You cannot wait that long; you had better cast in your lot with us and adopt our methods." Now, if they succeed in this line of argument, I am afraid the other facets of the value and ideological argument will have relatively little effect on the outcome.

But let us be quite clear about what we are trying to achieve in relation to these emergent countries. We are not trying to get them to imitate us or to emulate us. This would be presumptuous, even if it were possible—which it is not. What we are looking for is identification; we want to get a feeling of "we," not "we and they." But identification is a two-way process. It requires first understanding one's self, then understanding the other fellow, so that you can find the common element and make the most of it. The greatest obstacle to our achievement of mutual understanding overseas is of our making. It is our refusal to realize and recognize what we are, what our values are, and what our system really is and our creation

---

[2] Arnold J. Toynbee, "Communism and the West in Asian Countries," *Annals of the American Academy of Political and Social Science*, CCCXXXVI (July, 1961), 31.

Values for a Changing America

of an image of ourselves which is itself unreal. We thus make it impossible for other people to identify themselves with us.

The role of government.—Let me illustrate what I mean in specific terms. There have been many books written, articles, even college courses, government publications, and reports on our national values, our national objectives—what our system really is. They are all eloquent on the familiar themes of freedom, of individuality, private enterprise, and so forth. They are wonderful as far as they go, but the omissions in most of these books and statements leave an impression that is positively dangerous, for it is out of date in a changing America. You could read most of these books, and you would never realize that the United States government does, in fact, stimulate, regulate, police, and even subsidize American industry and agriculture in a thousand ways, large and small. You would never know that social insurance, social security, workmen's compensation, unemployment insurance, and the like exist in the United States—far less, that we have one of the most generous systems in the world. You would be quite unaware of the role played by organized labor, by federal tax credit and purchasing and fiscal policies, and by such agencies as the FTC and the FPC, and the FCC and the ICC, and the SEC and the AEC, and the CAA and the CAB, and the FCA and the HHFA, and the NLRB and the RRB, and the VA and the SPA. The economics of these books are much closer to Adam Smith [3] than J. K. Galbraith [4] or Arthur E. Burns.[5] The agriculture is closer to the Homestead Act than to the Soil Bank; and as for labor, we are made to seem closer to Walden Pond than to the Wagner Labor Relations Act.

Suppose we go to a country like India, with this picture of our values and objectives. What can India say? She will be driven to say, "We are sorry. It may have worked for you, but it cannot possibly work for us." India has few capitalists, few of the ingredients of a self-started, self-propelled, private enterprise system. She cannot

---

[3] Adam Smith, *An Inquiry into the Nature and Causes of the Wealth of Nations* (New York: P. F. Collier, 1901).
[4] John Kenneth Galbraith, *American Capitalism* (Boston: Houghton Mifflin Company, 1956).
[5] Arthur E. Burns, Alfred C. Neal, and D. S. Watson, *Modern Economics* (New York: Harcourt, Brace, 1948).

realize her ambitions for development without a substantial degree of governmental involvement; and if we, therefore, create the impression that a strong degree of governmental involvement in the economy puts her system beyond the pale as far as we are concerned, then our hopes of identification will have been shattered. And it is all our own fault, in spite of the fact that the public sector in India today stands at 5 per cent, while in the United States it is 20 per cent. We call them "Socialists"; they call us "Capitalists." If we let matters get into this position, we are guilty of one of history's most tragic and inexcusable blunders.

We *do* have a principle—the guiding principle of our government, business, labor, and individual relations. It applies equally well to the United States, to India, and to the other developing countries, and it can serve as the common ideological denominator between all of us. The heart of this concept is contained in a quotation from Lincoln, which in recent years has become one of his best known sayings. To paraphrase it, he says that the function of government is to do for people what needs to be done, but what they cannot of themselves do at all or do so well. When you transplant this principle to India, for example, you find, first, that there is much more that needs to be done for people, and second, there is a much higher proportion of it they cannot do for themselves. But the principle is just the same, although the facts are different.

This is not Socialism. This is the opposite of Socialism; this is the best antidote to Socialism in today's world. A Socialist is a person who says, "If something needs to be done for people, other things being equal, let the government do it." The Lincoln principle says, "If something needs to be done for people, other things being equal, let it be done privately. But if it cannot be done privately and it must be done and only the government can do it, then let the government do it."

There is a third principle—that of the reactionary. He says, "If something needs to be done for people—for their health, their education, their welfare—and it cannot be done privately and if only the government can do it, just do not do it."

This is not Socialism—creeping or any other kind, and it is not classical Capitalism of the time of Marx, either. Nor is it a mixture of the two. It is something new in a changing America. It is something made in America, and something of which we can be very proud. Let us see why.

Relation of government, labor, and business.—In classical Capitalism, only one force counted—business. Socialists came along, and they agreed there should only be one force, but it should be government. Then a third force came along—strong, organized labor. The old view was one based on an inherent antipathy between business on the one hand, and the other two elements on the other. The class struggle between capital and labor was accepted as a fact of life by both sides. On one side, the fanatical Communists were perfectly willing to burn down the very plant that meant their own jobs in pursuit of their goals. The classical Capitalist was supposed to have no interest in labor except to wring all he could out of it at the least possible price and throw the residue on the scrap heap. Likewise, the relation between government and business, by mutual agreement, was supposed to be inherent enmity. The employers dealt with the government on the assumption that *any* governmental involvement with business was necessarily evil and poisonous. The Socialists expressed the inherent antagonism between government and business, with which they agreed, in a different way—simply that government should destroy and take over business.

The new and distinctive contribution of American thought and experience is this: These three elements—business, labor, and government—in a modern industrial society are not fundamentally antagonistic but support and advance each other's interests. Rightly conceived with proper leadership, with an intelligent sense of self-interest all around, these three elements can raise the level of productivity and the standard of living beyond any point that any one of them could reach, even if given absolute carte blanche to do as it pleased. Let me give three examples of this mutual-interest theory.

Many business men formerly assumed, almost automatically, that they should be against social insurance—social security, unemployment insurance, workmen's compensation, disability insurance, and the like. Most of them now have come to realize that our system, our private enterprise system with its mass production, cash-wage economy, could not function without social insurance. There are many reasons for this, but let me indicate just one. Our high level of prosperity is largely a consumer-based prosperity. This in turn is based upon installment buying, especially the larger items, to a very great degree. Installment buying, in turn, is based upon the confidence that consumer purchasing power will continue. And that is based upon the fact that if wages are interrupted by unemployment, by illness, by old age, or by death, there will be a residual income from social insurance. Thus, you can safely take out an 18-month or 18-year installment contract and not have to worry that you are going to lose both the goods and the bank payments. Social insurance is not merely helpful; it is absolutely indispensable to the kind of cash-wage, consumer-based prosperity that we have.

Similarly, if you take the whole complex that is sometimes known as government regulation or government interference, depending upon your point of view, most of it proves on examination to be quite indispensable to the functioning of a complex economy like ours. How could there be a television industry, for example, if the government did not assign channels? If channels were grabbed on an every-man-for-himself basis, the industry would soon smother itself in a blanket of screeching, howling, overlapping signals. Or how could there be a packaged food, drug, and cosmetic industry without the confidence, born of government food and drug acts and inspections, that if you buy a sealed jar of shampoo or a jar of pickles, the pickles will not poison you or the shampoo burn your scalp off? Who would ride in a commercial aircraft if he could not rely on governmental ordering of traffic and checking of safety standards? Indeed, you could multiply these examples all up and down the line of the distribution of modern goods and services. Of course, the minute the government goes one inch beyond what is necessary for public protection, then indeed it is harmful and stifling, as it has been at some times and still is in some places.

One more example of this theory. The essential mutuality of interest between labor and management is becoming widely accepted as the distinctive contribution of American labor relations. The surface contest between the employer and the employee over wages and conditions of labor is obvious. There is also a contest between the housewife and the butcher over the price of hamburger and between

Values for a Changing America

the wholesaler and the retailer over the price of a refrigerator, but that does not mean that there is a class war going on between them. That does not mean that the dearest wish of each party to the contest is that the other should be utterly destroyed.

Marx, like most writers on economics prior to John Stuart Mill, was obsessed with the idea of distribution. To him, the economic problem was like an old cartoon; there was a big bag of gold, a fixed amount, and on top of it sat the Capitalist, with his familiar tall silk hat and big cigar. The whole idea of economics was to get him off the bag of gold and redistribute it to the more deserving proletariat.

At about the same time, Lincoln enunciated the modern theory that the real secret of prosperity for all is to increase the total stock of goods through added productivity. "Let not him who is houseless tear down the house of another, but let him labor diligently and build one for himself." Then came Henry Ford and his voluntary five-dollars-a-day wage, and the American pattern began to emerge. High production, good wages, widespread purchasing power as the mutual goal of both employer and employee—and it is this pattern that has set the pace in the world.

POST-WAR PRIVATE ENTERPRISE

I said at the outset that our values and our system have been active and positive forces for change in a changing world. This idea that Socialism and Communism are the "wave of the future" is an old-fashioned idea still upheld by a few propagandists like Khrushchev and people who have not read their papers since the death of Adolf Hitler. There was a time in the thirties when it seemed that everything done in Britain or France was going to be done here twenty years later. All that has changed since World War II. Now it is the other way around.

Look at the evidence. After the war, Britain started out to socialize various industries and services and had nothing but economic troubles. West Germany, Japan, and others went down the private enterprise path and had the lustiest national economic growth of any countries in the world. Britain took the hint, looked around, and not only reversed its nationalizing trend but actually tried to de-nationalize such industries as could be unscrambled.

Some significant information, however, came from a public opinion poll taken by Elmo Roper of the ten major foreign industrialized nations of the free world, including countries like Sweden, Argentina and others that are sometimes loosely referred to as "Socialistic." On the average 92 per cent in these countries were against nationalization of industries. Only 8 per cent were in favor of Socialism, according to its standard definition.[6]

In light of this crushing demonstration of world opinion, what becomes of the idea that the whole world is drifting to Socialism? Indeed, the Socialists themselves are abandoning Socialism. In 1957, for example, the Socialist Party of West Germany officially renounced state ownership of major industries. The most striking of all is the great paradox of our time—that the Russian Communists themselves are avidly copying our system, and that the areas in which they have had their greatest successes are precisely those areas in which they have, to the greatest degree, abandoned their dogmas and copied our practices. Let me give just three examples.

The incentive principle.—The first is the incentive principle, built-in as the very main spring of American life, with rewards for energy and ingenuity, penalties for sloth, but scoffed at in pure Communist theory, the ultimate expression of which is "from each according to his ability, to each according to his need." There is not an ounce of incentive in that. What is happening in practice? At President Eisenhower's Camp David meeting with Mr. Khrushchev, Khrushchev actually boasted to President Eisenhower that the Russians were making more use of the incentive principle than the Americans were.

Milovan Djilas tells us in his book *The New Class* [7] that the Communist's Secretary of the Rayon Committee, whom I take to be a middling sort of bureaucrat, gets 25 times the pay of the average

---

[6] *Where Stands Freedom?* A Report on the Findings of an International Survey of Public Opinion conducted by Elmo Roper for TIME, the Weekly Newsmagazine, February-March, 1948 (New York: *Time,* the Weekly Newsmagazine, 1948).

[7] Milovan Djilas, *The New Class* (New York: Frederick A. Praeger, Publisher, 1957).

Soviet worker. The Secretary of State of the United States gets 6 times the pay of the average American worker. Some Soviet scientists, the most important in the space program, may get $40,000 a year. Artists, writers, even ballet dancers, and others are treated very well indeed. But so exaggerated is this incentive that on the downward side, the common, ordinary proletariat who are supposed to be the chief concern of Communism get only a subsistence. Perhaps you read in the paper recently a fact that surprised many people, that the Soviet Union did not even provide social security for farmers until recently, while we have had it for years.

This money incentive principle is even extended to grades in school. Almost everybody in college is on a stipend. A person who gets "A's" gets a higher stipend than one who gets "B's"; one who gets "B's" gets a higher stipend than one who gets "C's." We used to get a nickel if we came home with a good report card. They have carried it to the ultimate conclusion. Where this incentive principle is operative, you see results. But when these results are held up to the world as evidence of the inherent superior power of Communist doctrine, it is time to expose the fraud. This is a practical willingness to betray Communist principles and adopt our methods when what is wanted is hard results and not propaganda.

Freedom of thought.—Exactly the same observation applies to the second pilfered principle—freedom of thought. Communist tradition, from Marx right down through Lenin and Stalin, has always called for the most ruthless control of thought in all fields, not just political, but economic, literary, artistic, scientific, or architectural. You recall how Stalin decreed the validity of Lysenko's theory of genetics.[8] And if some unfortunate geneticist's experiments and research tended to prove the opposite, he would have done well to suppress his observations if he wanted to live out his life in comfort. Three of the most prominent ones did not and landed in Siberia.

But in one area, this dogma of thought control collided with another of even higher level priority—the necessity (also supported by the writings of Lenin) to strengthen Soviet military and expan-

---

[8] Trofim Denisovich Lysenko, *Agrobiology; Essays on Problems of Genetics, Plant Breeding, and Seed Growing* (Moscow: Foreign Languages Publishing House, 1954). Translated from the 4th Russian edition.

sionist power through the most advanced weapons that science could produce. Stalin could perhaps play at omniscience in the field of genetics without damaging the arms program, but Stalin could not decree that rocket fuel A satisfies the party line and rocket fuel B does not if he wanted to get a rocket off the ground.

And so in one small, carefully circumscribed area of the natural sciences relevant to the arms or space program, the dread virus of freedom of thought was grudgingly turned loose. Once again we have seen the results, and once again we have seen the weird, upside-down claim that satellites and missiles prove the superiority of Communist doctrine.

Productivity.—The third principle borrowed from us is that of emphasis on productivity. We now find ourselves, from time to time, being challenged by Khrushchev to a race in productivity, measured by everything from box scores on pigs to pig iron. We have not heard quite so much lately, while the wheat deal was pending, but we will again. If Marx were alive today, he would bet everything he had in this race with Capitalism. Writers on economics, perhaps paradoxically, sometimes produce passages of rich, beautiful, purple prose, but none of them can compare with the almost lyrical praise heaped by Marx in the opening passages of the *Communist Manifesto* on the inherent productive power of bourgeois capitalism, and if you don't believe it, just get your copy of the *Communist Manifesto* and read it. You will find such passages as this: "The bourgeoisie, during its rule of scarce one hundred years, has created more massive and more colossal productive forces than have all preceding generations together." [9]

". . . It has accomplished wonders far surpassing Egyptian pyramids, Roman aqueducts, and Gothic cathedrals; it has conducted expeditions that put in the shade all former Exoduses of nations and crusades." [10] And so on and on. We sometimes forget that Marx's whole theory of the downfall of Capitalism was that it was going to come about because of too much production. Here is the exact passage:

[9] Karl Marx and Friedrich Engels, *Manifesto of the Communist Party* (Chicago: Charles H. Kerr & Company, 1908), p. 20
[10] *Ibid.*, p. 17.

> Modern bourgeois society with its relations of production, of exchange and of property, a society that has conjured up such gigantic means of production and of exchange, is like the sorcerer, who is no longer able to control the powers of the nether world whom he has called up by his spells . . . and why? Because there is too much civilisation, too much means of subsistence, too much industry, too much commerce.[11]

I am sure the Communists do not choose this passage as their text when they preach to the underdeveloped countries—which would undoubtedly be glad to take their chances on too much commerce, too much industry, too much production, too much means of subsistence.

So when Khrushchev boasts about the inherent superior productive capacity of Communism over Capitalism, we should just quote the *Communist Manifesto* back to him and let it go at that.

While I am talking about values in a changing world, I want to point out, specifically, that I have scrupulously avoided casting our values and our objectives in terms of a competition or race with the Soviet Union. The space race is a special case; I am talking about our highest values and our highest goals. We are not starting from the same point; we are not heading toward the same goal. How could we be in a race?

The problem that obsesses the Russians—sheer quantitative material production—we have long since, for all practical purposes, licked. By far the greatest Soviet production problem today is agricultural. What kind of a race does that pose for us? Half of the Soviet people work on farms and produce a diet which is still the worst in Europe, in spite of some improvement. About a twelfth, at the most, of the American people work on farms—probably less. They produce the best diet in the world; they export thousands of tons of food; and they still pile up such mountainous surpluses that it costs a million and a half dollars a day just to store them. The Soviet government is putting forth frenzied efforts, including breaking up the tractor stations, de-centralizing, copying Iowa farm methods, and putting in a whole new system of prices and rewards —all to increase agricultural production. The United States govern-

[11] *Ibid.*, p. 21.

ment is also putting forth frenzied efforts, including Soil Banks, acreage restrictions, payments *not* to produce, all to decrease agricultural productions. Some race!

Naturally, Khrushchev would like to announce a volume of production race under these circumstances. When the Russians announce, then, that they are going to overtake us in production, that they are even going to wave to us as they go by, let us just say, "More power to you." The best result that could happen would be a period of genuine concentration by the Russians on their very real internal problems, both because it would distract them from foreign adventures and because it would gradually help build up a body of opinion at home that has a high stake in stability.

Conclusion

This idea of a race, this idea of having goals to bring out the best in you is fine. But our race is not with Russia. Russia is puffing mightily along a leg of the race that we have long since completed. This does not mean that we should slump idly beside the track; we have a new leg of the race to run. It is hard to run a race not against an opponent but against the best that is in you. At the dog tracks, they tell me, there is always a little white mechanical rabbit that speeds out ahead of the greyhound to draw him to his greatest efforts. A miler will run his best mile if he is successively paced by four quarter-milers. But we, as a nation, have no mechanical rabbit to draw us on; we have no pace-setter. We must be our own pace-setter.

If we are to do this, the first requisite is to get rid of this phony idea that *we* have arrived and all that remains is for the rest of the world to catch up with *us*. The real truth is that we have reached only a precarious mid-point in the most revolutionary political and economic experiment in history, and there remain before us, if we can only see them, new peaks of achievement that are as high above today's levels as today's are above those of 1787. So let us lose no time in defining and articulating these values and these goals that are our objective on this leg of the race. They are not, as on the last leg, sheer material production and subduing a raw continent. Rather, they are greater self-expression; intellectual, religious, and cultural creativity; refinement and perfection of our freedoms; the fullest exploitation of the possibilities of science, of intelligence, of education; the perfection of economic arrangements which will not only elicit the increased production of which we are capable but distribute it in a way to bring the good life to all our people; and the construction of international devices and institutions that will put the rule of law in the place of the rule of force among nations and place all people on the road to prosperity, personal and national freedom, and enduring international harmony.

Values for a Changing America

RALPH W. TYLER [*]

THE POSSIBILITIES of this topic, general as it is, create a great temptation for any speaker. What I would like to do is to discuss briefly the values for a changing America from the point of view of the educational tasks, since we are here largely concerned with education at school or college. However, since the term "values" and the term "changing America" are both used in many different ways, they ought to be defined a little more clearly.

VALUES OF THE INDIVIDUAL

The values to be discussed will be approached from the point of view of individual psychology, that is, what human beings value or cherish that become active goals in their lives.

We know from experimentation with human beings that if they are denied some of the physical needs like food, or water, or opportunities for sexual expression, or opportunities for movement, that they will be strongly driven to make up for these needs. They will be driven to do things in order to get food, or water, or to carry on activities. There are also certain social needs that seem to be characteristic, at least of the primates, as well as of human beings. Primates, generally, evidence this in their reaction to other animals or human beings, their effort to belong, their need for affection and for recognition within social groups.

We know that if these needs generally are well met—these phys-

[*] Director, Center for Advanced Study in the Behavioral Sciences, Stanford, California.

ical and these social needs—that human beings are largely directed by values, that is by ideas they have learned after birth that have become significant to them and for which they will direct their major activities. Of course, you may value an object, or you may value an activity—an object like a car, an activity like dancing—or you may value an idea, like the idea of justice, or fair play. That human beings can develop strong attachment to values and these become dynamic and active in guiding their own behavior is one of their most important characteristics from the standpoint of their real potentiality as humans and from the standpoint of education. The development after birth of these values toward which men will act, the values by which men live, is the topic I want to discuss.

A Changing America

Now look at the other aspect of this title—a changing America. We know, of course that the world does not stand still and that America is actively on the move. Those aspects of our changing country which seem to me particularly relevant to our concerns as teachers and administrators have been chosen for comment. What are some of these?

INCREASED POPULATION

The most obvious one, of course, is the rapid population increase. This is affecting us as we provide more space and more teachers and more other resources for school and college.

TECHNOLOGICAL DEVELOPMENT

A second aspect is the rapid technological development. This has at least two major implications in connection with our concern about values: One is the shift in the labor force. For example, when I was born, 38 per cent of all of the gainfully employed in the United States were engaged in agriculture. Now only 8 per cent are in this field, because the applications of science and technology to agriculture have resulted in the better understanding of growth processes in animals and plants, the development of new hybrid species, the construction of machines for handling the ground and for sowing and reaping. This has made it possible for us to produce food and fiber for the nation in unprecedented amounts, using only 8 per cent of our labor force, and the percentage is dropping every year. Agriculture is only one illustration, for there are other shifts in the labor force, such as the 40,000 persons who last year were engaged in operating elevators in New York City and who are no longer so employed because of the automatic elevators.

The tremendous implication of this for education lies in the fact that the jobs which are being eliminated are largely those that required little or no education. When I was born, 26 per cent of the labor force was unskilled; now only 11 per cent is unskilled. The proportion of skilled labor has dropped slightly as well. The great increases have been in areas like science, engineering, teaching, the health services, the recreational services, accounting, and controlling. The jobs which are expanding, you can readily see, require a higher than average level of education, for they demand understanding and skill far beyond that of the jobs which no longer exist.

With this development of technology there has also been a sharp change in the patterns of consumption. When I was born, 85 per cent of all consumption was material—food, clothing, shelter. Now this represents only about 26 per cent of our consumption. What has become possible as we have been able to produce material things with so little of our labor force has been to provide more adequately for health, for education, for arts and music, and other recreational activities. But the demand for these non-material things is not increasing as rapidly as our ability to produce them. This creates an educational problem of developing consumption patterns that parallel what we can now produce; that is, we need to shift our desires to take advantage of the availability of non-material things. This requires a value shift.

INCREASED URBANIZATION

The third aspect of our changing America relevant to this topic is increased urbanization. A majority of our people live within great

Values for a Changing America

metropolitan areas. At the turn of the century, only 22 per cent lived within such urban areas. Now, in place of having largely a rural America, we have largely a city America with the increased anonymity of urban society and with the increased need for integration among the parts in order that they may work effectively. This is in contrast to a society in which a good share of the population lived on the farm and were able to produce their own subsistence; the money exchange was largely the surplus. Today the fact that most of us get from others all of the things we need other than what we produce in our occupation results in an interdependent society largely engaged in interchange, but the individual is so anonymous that he is not aware of the people involved with him. They, too, are anonymous.

WIDE-SPREAD COMMUNICATION

A fourth aspect which has implication for values is the great development of communication. Obviously, communication was very important in the early days of this country, and the publication of *The Federalist Papers* and other pronouncements of our founding fathers had great influence upon the small number of people who had contact with their writings and listened to their speeches. Now, the development, not only of various ways of reaching the people through the printed page, the newspapers, magazines, and books but also through radio and television, has made it possible to reach many, many people. It is increasingly difficult, for example, to recognize the differences in speech between Massachusetts and Philadelphia, or even between the middle South and the North, as the television and the radio help establish a more common accent.

This means that we have increasingly a larger society. It is no longer easy to blame one section of the country for the ills of another, because all sections are "listening in" to mass communication. It is also more difficult to maintain deviant values among different groups.

In summary, I have directed attention to the values of the individual—the things he cherishes and toward which he directs a good deal of his activity, and I have noted that a changing America is characterized by its high rate of population increase, its rapid technological development with changes in the labor force and the consumption patterns that go along with it, and its great network of communications.

Contemporary Value Problems

What are the critical problems today in relation to individual values in this kind of a changing country in which we live? Some three of these critical problems will be discussed.

RE-INTERPRETATION OF OLD VALUES

The first is one that has frequently arisen in the past even though changes occurred more slowly. Values require re-definition and re-interpretation to make them appropriate to changing conditions. This is not new. You will recall that the Jews were told in the Messianic law, "Love thy neighbor as thyself," and Jesus was asked, according to the Gospels, about who was one's neighbor, and He re-interpreted it to mean not simply the person who lived next door but the Samaritan—someone who was an "outperson," one who was not one of their own people. This need for the re-interpretation of the value of neighborliness was recognized 2,000 years ago.

What are some of the values cherished in our society today that require re-interpretation?

Kindness.—There is the value of kindness, or consideration for others. We hear people professing friendliness, but who limit consideration to members of their own group and see no inconsistency in supporting war or other inhumane treatment to persons who are out of their group. Can we live in a large urbanized, closely-knit society without re-interpreting kindness and consideration? You may recall that the Anglican Bishop of Johannesburg, who was finally forced to leave South Africa, commented that he was being told continually, "Well, are you going to desert your own?"

"As though," he said, "my own were people who happened to have the same skin color, but who have very different beliefs and did not hold to the kind of love and affection that seemed important to me." He said, "I have to re-interpret 'my own' as persons who hold humanitarian values, and they may have very different skin color." This is a re-interpretation of an old value.

Loyalty.—Correspondingly, loyalty requires re-interpretation. I taught for three years (1926–29) at the University of North Carolina, and I was impressed then that in the history texts of the state great emphasis was placed on loyalty—loyalty to the state and loyalty to the South. There was no mention of loyalty beyond those areas. What is loyalty for? To whom are we loyal? Are we loyal only to a small group, to a particular area, to the world of humanity? This value must be re-interpreted in terms of our present conditions.

Fair play.—This value, equivalent to justice, is commonly cherished by our people. Now to whom are we to exercise fair play? Is it only to those with whom we are immediately in contact? Do our actions affect others that are unseen? Questions of this sort will be answered differently now from a century ago.

Honesty.—Many people who are very honest in their relations within their own group see nothing wrong in trying to take something from a storekeeper that they do not know, or from the government or a corporation that seems to them an impersonal entity. Honesty is another important value which requires re-interpretation to be meaningful in the kind of society in which we live.

Pride in craftsmanship.—This value has always been important in the development of our society—pride in one's work, getting satisfaction from being skilled in one's craft. It seems easy to feel pride in the cake that you baked or the object you have made in the shop. But what is it to be skillful in the kinds of jobs that most of us hold where we do not turn out a particular physical object? Can we develop the same pride in craftsmanship as teachers, as administrators, clerks, factory workers, as persons generally engaged in the complex occupations in our society?

Initiative.—We have been proud as a people that we came to this country and that we were able to take initiative in conquering its frontiers, in developing a great technological society. The initiative shown by a person who went into the forest and cut down the trees and turned these wastelands, or these forests, into farms is obvious. But what is the corresponding interpretation of initiative today? How do I take initiative in this large society, initiative in civic matters, initiative in my occupation, initiative in social affairs? Certainly initiative is possible, but have we re-interpreted it sufficiently?

Responsibility.—This has long been emphasized as a value basic to the family, the job, and the community, but it clearly needs re-interpretation for our times. In what way can we be responsible when we are not completely carrying out the total activity, when one is only part of an organization, or part of some large enterprise?

The first problem of values as we look at our changing society is the problem of re-interpretation.

ACQUISITION OF NEW VALUES

A second problem arises from the fact that changes in modern life require some new values that were not commonly recognized as part of the American tradition.

The application of intelligence.—As we see the way in which science and technology are continually changing the world, we come to value study and the use of disciplined intelligence in finding answers to problems as they arise rather than placing our faith in the answers that were worked out some years ago. We do not have final answers to some specific problems. We do not know precisely what to do about such problems as racial conflict, the population increase, war and peace, and better integration of our industrial society. Our faith cannot be placed in some outmoded answers that were appropriate 50 or 75 years ago. Our faith must be in the ability of our people, properly organized through study and intelligent applications of our knowledge, to find solutions, to recognize that these are continually changing and that new answers need to be provided. This emphasis is not upon answers as our value, but upon intelligent study and the application of intelligence as a mode of dealing with new problems as they arise.

Tolerance of ambiguity.—A second new and important value today is tolerance of ambiguity in contrast to clear "blacks" and "whites." Very often young people are reared with the notion that one can easily make a distinction between right and wrong, correct and incorrect. But we are now in a society in which problems are being worked on and no final solutions are clearly evident. We need continually to recognize the tentativeness of our views and our actions, and we need to tolerate ambiguity, that is, to recognize the possibility that our present notions may be incorrect and that further study is needed. This is very difficult for some individuals who want immediately to come to some conclusion. Yet, this value is a very necessary one if we are to continue to move ahead using knowledge to bring about improvements in our world.

Enjoyment in cultural diversity.—The third new value which is clearly important—it has always been a part of the value system of some leading religions but yet has not been universal—is enjoyment in cultural diversity. It is probably true that America has benefited, perhaps, more from the fact that we are a culturally diverse people than from any other characteristic of our society. We have worked and played together with people from many parts of the world who come with many different backgrounds and patterns of living; we have incorporated them so that we have been able to enjoy the music and art from various parts of the world; we have been able to benefit from the religious beliefs, from the practices of charity, from a whole range of science and technology from these many peoples. Yet this is often done with a kind of restiveness, a kind of feeling which fortunately has never been embraced by a majority in this country but which characterized Nazi Germany, the feeling that only as we are of one type could we survive. It is increasingly clear that this is not the nature of our society and that a strong society is not simply made up of one type—everyone having the same beliefs, the same ways of doing things, the same patterns of behavior. We need increasingly to recognize the importance of diversity; we need to appreciate and enjoy diversity. It is a necessary value in a modern urban society and in a world society where peoples are coming closer together through rapid transportation and communication.

These three new values—the application of intelligence, tolerance of ambiguity, and enjoyment in cultural diversity—combined with olden values re-interpreted to fit modern conditions are important to our society.

CONFLICTS OF VALUES

A third problem of values in our changing America concerns the conflicts that arise among them. Some values are not obtainable without sacrifice of others, and the individual must make choices when conflicts arise. Two illustrations are mentioned here only as examples of a number of others.

Material and non-material values.—Perhaps the most obvious conflicts today are between material and non-material values. Our newspapers, magazines, radio, and television all focus a good deal of attention, through advertising, on material values—this new car, this kind of beer, this sort of dress, these other products. Most of us cannot afford all of these material goods, particularly if we are to obtain many of the non-material values. We must ask. What price are we willing to pay for education? What price for better health? What price for art and music? This kind of question arises again and again, because we do not have the resources to provide for everything we want. Commonly, we must sacrifice some material values to obtain non-material ones.

Narrower and broader loyalties.—Another illustration of conflicts in values is between the narrower and broader loyalties. Can we be loyal to our family, to our neighborhood, and at the same time to the larger community? This often sets very real problems. It certainly must be a problem in the South these days in connection with civil rights. Is one loyal to Macomb, Mississippi, as the majority of people there might feel or is one loyal to a broader social group than this? These two illustrations will suggest many others. Our conflicts in values create problems in various areas of life.

The Development of Values

We know that persons are not born with values. They are born with physiological drives and apparently with certain social drives, but the values we have been discussing are acquired after birth. We know *some* things about the process, although this is an area where a great deal of research is still underway, and much is *not* yet known.

ACQUIRING VALUES

From parents and friends.—We know, for example, that the child is likely to value the things his parents and friends value and seem to get satisfaction from, and he accepts and shares them. This attitude is reinforced by the fact that others to whom he looks as having some authority also hold these values.

From experiences.—We also know that an individual can acquire values different from those of his parents or friends when he has had satisfying experiences with these particular activities or objects. Thus, a child or youth may find satisfactions in books which were not in his home, or in music or art which his friends do not enjoy, because he had experiences with these objects which were enjoyable. Like other types of learning, experiences that are satisfying are continued and become a part of the child's behavior. In this way he learns to value these things.

From rationalizing inconsistencies.—A third process in acquiring values is stated quite completely by Festinger [1] in his little book on dissonance. As one grows up, he finds it difficult to hold conflicting values or to believe in things that are not in harmony with what he has found to be true. He puts effort to bring about consistency and to get rid of this conflict within himself. This also may result in changing some of the values involved. It is suggested that a good deal of the current concern for civil rights has grown out of persons recognizing the inconsistency between their religious beliefs about brotherhood and their acceptance of the inferior status of certain groups. Internal pressure for consistency is a part of the means by which values tend to be changed and become more consistent.

From outside sources.—In looking at these, we see that a good many of the values we have been talking about are initially developed before youngsters come to school, when they have an opportunity to share in the values that their parents hold, or their friends hold, or the neighborhood group holds. One of the problems in our society

---

[1] Leon Festinger, *Conflict, Decision and Dissonance* (Stanford, Calif.: Stanford University Press, 1964).

is that, in contrast with earlier ones, it is difficult, if not impossible, to insulate the child from the values that are being portrayed and exemplified and made to appear more exciting and interesting outside the home. Television often depicts values, either in the advertising or in the programs, which may not be in harmony with what the parents would like to have their youngsters cherish. The newspapers are more concerned with selling newspapers than they are with the effort to contribute to important social values, and they often present somewhat attractively values that are in conflict with those of home, church, and school.

THE SCHOOL'S PART IN DEVELOPING VALUES

This brief listing of some of the chief ways in which children develop values suggests that the school normally plays a role in the process, but it is not by any means the sole agency. The school can certainly see that such values as fair play, respect for the individual, application of intelligent study, and aesthetic values are exemplified in the school and that the youngsters get satisfactions from them, but it must be recognized that the school alone could not be responsible for developing some important social and ethical values that are significant in personal life and in good citizenship. The home, the church, and other community agencies must do their share, or the task will not be done. Nevertheless, the schools do have certain particularly significant contributions that are not likely to be made elsewhere.

The curriculum and the school environment.—In the case of aesthetic values, they can provide youngsters with a chance to hear music, to see art, to read literature, to read and respond to plays that are often not generally available in many of our communities through the normal processes of the home or the community itself. The schools have an important role to play in connection with the development of aesthetic values.

They also have a similar role to play in intellectual values. There is much shoddy thinking and writing in our newspapers, radio programs, and television, and in general conversation and communication. The school has a responsibility in helping youngsters discover the significance of well-done intellectual work, the meaning of closely-reasoned argument, the significance of evidence to support facts, the way in which a good intellect operates in dealing with problems and in seeking to marshall information about them. This development of respect for intelligent attack and for study is one of the values for which the school and college must take major responsibility, for it will not develop otherwise, and it is very important.

In the field of moral and social values, the schools and colleges have not only the responsibility of providing an environment in which these values have a chance to be exemplified, where youngsters can discover such satisfactions as being kind to others and recognizing others, but it is also the school that is usually in the best position to help them re-examine values in the light of critical intelligence and to bring a better alignment between what they know to be the facts and what they believe and cherish.

For the youngster who is in a neighborhood where there is a great deal of stealing and juvenile delinquency, there is an opportunity for the school not only to represent a different kind of society from that he finds outside but, as he grows older, the chance to think about or reflect on what he has observed and what its consequences are, to deal intellectually and rationally with the values that he has experienced and what they mean.

We know that schools and colleges do a good deal in the development of values now, but much of this is unconscious. The educational influence can be increased by careful planning of the curriculum and the school environment so as to exemplify these values and make provision for intellectual examination, reflection, and interpretation of them.

The school's own values.—In addition to this, we find that schools and colleges affect the values of children and youth in other ways. Students usually have a notion about what the prominent values are in their school or college and what it really stands for. Interviews of children regarding what they think the teachers or the principals would value in their work reveal some interesting differences among schools. In some, it is quite clear in the children's minds that justice, fair play, pride in craftsmanship, and so on are behaviors the school expects of them. There are others where the children have the notion that the school does not care what they do so long as they keep "their necks in" and "their noses clean," and that there is no expectation that students will raise questions, get new ideas, or become intellectually excited. You are no doubt familiar with the work of Pace[2] and Stern[3] in characterizing the different college environments. The school or college expectations of the students have an influence with developing their values.

The peer group.—The second way in which schools and colleges influence values is through the friendship groups of children and youth, and what his peer group considers important is a potent factor in the child's value system. There appears to be quite a diversity even within the same school or college. Different cliques in school or fraternity groups in college may stand for different things, and thus have different influences on students within the same institution. I am not proposing, as a practical means, that an administrator or a teacher should simply tell a group it should not have these values, but it is possible to have a real influence on the friendship groups of children and youth, helping them discover important values they have overlooked so that the value systems of the fraternities or the friendship groups are changed.

Identification.—A third means by which values are influenced in school and college is by personality identification. A young person is greatly influenced by attractive personalities that seem to him the kinds of persons he would like to be. The small child picks up a small broom and tries to sweep as she may have seen her mother do or tries other activities that her mother does because the mother is an attractive personality that she would imitate. As we go on through life, the teacher may stand out, or the principal, or some other adult.

The personalities that stand out, that seem attractive, are not

---

[2] C. Robert Pace, *They Went to College* (Minneapolis: University of Minnesota Press, 1941).
[3] George Stern, Morris L. Stein, and Benjamin S. Bloom, *Methods in Personality Assessment* (Glencoe, Ill.: Free Press, 1956).

Values for a Changing America

the same for all youth, because it is hard for a big, lanky boy to be attracted to the personality of a little, short, female teacher. For this reason there should be some variety in the personalities in a school. But all of them ought to exemplify some of the basic values, so that as the youngster seeks to be like or to emulate his ideal, he is taking on some of the basic attitudes and values. Schools and colleges do not often recognize the extent to which the teachers actually reflect the values that they say they hold. These should be particularly the values for which the school has major responsibility—the value of study and reflection and other intellectual values, aesthetic values, social and ethical values.

In summary, the school has a significant part in the development of values. In the curriculum, it can provide opportunities for students to have experiences otherwise not available in the home or community; it can stimulate and guide reflection upon and interpretation of values that they have experienced, both good and bad. The school can also furnish a climate in which youngsters sense that certain positive values are desired; it can encourage social groups within the school to reflect some of these major values; and it can select and support teachers whose personalities are attractive to students and who reflect these values. When these things are done, schools and colleges do a great deal in developing the values that are relevant in the changing America.

WORKING WITH THE COMMUNITY

The school is not doing all that it can do if it does not do something in the larger community. This has become clear in the studies made of the slums of large cities. What the children see outside the school in these slums does not represent values that are important for their best development; in fact, these are often negative ones. The school has a part to play in helping communities utilize their youth-serving agencies, in helping get the co-operation of persons who operate business enterprises and others who deal with youth, for only as the community environment is more largely mobilized can constructive values be developed by many youth.

Conclusion

The values of people are important in shaping thought and action. In our rapidly changing society, there are serious problems in the field of values. Some of our older ones need to be re-interpreted in order to make them vital today. Certain new values are needed that are especially important for dealing with the kind of changing world in which we live. Furthermore, our children and youth need to recognize and deal more effectively with the conflicts of values so that they can make wise choices among them. Finally, the schools must clarify their part in the development of values so as to become a more effective means for helping young people build a constructive value system.

II

Contemporary Approaches

Teaching Moral and Spiritual Values in the Public Schools: the Philosophical Issues

ROBERT E. MASON[*]

The remarks which follow have been organized in three divisions. Because of the special relevance of personal bias in a discussion of this particular topic, the first part includes my life history in those dimensions which, it seems to me, may have had something to do with shaping my views on this subject. In the second part, terms are defined, and this essay in definition really makes up the main part of the paper. The third division, however, makes reference to the contemporary situation in the light of the recent court decisions and assesses the possibilities for teaching moral and spiritual values in the public schools within the letter and spirit of those decisions.

INTRODUCTION—PERSONAL BIASES

Although the words *religion, church, temple, synagogue,* or *worship* do not appear in the title, it may be assumed that the topic concerns religion and the place of religious education in schools, particularly public schools. For despite a great library of works in philosophy and ethics treating ethics, morality, and moral education as autonomous and not dependent upon religion and despite occasional suggestions that spiritual experiences are not dependent upon conventional religion for their initiation and sustenance, not only the general public but also professionals familiar with the specialized literature persist in making the connection. It has been

[*] Professor of Education, University of Pittsburgh, Pittsburgh, Pennsylvania.

assumed, therefore, that the central concern is about religion in the schools.

Much of the discussion will be directed to questions of how moral and spiritual dimensions of education may be preserved and extended in public, hence officially religiously neutral, schools. But since there will be this understood reference to religion assumed as a part of the context, it is only fair to indicate something of my own ethnic and religious background. For it is the intimately personal influence of family, kin, and tribe that sets the religious context of life. A man gets his religion from his mother and father, his grandparents, aunts and uncles, and the village or neighborhood which provides his social nurture in his formative years.

The phenomenon of conversion, which some claim to have experienced, and the faith that results have sponsored many noble missionary ventures. I wish to respect it, for religion and religious experience must always be respected and treated with great delicacy, but religious and ethnic nurture are of more fundamental importance than conversion in extending religion among men. It is proper and authentic that replies to questions about religious commitments so frequently take the form, "I was brought up in the Catholic Church," or "I was raised a Baptist," or "I grew up in an Orthodox home." For mostly this is the way religion is perpetuated, conversion often being a conscious renewal of devotion on the part of one who has wandered away or a studied critical commitment to an aspect of one's tradition which has been defined with special meaning in a variant sect.

Here, then, is a little of my own religious nurture, for this is needed in order to evaluate what follows. No matter how coldly objective a writer on religion may try to be, his critical scholarly efforts will inevitably partake of the context in which his mind and personality were nurtured.

My nurture was close to the stereotype of the midwestern cornbelt village boy growing to maturity in the years between the wars. My parents and all my relatives were devout, Bible-reading, evangelical Protestants. We went to church and Sunday School every Sunday, and usually Mother and Father attended mid-week prayer meeting on Wednesday or Thursday evening. It was wrong to go to

The Philosophical Issues 47

movies or dances. It was wrong to play cards, drink, dance, or smoke. The Bible was the word of God. But you could also speak with God—ask Him questions and get answers from Him—if you would close your eyes, kneel down, and concentrate, actually speaking the words. These notions were just as much facts of life as the characteristics of the seasons. There was much arguing about the fine points of theology and the details of the moral casuistry (for example, it was finally determined that you could play "catch" on Sunday, but that it was wrong to get up a ball game; you could buy gasoline on Sunday, but not a loaf of bread or ice cream). Yet despite the continuing challenge of keeping the casuistry up to date in the rapidly changing society of the years between the wars, the basic elements of the faith were never questioned.

Moreover, we had lots of fun. I am neither bitter nor supercilious about this nurture. In fact, the standard pose of superiority and the thread-bare wisecracks which middle-class intellectuals make about Bible-belt Protestantism bore me. There were wonderful Sunday School picnics and pot-lucks that would make a seven–dollar-a-plate smorgasbord look skimpy. There was a jolly folk humor and good nature quite like that which Sam Levenson has so joyfully shared with us from its quite different origins in the Great City. There was a very high level of native intelligence, and everybody looked upon the universities at Ann Arbor and Lansing as their own community property, which indeed in a sense they were. There was good neighborliness, compassion, and a very high level of day-to-day morale. People were really cheerful—consistently so. And this did not change during the depression years, even when all the banks in Toledo closed and two of the three in our little town collapsed, taking the savings of half the people with them. It was tough luck, and so one automatically tried to buck up and help his neighbors do likewise. The closing of the bank was, to a person who had his savings there, like a major crop failure, a fire destroying the house or barn, a bad automobile accident, or "losing the farm because the bank had to foreclose." These were experiences with which the people had long-time intimate familiarity. So they took the Depression in stride; but some of them did grieve when they lost the money that had been saved to take the boy through the first year at the university at Ann Arbor or when the daughter had to come home from Ypsilanti, because she could not find a job to pay her way through the normal school.

The specific theology of this nurture has raised questions in my mind. I have not succeeded in preserving belief in the specifics of the supernaturalist creed. Moreover, the elements of the moral code—that is, the explicit prohibitions of specific acts—in reality expressed peculiar and probably unjustified social taboos. Again, the claim to possession of revealed knowledge was unwholesome in that it encouraged a type of bigotry and closed-mindedness that was not good. With these important disclaimers, however—and they are indeed important—I would proclaim my continued high respect for and appreciation of the nurture which my midwestern rural village origins gave me and would freely grant that my ways of interpreting and responding to my world are, to a considerable degree, products of it.

Definitions of Terms

The stated topic includes two key terms—"moral" and "spiritual." The connotation of these so strongly suggests a reference to religion that we assume its presence; hence the three key terms are, namely: "moral," "spiritual," and "religious."

MORAL

The moral dimension of education is the "So what?" of education and can be distinguished from the purely descriptive or informative dimension, although it is not so easily distinguished from the interpretive dimension. For instance, a child knows that school begins at 8:30 a.m., that he is duly enroled, and that the school rule is that he is to be in his room, seated at his assigned place, at 8:30 a.m. daily when school is in session. These are all items of information, and they can be and are taught as such. Yet a child can know all these things and can still ask, "Why should I go to school now?" when it is time for him to leave home.

And you can tell him, "Because you will be late."

The Philosophical Issues

But he can reply, "Why should I not be late?"
And you can tell him, "Because it is the rule to be on time."
Yet he can still ask, "Why must I obey this rule?"

At about this stage, particularly with young children, some parents and guardians close the argument by resorting to force—overt physical compulsion, threat, or appeal to established authority, e.g. "Because I say so"; "Because it's the law"; "Because if you don't the attendance officer will come and get after you."

Similarly, a child can know that in writing the name of a month, the first letter is to be capitalized. But he could, conceivably, decide that he likes the looks of the word better with a small letter, or he could say that it is too much bother to use capital letters. Why *should* he capitalize the name of a month? Now if anything is worth teaching as information in the first place, it is worth teaching in its moral dimension. That is, if it is worth the time to teach youngsters that *October* is spelled with a capital *O,* it is worthwhile to teach them *to* spell it that way. Yet, the two kinds of teaching are subtly different. To know that *October* is spelled "October" is not quite the same thing as to spell *October,* "*O*-c-t-o-b-e-r," themselves. A youngster can know that it is spelled "*O*ctober" and can still ask us why he must do it that way, since he likes the word better spelled with a small *o*. We are then faced with the problem of how to convince him that he *ought* to spell the word the way it is customarily spelled.

The moral dimension in education is the part designated by the word *ought*. It confronts us at the point where we decide, or take part in deciding, what to teach in the first place. Then it confronts us all the time as we struggle to get youngsters to accept what we teach them and to incorporate this into their lives.

SPIRITUAL

The spiritual dimension of education mainly designates feelings. We want youngsters to feel a certain way when they see the flag and to feel another way when they are taught about children suffering from malnutrition in city slums. We consider that an individual's education has been deficient if he does not experience a certain ecstasy in response to one or more of the following: (1) the discovery of an inlet from a cold spring six feet below the surface of the lake where he swims; (2) the sight of Mount Rainier on a perfectly clear day; (3) a little girl done up in her very best for an important party; or (4) coming up on Lake Michigan, stretching endlessly from the very edge of a meadow on which Wisconsin dairy cows are grazing.

We consider that something has gone wrong in a person's education if he experiences ecstasy—a feeling similar to that some of us have had in situations like those suggested above—in setting fire to a cat, slashing the tires on a new car, beating a child, or smashing a store window to steal the watches left on display there. Spiritual education, then, involves getting youngsters to *feel* good, to "get their kicks," to *be joyful* in experiences of which we approve. That is, to use the simplest of the examples, to enjoy and really feel good about spelling *October* the way it *ought* to be spelled. The spiritual dimension in education is an emotional part. It involves nurture of feelings which make the right things enjoyable, the wrong things distasteful.

RELIGION

Recall that the word *religion* does not appear at all in the title, but I am putting it in because the juxtaposition of the reference to moral and spiritual values immediately suggests religion. Now, what is religion and how is it that whenever we see the reference to moral and spiritual values we think of religion? Of course, there is a library of literature on this theme, so one must take care in stipulating his own definition. Yet I should like to venture one, for otherwise the conventional meanings are so disparate and vague that misunderstanding might indeed be complete.

Religion is how you answer the following questions: (1) Where do babies come from? (2) Why do young people run off and get married? (3) Where do you go when you die? That is, I propose that religion refers to a way of responding to the mysteries of life, love, and death. It includes both the ritualistic and symbolic modes of response, as well as a body of critically formulated cursive statements about these matters.

The Philosophical Issues

What, then is the relationship between religion, spiritual values, and moral values? One way—and this may be taken as the position of the advocate of religious education—is that how you explain life, love, and death determines which things are important enough to teach the young. Then, you try to get them to enjoy and take satisfaction in putting into practice what you teach them. Or again, "morals" means "doing right"; "spiritual" means "wanting to do right and getting enjoyment from doing so"; "religion" means "a way of determining what is right according to accepted beliefs about the ultimate realities."

On the other hand, the secularist makes the proposal that while moral values are of central importance, especially in the work of the lower schools, spiritual values are luxuries, not educational necessities, and religion is unnecessary. The position of the secularist is established on the bases of the foregoing analysis:

(1) Automatic responses making use of the spoken and written language and partaking of socially established ways of dressing, walking, meeting people, caring for property, and amusing oneself must be instilled in order for a person to participate in his society. That is, one has to get people reasonably civilized in order for them to be dependable workers or to profit from going on to college and university. They must have established a repertoire of fixed automatic responses in reading, writing, arithmetic, and social courtesy in order to be "turned loose." The lower schools must have taught them to read, write, compute, and behave properly in order for them to be tolerated in college, university, or in the larger community.

(2) Spiritual values are not necessarily involved in moral education. It is possible to achieve moral education by force and imposition so that the right way of doing things is stamped in with little or no emotional concomitant. Moral education can be quite successful when it is highly disciplinary and routine. This could be argued by giving examples of a range of school atmospheres, from the coldly disciplinary efficiency of a military boarding establishment to the sentimentality of a Pestalozzian primary school. But I doubt very much that we could establish, empirically, that a spiritual dimension is a necessary condition of moral education.

It is possible to achieve moral education by processes like those described currently by proponents of operant conditioning—where situations are so meticulously set up that only the preferred response is reinforced, thus eventually established. Or again, Orwell's *1984* [1] did, indeed, describe an efficient, workable educational program, whether we like it or not.

(3) Religion is unnecessary because it is possible to set up an entire school program on the passing routines of life. Mostly this is what we are doing nowadays. Our Ph.D.'s know little more about life, love, and death than our first graders. Our education deals almost entirely with the foreground of existence. Here in Western civilization we have built up such an enormously complicated scheme of superficial routines that it is possible to remain very, very busy, giving no attention to the mysteries of reality. This way, we do not need religion, because we decide what we ought to do by determining what is being done, and there is no more of a spiritual dimension in morality than in pressing the brake to stop the car—the machine is just made that way. If you are going to drive the car, it is *right* to press the brake to stop it, and there is not much to get excited about either *pro* or *con,* because this is just one of the facts of how the machine is put together.

Let us venture one more attempt to re-state the argument on this point. In one sense, the guidance of religion in rendering explanations of the meaning of life, love, and death is absolutely fundamental in education, because only if you start with clear ideas about these fundamentally important matters can you decide which things are worth teaching at all. Thus, by the illumination of religious insight, the moral choices of things worth teaching are made. All education, thus, becomes moral education and partakes of a spiritual quality. Youngsters and their teachers practice what is taught and thus celebrate what is learned as derived from and supportive of explanations of the great realities of life, love, and death provided by religion. Some such rationale supports parochial education.

A statement of the secular view, on the other hand, is that there is no point in wasting time thinking about life, love, and

[1] George Orwell, *1984* (New York: Harcourt, Brace and World, 1949).

The Philosophical Issues

death. There is no evidence; people disagree radically; and anyway, since we have no dependable knowledge about these matters, why dwell on them at all? Thus, the source of educational authority becomes the civilization which the school has grown to perpetuate. This way, the education of younger children is highly moral because they are not only being informed, but they are being trained and conditioned so that the culture ways are fully and completely internalized. In this process, how they feel about various elements of this training is somewhat unimportant, for what is being imposed upon them is the ways of their civilization—these are to become a part of the very warp and woof of personality, scarcely subject to the contemplative awareness which characterizes spiritual experience. Thus from the secular point of view, the civilization takes the place of religion as a final source of authority; a process of moral indoctrination in which schools for children and younger adolescents carry large responsibility is really a process of socialization or enculturation; such a process of socialization or enculturation with the culture accepted as authority has no necessary relationship to or dependence upon spiritual values. The attitudes of wonder, awe, respect, and reverence which characterize spiritual experience have no necessary part to play in personality formation seen as enculturation.

I propose these two characterizations as designating the contrasting perspectives of religious and secular education. Moral values are fully as central in education for the secularist as for the religionist, but for the secularist moral education is a process of socialization, while for the religionist it is a process depending upon spiritual reinforcement in the light of religion.

The Contemporary Situation

THE RELIGIOUS ISSUE

Before World War II, there had for a long time been relatively little heated discussion about religion and the public schools. After the Civil War, the nineteenth century public schools in America had grown as Protestant Christian institutions, with specific catechetical instruction in the faith of the sect to which the child belonged left to homes and churches. A range of explanations have been given for the intense revival of the religious issue in public education in the last twenty-five years. Most of these represent variations on the theme of the decline of the Protestant majority in the country. By 1940, the children of the millions of immigrants from Eastern and Southern Europe who had flooded through Ellis Island between 1890 and 1920 had become established citizens and taxpayers for whom a Protestant school system was not entirely satisfactory. The old white Anglo-Saxon Protestant domination of the schools has increasingly come in for challenge.

Since World War II, the religious issue in public education has been discussed almost *ad nauseam* and has, one way or another, become entangled in a range of educational issues, some of which have been blurred by the entanglement. This year, we meet in the afterglow of public indignation over the New York State Regents' Prayer, the Pennsylvania and Maryland Bible reading and prayer decisions of the United States Supreme Court. The greatest outcry came, as we recall, in response to the decision affecting New York State policy, with formal efforts to move to impeach the court or amend the Constitution. Only a few months ago, the high court rendered its decision against Bible reading and the Lord's Prayer in the public schools of Abington, Pennsylvania, and Baltimore, Maryland, to which there was, apparently, somewhat less public outcry than in response to the earlier decision. The latter decision has the effect of prohibiting compulsory recitation of the Lord's Prayer and Bible reading in public schools on the ground that these are religious practices constituting a religious establishment, and therefore unconstitutional according to the First Amendment. In this eight-to-one decision, the court stated that study of religion or study of books deemed holy by religious groups, for example the *Bible,* are legitimate when treated as objective phenomena of secular history and literature, while stressing that the state is, nevertheless, firmly committed to a position of neutrality on religion.

These decisions, without question, support the perspective of secular rather than religious education as characterized above. There is to be no worship in school, either in the form of prayer

The Philosophical Issues 55

or devotional reading. Moreover, the sort of spiritual experience which depends upon or arises out of religious devotion or contemplation is not provided in any way. On the other hand, if the knowledge about churches, synagogues, and temples, why people support them, and what they stand for should in some instances issue in spiritual experiences as concomitants, we have no court ruling making this phenomenon unconstitutional. At once, nevertheless, it would seem that a deliberate effort on the part of a teacher to induce spiritual experience as religious experience would be deemed an infringement of the ruling.

SPIRITUAL VALUES

Now, consider again the reference of the designation "spiritual." You remember the examples used—swimming, traveling in the mountains, a vignette of childhood, the country. What about the satisfactions of special intensity that we find in our contacts with nature, works of beauty, and our fellow man? Are these aesthetic, or moral, or spiritual, or religious, or what? The problems of theoretical analyses involved here will only be touched upon briefly:

(1) There is no clear demarcation between aesthetic values and spiritual values. So long as there remains a concern in the secular society of music, art, and the humanities, to make up a strong enough consensus so that taxpayers will have their school money used to support teaching in these areas, the spirit of wonder and awe engendered by things of beauty may occasionally be nurtured in the schools.

(2) In intellectual work, there occasionally emerges a kind of insightful understanding accompanied by the same spirit of awe and wonder. These experiences sometimes occur as students sense the intellectual elegance in a mathematical formula, find excitement in a laboratory phenomena in chemistry, or uncover the heart muscle in dissecting a frog. This is more than gross excitement; there is something here that borders on aesthetic or even spiritual experience. First-rate teaching will produce such experiences; if these are spiritual, they remain within the secular pale unaffected by the court rulings.

We conclude, then, that if spiritual values designate those and only those experiences produced by religious worship as such, the schools are not to educate for them. If, however, spiritual values mean those experiences which come out of aesthetic confrontations of nature, objects of beauty, and examples of intellectual elegance, spiritual values of these non-religious sorts will continue to be fostered in the schools. However, the overwhelming push for speed-up and increased efficiency in schooling threatens even this secular dimension of spiritual experience. The artistic and humanistic studies demand some leisure time for contemplation, and the spirit of wonder in intellectual domains is dampened in a school atmosphere which demands pushing on immediately to the next unit. What I mean to suggest is that the currently popular tendency to push youngsters to the limit in an effort to accelerate quantitatively measurable learnings is a movement which is antithetical to the spirit of wonder, awe, and appreciation of the beauties of our world. If the race with catastrophe has become so desperate that time for wonder no longer can be afforded, I fear that the catastrophe may already have overtaken us. There is no place for the wasting of time, but there must be time to grow, and in working to eliminate inexcusable wasting of time, we must take care not to force growth too much.

MORAL ASPECTS

The moral dimension remains. If the advancement of civilization depends upon the advancement of learning, the perpetuation of civilization from generation to generation so that we do not slip back to barbarism depends upon effective transmission of the mores—upon the unequivocal internalization in the young of the approved ways. Moral education always begins with the approved ways—with what the Greeks called *Dike* and *Themis*—what has been pointed out and what has been established. However, older adolescents and college and university youth should be encouraged to make critical reviews and tests of the ways which have been established. This is the reflexive turn in moral education. It is education as nurture, turned back upon itself and become education as moral criticism.

There are three elements or factors in this process, and the process of criticism is hierarchical: (1) At the first level there is moral education as enculturation or socialization, with the child having been trained to live the elemental ways of his group—to speak and write its language, to make effective use of its system of calculation, to observe its social rituals. (2) When the reflexive process begins—the process of systematic self-criticism—the criteria of judgment are drawn from consideration of the necessary conditions for physical and emotional well-being. Thus may cruelties and injustices in the established ways be identified. This is the second element and the second stage in moral education. But criticism of the established ways in the light of consideration of the well-being of the masses of suffering humanity is not finally conclusive. For to overturn established ways in humanitarian enthusiasm does not necessarily establish viable new ways. Too many enthusiastic young liberals do the cause of lasting liberalism a disservice by persisting in the second stage of moral education. These are the wholesale rebels, the iconoclasts, the vigorous exponents of "throw the rascals out." (3) Responsible moral nurture will encourage vigorous social criticism and will work to expose evils and deficiencies in the established ways. But it will proceed to the third stage of moral education in which the full energy of scholarly criticism will be directed to problems of implementation. This third stage I should like to designate as scientific criticism—not scientific in the sense of always precise experimentation and measurement—but to use critical methods appropriate to human and social phenomena. These cannot always be the precision balances of the physical scientist's laboratory, nor even the mathematical tools developed by the statisticians, valuable as these have become. In this way, the morally responsible social rebel will be taught to stand upon his rebellion against established ways and to propose viable alternatives. Proposed alternatives are then to be weighed and criticized against the old ways, with full effort to weigh assets and liabilities. Sound and responsible moral education encourages rebellion, then imparts the responsibility for formulating proposals of alternatives to that situation against which rebellion is directed. It then imparts the habit of critical evaluation of proposed alternatives among themselves and with the status quo, making use of all relevant research data and techniques. Thus is rebellion transformed into responsible moral leadership.

Conclusion

Moral education remains a central responsibility of the secular school, even after the realm of the spiritual has been merged with the aesthetic, and religious worship has been forbidden. Moral education involves, first, teaching youngsters to practice the approved ways of the society. But with this part of the task fulfilled, moral education returns upon itself to examine the ways taught, asking always whether the ways are at all those points which make for the well-being of mankind. It then encourages rebellion against those ways which seem not to be best, but challenges the moral rebels to come up with positive proposals for improvement. Finally, it teaches them to evaluate the various proposals for change against the status quo, making use of all relevant available scholarly techniques. It supports and encourages advocacy of responsible, critically examined, new alternatives. It affirms the old adage, "Nothing ventured; nothing gained," but emphasizes the importance of making sober, critical selection of that which is to be ventured, with full respect for failures and successes of ways used in the past.

In this manner, significant contribution can be made to moral education under a school policy which reserves worship and the related spiritual experience to home, church, and synagogue. Given some free time to spend at home and at voluntary places of worship, this may be a better way to cultivate the religious and spiritual values in children, anyway. These values are among those so intensely personal that we may better wish to cultivate them in the sanctity of home and chosen place of worship rather than in a public facility.

Summerhill: A Radical Approach to Education

GEORGE VON HILSHEIMER*

INTRODUCTION

Neither Summerhill, nor the American schools inspired by it, are truly experiments. Despite the title, Summerhill is a school demonstrating a well-conceived, adequately proved, and essentially conservative philosophy of education. Summerhill was not and is not an isolated phenomenon. It exists in a tradition that includes the Ford Republic and the Little Commonwealth, The Gorky Colony, The Ferrer Modern School, Finchden Manor, Prestolee (a Lancashire County School) and many others.

These schools have demonstrated, over decades, the adequacy of their pedagogy, both for their stated goals—well integrated and happy people—and the goals of public education—the intellectual and functional training of citizens for economically and politically valid roles in society.

Briefly, the Summerhill idea postulates a school in which (1) the adults' legitimate rule-making authority is limited to health, safety and the requirements of public law, (2) adults and children have an equal voice and vote in the establishment of all other rules, (3) a sort of basic bill of rights limits the kinds of rules the school community can make (i.e. no bill of attainder or *ex post facto* laws, etc.), (4) children are not compelled to attend classes, and (5) the staff's primary goal is a healthy psychological and social climate, and only incidentally intellectual education.[1]

---
* Headmaster, Summerlane School, Mileses, New York.
[1] A. S. Neill, *Summerhill—A Radical Approach to Child Rearing* (New York: Hart Publishing Co., 1960).

The Summerhill concept assumes that co-operative, loving, social, and constructive behavior are a natural and healthy potential of children. It is not to say that children are *intrinsically* good. Children are not *intrinsically* anything other than the potentials permitted them by their societies. There are societies in which no children, other than those with organic pathologies, are antisocial. Our society is obviously not included. Fortunately, there have been few societies like ours in which all children, particularly adolescents, seem to be expected to be antisocial.

It is a sociological cliché that children gain their values from their peers, rather than from their parents and other adults. This is objectively true in much of our society. The point that children do not exist in a vacuum seems rather harder to make. If children get their values from other children, it behooves educators to concern themselves with the process by which values are mediated to those other children. The social reality that has made this ridiculous cliché respectable is the fact that children no longer live in a community. The adult values are, therefore, communicated only as formal and distorted ritualistic gestures. Fathers spend less than a few minutes in each week alone, purposively, with their children. There are few moments of family interaction as a self-conscious, integrated entity. Few children see their fathers at work, at play, or in any significant relationships. Shopkeepers, artisans, neighbors, older children, and older people are geographically, socially, and psychologically removed from children's realities. Children are raised by women barely older than themselves, in an age and social ghetto unrelieved by people with perceivably valuable and comprehensible things to do.

American Public Education

The most valuable contribution of America to political history has been the idea of a free, universal, public education. One of the ironies of Admiral Rickover and Company is that, in asking us to copy Soviet education, we are being asked to copy a copy of ourselves. The Soviets, capable as always of borrowing a good thing, sent scores of educators to investigate American education in the nineteen twenties. Their system was established as a copy of ours. American

Summerhill: A Radical Approach to Education

education was, and is, the leading educational system in the world.

The world in which American public education was developed no longer exists. An educational structure designed for the mass education of an illiterate, poor, and educationally well-motivated population, living in vitally interrelated communities, has diminished relevance for a literate, affluent population, conditioned to entertainment and advertising in a community-less society. It is perhaps too long since the root assumptions of "comprehensive, centralized, public" school were re-examined. Dr. Conant notwithstanding, the need for elaborate equipment does not justify the central school with its huge student body. Schools like Summerhill, and many other much more conservative schools, have demonstrated for half a century that elaborate laboratories, audio-visual equipment, and the rest of the entertainment-related paraphernalia of modern schools are not needed to educate students competent to compete with graduates of the "best" schools. In fact, overwhelming evidence suggests that such administrative crutches hinder good teachers.

The mass school exacerbates the poverty of real persons in a child's life. Even though, on paper, the central school presents a richer display of resources, it is, in fact, culturally poverty-stricken as it is perceived by the child. It was difficult enough for the one-room school teacher to get to know her children. She had, however, the tremendous advantage of being forced to leave the children to their own devices, within the structure of the school, for the majority of the school day. She had the tremendous resource of the social authority and knowledge of older children to share with the little ones. She had, in most cases, a continuity of years in which to know, and most important, to be known. Even if a child came from an isolated farm in which he was the only child, he found in this structure of schooling a vital and real community.

SOME CHERISHED MYTHS

It is not necessary for us to tear down the central school to revert to older standards of teacher preparation, curriculum, and pedagogy, or to dismantle the entire megapolis culture we have grown in order to realize the advantage of a schooling rooted in community.

It is necessary merely to discard some cherished myths about schooling.

Why do children go to school at age five or six? Is there any objective evidence that this age is the best? If there is such evidence, is it reasonable to assume that, unlike all other human phenomena, this one readiness occurs in the entire population of six-year-olds on the same day in September? Would it really be administratively so difficult to allow variation? Is our nation so poor that it cannot truly afford choice? Is it necessary so thoroughly to distrust parents and children that their opinions about readiness must be discounted in every case? The evidence demonstrates that children who escape school until they are eleven or twelve or older catch up with otherwise similar children in six months to a year. What are we doing to the other children in those first six years if educationally we can accomplish the same thing in six months?

Is the optimum period of instruction thirty minutes? Six hours? Experiments have shown that children learn more when taught the same content for five minutes rather than ten. The average adult attention span is eight minutes. It is rather shorter for children. Are our schools really overcrowded, or do we send children to them too soon, for too long at a time, in too large groups? What would happen if, instead of thirty children five days a week, a teacher had six different children one day each per week?

Of course, these questions and the thousand similar ones that might be asked assume that the purpose of the school is to provide a place in which children may grow most adequately. As the headmaster of an idealistic school supported by dedicated parents, I can afford such quaint notions; I can afford largely to ignore the political realities that public school systems must face. Still, if public education cannot be made perfect, it can be perfected.

Children's Self-Determination

When Homer Lane was director of playgrounds in Detroit (1906), his city voted a large expansion of facilities, with funds for professional staffing. At the same time, Cleveland expanded its facilities but did not provide for staff. Lane was jolted out of his complacency when juvenile delinquency began to go down in Cleveland, but to rise in Detroit. He spent many days on the playgrounds and slum streets of both cities, determining finally that the recreation program itself was, as it appeared, responsible for the increase. When adults inflict their agenda on children, with small regard for the interests and needs of children, something has to break down. Children must be importantly involved in the determination of their own activities and social regulations. This insight of Lane's became the central idea of The Little Commonwealth, a school primarily for juvenile offenders. These young criminals were *forced* to accept the responsibility of choosing their work, their activity, and the kind of social regulation they would live by. Adult staff members were participants and facilitators; they did not abandon the children, neither did they mistakenly assume that they knew what was best for them.[2]

THE ADVENTURE PLAYGROUNDS

Lane's experience is reflected in the modern development in England and Scandinavia of the Adventure Playgrounds. A fenced-off area and building supplies and tools are provided, with only one adult— a sort of facilitator, not a program director—as the entire facility.

The evidence is clear that children can be left alone productively, safely, with good pedagogical results. It may be of interest to note that the insurance rates on Adventure Playgrounds is now less than that of orthodox playgrounds. They are not only more fun; they are safer. The Tom Sawyer image of our past, and the real past of nearly everyone who reads this, saw children exploring, playing, roaming freely for many hours each week in the company of others, older and younger children. The last twenty years has produced the first generations of Americans that do not importantly associate with, rely on, and assume responsibility for unrelated children in large numbers and of different ages. The objection that our urban society will not permit such freedom safely cannot seriously be taken. The Adventure Playgrounds have been measured by the quite unsentimental standards of insurance actuaries.

[2] Homer Lane, *Talks to Parents and Teachers* (New York: Hermitage Press, Inc., 1949), pp. 207-212.

THE SETTLEMENT HOUSES

Nor have our educational attempts to reduce the dangers of urban life been at all helpful. Juvenile delinquency has increased in every area in which a well-funded program has operated in this country. The University Settlement House, the first in America, is in the center of the worst drug and conflict problem in New York City. Henry Street Settlement House, perhaps the best known of its kind in America, watched Henry Street become known as "Blood Alley," an epithet removed only with the large scale demolition of the neighborhood and the "progress" of gangs from fighting to drug addiction. It is not a coincidence, nor simply a function of enthusiasm, that nearly every small, understaffed, underpaid storefront project, does in fact reduce delinquency and help a substantial majority of its cases enter the productive world. Economic and social realities force such programs to rely on the children. The adults are facilitators offering facilities to children. They focus on the children and not on their theory of education, rehabilitation, or social welfare.

THE "CONSERVATIVE" SCHOOL

Given the educative strengths of a vital community, given the social ability of children in a supportive community, given the biological and psychological disposition to growth in all organisms, a school which structures itself to take advantage of these root abilities is indeed a conservative school. The simple process of providing facilities for children, with adults who have the maturity to remain adults and to set aside their preconceptions in order to facilitate growth and not direct a curriculum, is demonstrably valid. The curriculum-obsessed, theory–centered, classroom–focused school is indeed the radical attempt to force a new and unnatural psychology on the child.

Most of the pressures inflicted on children are caused by adults' inability to remain adult. Biologically, the job of children is to play and play and play. Physically, they are about the task of differentiating nerve endings, sophisticating muscular control, learning all the complex activities that go into mature abilities. Social conventions, manners, and intellectual disciplines are no more difficult, biologically considered, than speaking, running, balancing a broom, or climbing a tree. Conventions taught by rote cannot become integral, nor can intellectual disciplines learned in fear of failure become vital. It is interesting that, uniformly, the students of Summerhill and other child-centered schools are regarded as almost courtly in their social bearing away from the school and toward strangers at the school. Their intellectual curiosity and discipline is awesome to behold and to try to serve, once the period of regurgitating artifically induced motives is over.

Summerlane School

At our school no attempt to encourage manners is made in a self-conscious way at all—although an adult, or a child, has a perfect right to ask someone to take offensive behavior out of their room, or out of public rooms. No attempt to persuade intellectual interest is made. A teacher may demand discipline as a requisite of a class—the student does not have to attend. Since we pay a great deal more attention to pedagogy at Summerlane than at some schools, I cannot say that intellectual interest is not encouraged. The encouragement however, is encouragement by competence, relevance, and interest. It is not moral suasion. The only regular complaint about classes at Summerlane is that there are not enough—despite the fact that, for teen-agers, classes go on in the evening as well as during regular school hours.

The necessity felt by most adults for compelling children to moral behavior, to productive behavior, and to learning is predicated on the assumption that children are inherently antisocial, wasteful, and willfully ignorant. This assumption has to be predicated upon vast feelings of inadequacy in the adult himself. An adult who is confident of his own identity has no need to enter what amounts to an ego struggle with a child. We are aware that irrational feelings of inadequacy, irrational needs to protect ego, irrational values and behaviors afflict everyone. It is necessary to build into the structure, the ethics of the school protections against our inevitable adult failures.

DEMOCRATIC EDUCATION

The Summerhill school takes seriously the political history of the West in recognizing that democracy is a process that does not depend on superior personalities to make it work. Indeed, democracy has demonstrably worked with quite mediocre, even venal, personalities at the helm of national states. By granting the child the franchise, Summerhill guarantees correction of the abuses of power. A teacher who exceeds his authority can be disciplined. Indeed, the superior teacher in this school deliberately takes actions that will guarantee her being disciplined when she suspects the children are taking her too seriously. So long as a teacher can remember that her job is not to have a popular classroom, or even to be loved or liked, but to guarantee that children begin to assume self-responsibility, she will be able to remain adult. We do not straighten the clothes of our adult peers, nor spit-bathe them, nor make their beds, nor correct their grammar, nor offer them serious criticism of their behavior before others—if we wish to retain their friendship. How much less respectful of the integrity of children are we? We do not expect them to be competent, and lo, they accommodate us. It is not necessary to assume that children are knowledgeable, experienced, or as competent as an adult in order to behave toward them as if we had the advantage of some civilization ourselves. Nearly everyone has had the experience of gladly suffering a fool. None of us treat adult ignoramuses, boors, or incompetents rudely until they have exhausted all patience. The Summerhill idea might be summed up simply as intending to act toward children with the same courtesy we grant our peers.

Decision-making.—The function of democratic education is to teach the effective, knowledgeable, responsible making of decisions. In a democracy it is imperative that the citizens respect authority only when it is based on knowledge, responsible power, and competence. A teacher must let the child know that his authority comes not from being older and bigger, or being dressed in a suit, or having a title, but from the mastery of his subject. A teacher must be capable of deliberately making mistakes, of being wrong, and wrongheaded, of being set back without rancor, of being chastized in good humor, and also of being quite unreasonable and stupidly so. Otherwise, the child will trust simply in the teacher and not look to the facts, the experiences, the realities of the living situation. A child who is taught that authority flows from position, that respect is due age without competence, cannot be taught the intrinsic and superior worth of discipline, order, or courtesy, but simply obedience.

The responsibility of freedom.—Children were more rebellious, more independent, less respectful of arbitrary and incompetent authority a generation or so ago. My most difficult task as a headmaster in a "free" school is to create situations in which the children will rebel. It seems as if the only freedoms American adolescents even recognize any more are to stay up late, to smoke, to drink, and to make noise. Children everywhere have been conditioned to incredible indignities. Not only do they not want freedom, they are terrified of it.

Now some critics will think they have utterly destroyed the arguments for student-centered schools by insisting that children do not want freedom. Precisely! Some inmates of Auschwitz were brought to the state of loving their keepers. Not only is the objection irrelevant but is indeed ironic, coming from proponents of disciplinary education who advocate giving children what is best for them.

Our school requires the student to stay at the school for at least a year—with reasonable exceptions—for exactly the reason that children will seek the escape valve of their queerly permissive authoritarian home and public school in order to avoid the responsibilities of freedom. We insist that children not go home for weekends. They will stay up late into the night for a week and then run home, where Mama will make them sleep. When they are *required* to face their own need, they begin to discipline themselves. Although it may offend common sense, the disciplinarian family is often the most indulgent. There seems to be a rigid psychological consistency, if not a necessity, in those families which most often inflict irrelevant disciplines on their children—clothes, cleanliness, noise, deportment —to most easily collapse when a serious conflict such as, wanting to leave school, getting married, buying a car arrives. It is ironic that as a headmaster of a free school, I far more often counsel parents in how to say, "No," than otherwise.

The "permissive" philosophy.—The Summerhill philosophy, at least as we practice it at Summerlane, is not a "permissive" philosophy. Nor do I think it legitimately belongs in the Progressive tradition. Progressive education was preoccupied with curriculum and pedagogy. Summerlane is preoccupied with community and values. It is our contention that, in a cultured community, intellectual education is safely subsumed.

One of the reasons the Summerhill philosophy is not a permissive one is that adults do not have the authority to permit. Children, particularly new students, frequently come to ask me for an exception to a school rule. I can only say, "'The law is such-and-so, and I am only the headmaster—that is to say, I am the head teacher; I am a teacher, not a cop." The only "permissions" I can grant are violations of my own privacy or integrity, and as an impatient and perfectionistic personality, I am not likely to do so.

Of course, most of the behavior of children that causes Summerhill to be regarded as "permissive" is simply beneath the attention of a serious teacher. Americans must be the most guilt-laden people in the history of the world if their handwashing obsessions and related neuroses regarding dirt, messiness, haircuts, proper clothes, and noise are any indication. This obsessive concern for irrelevant issues is well on the way to destroying teaching in America.

The teacher's position.—Despite the fact that a teacher at Summerlane must have the maturity to intend to be wrong, it is important to say that, in all the community and personal relationships, the teacher cannot see herself as a manipulator. Technique is valid and necessary in the classroom (and a school meeting, particularly in the beginning, is a classroom), it is out of place in honest friendship. Honesty, even of the most personal sort, is possible in this community; we have increasingly found that our opinions can safely be shared with students; misbehavior can openly be reported and discussed; other issues usually regarded as private and protected by the staff are not by children and do not need to be. A teacher must be willing to admit her mistakes and to accept the consequences of them. It is vital that she not importantly see her living relationship with children as manipulative.

The teacher has a legitimate and necessary function in the school and the community. However, a curriculum-centered pedagogy is as impractical as a surgery that strictly follows a chart of average human anatomy. This is quite as just an analogy of creative curricula as of static and traditional curricula. A public education that requires most of the teachers to file daily lesson plans rejects the reality of all good teaching experience. I can guarantee the most conservative principal that I will cover reading, writing, and arithmetic in the course of a day of teaching; but, if I take seriously a developmental lesson plan, I ought to turn in my license—which, is, of course, why most teachers do not take them seriously.

The curriculum and technique.—Paul Goodman has a lovely line in *Empire City* in which he says, in effect, that the job of a school is to make a person at home in the city and to subvert it.[3] That is, a valid education gives a man the skills and knowledge necessary to utilize his culture fully, to evaluate it clearly, and to take action to change it. This presumes a great deal more than the curriculum of most public schools. It is the presumption that we make at Summerlane, and that our experience and that of other Summerhill-variants have proved possible.

One of the great disappointments to most teachers in Neill's books is that these contribute little to classroom technique. This is so, because he is convinced that a happy child in a literate culture will be literate and intellectually competent to carry out such tasks as he might want to. In a culture in which unhappiness is almost the stigma of membership, Neill believes it is necessary to overemphasize the techniques of remaining happy.

I would borrow from Sylvia Ashton-Warner the term "organic education" to describe the teaching technique and curriculum organization that ideally is practiced at Summerlane, and, so far as I can determine, at Summerhill.[4]

I have not yet encountered a child that will not learn to read, and read well, if left alone in a *literate and vitally interrelated community*. We have enjoyed numerous controlled experiences which indicate that the improvement of intellectual abilities continues in our school even when the students avoid class like the plague. Two girls, aged eight and eleven, attended from September to Thanksgiving last year.

[3] Paul Goodman, *Empire City* (New York: Macmillan, 1964).
[4] Sylvia Ashton-Warner, *Teacher* (New York: Simon & Shuster, 1963), p. 27 ff.

They returned to their former public school and to the same group of children where they had been the previous year. One had been a mediocre student; she re-entered at the top of the class. The younger had been at the top of the class and re-entered there, but neither one had attended a single "class" at Summerlane. This might simply be evidence that nothing is really taught in a superior suburban school between September and the end of November; however, I submit that real education goes on in any literate community as long as adults are freely available in real and living situations.

For the education of adolescents who have been brought up in Summerlane, there is little the teacher does that is not an ordinary part of the interaction of an intellectual community. That is, someone writes, produces, directs, and plays a drama. The school plays a Shakespearean drama. The events themselves are comparative and evaluative. There is discourse, argument, and ego-protection. The disciplined, cultured, knowledgeable individuals in the community exercise the authority of their discipline, culture, and knowledge. They can not fake it in this kind of living community. Individuals read and read and read. They talk. They debate. An authority delivers himself of a new idea, buttressed by such evidence as he can marshall. The community reacts.

Essentially, once a child has learned to read and to compose and to put some distance between criticism of his effort and his personality needs, there is little you can do as a teacher other than to enjoy the growth and cultivation of another unique and precious individual. The amount, intensity, and catholicity of reading at Summerlane is incredible. Impressive, as well, to more conservatively-minded evaluators is the 10 to 20 per cent increase in scores on reading and intelligence tests that occurs with the average student in the first semester. High school education at Summerlane is ideally tutorial, scholastic, self-disciplining, and productive. Each new adolescent, however, apparently must go through the process of finding superior alternatives to the lecture-class he has been taught to recognize as education.

Elementary education.—Elementary education, however, is a valid profession, even at Summerlane. The elementary classroom always has at least two teachers, often as many as ten. The number of

Summerhill: A Radical Approach to Education

students is always under thirty. The room is large and has an easily accessible half-second-story for reading and solitary, quiet study, or sloth. The main room is organized with messy corners, book corners, and display corners, and it leads into a small shed with a shop and very messy things (predominantly carcasses). The two core teachers establish themselves as activity and emotional "poles" in the room.

Without directing the children to either teacher, each teacher moves into his own activity as the day begins. One is active, outgoing, louder, attending to painting, clay, building, and rambling outside. The other is quieter and more passive, the reader, writer, and builder of songs and other scholarly activities. It is important that these divisions not be made in a merely mechanistic fashion, and that either teacher may perform any task in the schoolroom. Every effort is made to associate books, schooling, reading, with a relaxed purposiveness.

This dynamic structure of classroom, freely offering children emotional and experiential choices, seems to me essential to accelerated learning. While the size of our class is obviously helpful, it is not necessary. I have established three teachers in a bare classroom, 50 x 40 feet, with 100 illiterate migrant children and have accomplished much more than would have been done with three classes of 30-plus each. While large classes are more difficult than small, they are not an excuse for less freedom but an imperative and opportunity for more.

Reading periods are about the same time each morning. They are sometimes skipped entirely as the teacher senses the tone of the children—or they tell her, "None of that stuff today." Sometimes reading classes consume the day. The littlest children are asked what word they would like. It is printed on a card and given to them for theirs. Or it is written on the board, and the teacher builds a sentence suggested by others, sometimes grammatically and developmentally, sometimes working the sentence out from the middle or ungrammatically. Proper word structure is seen as a function of the culture of the community. Understanding of proper structure is seen as a function of linguistic analysis, which goes on from the earliest class.

Once the child learns—quite quickly, given the presence of children who have been at the school before—that the teacher will not judge or punish his production of words, a large number of obscene and scatological words are produced. So long as the teacher maintains a neutral attitude toward the words, treating them no differently from others, the obsession disappears, inevitably to return when visitors or trauma approach the classroom. Like so much of childish behavior, cursing has little or nothing to do with its obvious motive, sex or religion, but everything to do with power over adults. So long as adults behave as immature and unprofessional "fetishists," children will periodically be obsessed with such words. Our attitude at Summerlane toward teachers who are shocked by these words and this process of learning is quite as if they were medical doctors who refused to treat "private" portions of the body.

Writing is developed in much the same way. Children write what interests them, and read the writing of others. Tape recordings or transcripts of their own little stories, or nonsense, or refusals are made, typed, or mimeographed, and reading proceeds apace. There is no "Up, Up, Up, John" at Summerlane. Illustrations of words made by the children, collages of words and illustrations, "dada" stories made up by pasting word cards, and other techniques well known to all good teachers are a part of our regular armament.

Sociology and political science are ridiculous subjects to offer students who have not been shepherded through and in vital contact with their society. The city, no less than the countryside, is a vital and necessary classroom, and this does not mean guided museum tours. Quite young children can see the dramatic change of neighborhood lines, the abrupt economic change at a state line, the significant flow of foot traffic, the flow of vehicular traffic seen from the street and from a high building, the difference in taste of a commercial bread and a home-baked bread or salad dressings. They can ask and answer penetrating questions about the reasons for such phenomenon. Why are almost all the trees from Boston to Cleveland the same size? Why are the trees in that field all different in size, but the majority of trees the same size? Why are trees here regularly placed? Why are farms here and abandoned buildings there? Where is the soil more fertile? Why? Why do chicken farmers have little round houses?

The function of the teacher is to point, to pry, to prod, to prick, to question, and always, always to draw back from and to look and learn from what the children are seeing and asking. A cultured teacher, living in a community of cultured persons, cannot avoid communicating that culture to children when she is actively involved with the children. The only textbooks she needs are the ones which she uses for herself.

Silencing the critics.—It is possible to say, "Yes! Yes!" to all of this and then to object, "But you have the children all day, every day; but you have dedicated teachers in an incredible ratio to children; but you have only sixty children."

I have taught in every cultural level in America from migrant farm workers to Scarsdale, New York. I have taught in Chicago's Black Belt, in middle class St. Louis and Miami; I have suffered Army brats in Germany, have been the visiting counselor for a religious education program covering the country east of the Mississippi and have run remedial programs in the Lower East Side and Harlem in Manhattan. I have worked with a well-qualified professional staff, with middle-class volunteers, and with illiterate volunteers and staff. I have not yet found a situation in which it is impossible to focus on the needs of the student as expressed by himself and to use this technique as a superior means of education.

We discovered, despite the official pessimism of the board of education, that it is possible to teach absolutely illiterate Puerto Rican delinquents to their age equivalent in six months. Of course, we had to begin by having them read Spanish comic books. In fact, we found that Puerto Rican children (even forty to the class) can be taught to read English in one or two hour-sessions once they have been taught to read in Spanish (which is always easier). We found that comic books are faster than textbooks and more rapidly raise the level of vocabulary. We have done this with professionally trained people and with personnel totally untrained before joining a volunteer staff.

At Summerlane, a fifteen-year-old boy, doing the seventh grade or the third time, has come to us for three months, *has taken not a single class,* and has returned successfully to a ninth grade class in public school.

Individual teachers, trained in our program, have taken New York City classes and accelerated them to average standing, despite the fact they started with basically illiterate slum classes, overcrowded, and inadequately supplied. It is not necessary to have a whole loaf in order to improve.

New York State has more administrators in the school program than all of Western Europe; New York City has more than France. One wonders what would happen to the teacher/pupil ratio were these administrators returned to the classroom. One wonders how much greater time for teaching the teacher might have without the advantage of all that administrative overburden.

In East Harlem, a program of volunteer teachers, meeting with as many as thirty children in slum apartments, was able to bring the majority of children to within 80 per cent of their national percentile in basic skills within two months. In Trenton, New Jersey, Princeton college students working in slum homes were able to accomplish much the same thing.

Let us grant that all experiments accomplish a great deal simply because someone is paying exceptional attention to the subjects; let us grant that enthusiasm and novelty are great accelerators. Having granted that, let us recognize that experimentation, undue and unusual attention, enthusiasm and novelty, and the use of many non-professionals are essential parts of a vital curriculum.

Operation of the school.—Summerlane differs from other Summerhill-variants in that it is owned co-operatively by the staff. The staff hires no service personnel. Every teacher is seen by the children, helped by the children, in daily living tasks vital to the ongoing needs of the community. Inevitably, some teachers are forced to specialize outside the classroom in carpentry, cooking, or other jobs. Still, their classroom work does not suffer. Indeed, they have a new authority with the children because they are real and vital people, not simply because they are formally appointed "teacher." Indeed, when new staff have difficulty with their own self-regulation and shirk their non-academic work, they are rejected by the children as teachers until they do become more vital to the community.

This interaction of the working and academic aspects can be achieved in public schools. The Lancashire County School at Prestolee is a vital example of this. There are no closed classrooms. Classes may be held in the hall as likely as in the room. Few books are bought in duplicate. The entire town is the school, and the school belongs to the whole town. It is open day and night. All the citizens are its students and teachers. The public school has been made truly "public." The official teacher pupil/ratio is worse than in New York City, the budget is smaller, even considering differences in national economics. The administrative problems in an English industrial town are quite as difficult as anywhere else, yet, the school is a vital and challenging center of the community.[5]

The profoundly disturbing thing is that superior techniques of administration, teaching, and school structure have been demonstrated at every conceivable class level, in every sort of social situation, in many countries, for many years. Even if one is simply interested in better scores on tests, it has been clearly demonstrated that the superior pedagogy is one that allows the student maximum choice. Yet we persevere in enthusiasms for minor curriculum changes, abominations like ETV, and the proliferation of administration isolation. It is a wonder that our children survive us!

[5] Gerard Holmes, *The Idiot Teacher* (London: Faber and Faber, Ltd., 1960).

A Descriptive Analysis of Approaches to School Desegregation

PETER H. BINZEN *

"THE PROBLEM of the Twentieth Century," W. E. B. DuBois wrote prophetically in 1903, "is the problem of the color-line." [1] Sixty-one years later, DuBois' words ring true almost everywhere in the world. In Africa, in Asia, certainly in the United States, the problem of pigmentation is paramount.

For a long time, white Americans viewed the race problem as a regional dilemma. We in the North pointed an accusing finger at the South. Impatiently, we implored it to do something. We seemed to think that if only the Southern states would exhibit goodwill and compassion, all of our worries about the American Negro would vanish.

We cheered when the United States Supreme Court on May 17, 1954, interpreted the federal Constitution in a new way, thus forcing the South into steps that it had refused to take voluntarily.[2] The court's historic ruling overthrew a cherished article of faith in the Southern way of life—the belief that schools are social institutions and that the races should be separate in all things social. Specifically, the court found unconstitutional laws requiring racial segregation in the public schools of 17 Southern and Border states—laws that had been implicitly authorized by the same court 58 years earlier.

---

* Education Editor, *The Bulletin,* Philadelphia, Pennsylvania.
[1] W. E. B. DuBois, *The Souls of Black Folk* (Greenwich, Conn.: Fawcett Publications, Inc., 1961), p. vi; originally published Gloucester, Mass.: Peter Smith, Publisher, 1903.
[2] *Brown* v. *Board of Education,* 74 S. Ct. 686 (1954).

The 1954 decision said nothing, however, about segregation that existed in fact, but was not required by law, in schools of Pennsylvania, New York, New Jersey—most states outside the South. And the court's failure to take cognizance of the larger problem tended to reinforce our mistaken impression that there was no larger problem. Events of recent months and years have made clear how wrong we were. At last the race problem is seen in its totality as one transcending regions and confronting the entire nation and world.

A Means of Social Change

Public education finds itself at the heart and center of the race problem in this country, and if solutions are to be worked out, they may come through the schools. For strong pressures are now being exerted to use the schools as instruments of social change. One sees this in Philadelphia, where the Board of Education has pledged to work for integration. One sees it in New York, where a major effort at reassigning children to other schools simply for the sake of racial balance is now underway.

It is worth noting that this role of the schools—as instruments of social change—is historically unusual. More often, American public schools have been used to guard against change rather than to promote it. Merle Curti, in his book, *The Social Ideas of American Educators*, wrote:

> We tend to think of our American system of public schools as having been founded out of a great zeal for the welfare of the plain people. But actually this zeal was tempered by zeal for the welfare of the employers of labor, by zeal for maintaining the political and social *status quo*. These economic motives were frankly recognized in the days of the founding. Now, however, looking back, we tend to rationalize, and to recognize only the more idealistic motives, which were of course also operative.[3]

Daniel Webster, in promoting public schools, said they would support society against the "slow but sure undermining of licentious-

---

[3] Merle Curti, *The Social Ideas of American Educators* (Paterson, N.J.: Pageant Bks, Inc., 1959), p. 85.

ness" and "open violence and overthrow." [4] Edward Everett favored educating mechanics since "an intelligent class can scarce be, as a class, vicious." [5] David Page's *Theory and Practice of Teaching,* which for half a century was widely used by teachers, emphasized their duty to make children aware of the "sacredness of all property." [6]

Curti thinks that the social evils of industrialism in the early nineteenth century helped spread a wave of humanitarianism, paving the way for establishment of tax-supported schools. But to win their fight, says Curti, such humanitarians as Horace Mann had to convince the ruling classes that universal education would save them money and assure their continued domination.

A similar argument was advanced by Sidney L. Jackson, writing in the *Pennsylvania Magazine* of July, 1942. "That education should serve as a means of social control was the design, apparently, of those who most vigorously promoted it," said Jackson.[7] He thought public education was supported primarily by the political right rather than the left. "Though, curiously, education was sometimes advertised by left-wingers as a good investment for those who feared social change," Jackson added, "it was more generally considered 'the only *sure foundation* of freedom and public safety,' and 'the palladium of our liberties.'" [8]

The Supreme Court's Decisions

Seen in light of this history, the Supreme Court's 1896 decision in *Plessy* v. *Ferguson* [9] appears a model decision for social control, while the 1954 ruling in *Brown* v. *Board of Education* breaks precedent by requiring Southern schools to affect social change.[10]

The contrasting language in these two opinions makes interesting

[4] *Ibid.,* p. 86.
[5] *Ibid.,* p. 87.
[6] *Ibid.,* p. 85.
[7] Sidney L. Jackson, "Labor, Education, and Politics in the 1830's, *Pennsylvania Magazine,* LXVI (July, 1942), 292.
[8] *Ibid.,* p. 284.
[9] *Plessy* v. *Ferguson,* 163 U.S. 537, 16 S. Ct. 1138 (1896).
[10] *Brown* v. *Board of Education, op. cit.*

Analysis of Approaches to School Desegragation

reading. Actually, of course, *Plessy* v. *Ferguson* dealt with racial segregation on railroad trains, but the court took the opportunity to endorse school segregation as well. And in doing so, it cited, no doubt with relish, an 1849 decision by the Massachusetts Supreme Court upholding school segregation in the Yankee stronghold of Boston. The Massachusetts Legislature outlawed segregation in 1855, but the U. S. Supreme Court still dragged the Bay State precedent into federal jurisprudence, albeit by a side door. Said the court:

> Laws permitting, and even requiring, their separation (of the races) in places where they are liable to be brought into contact do not necessarily imply the inferiority of either race to the other, and have been generally, if not universally, recognized as within the competency of the state legislatures in the exercise of their police power. The most common instance of this is connected with the establishment of separate schools for white and colored children, which has been held to be a valid exercise of the legislative power even by courts of States where the political rights of the colored race have been longest and most earnestly enforced.[11]

The court went on to deny the argument that compulsory segregation of the races stamped the Negro with a badge of inferiority. "If this be so," the justices held in 1896, "it is not by reason of anything found in the act, but solely because the colored race chooses to put that construction upon it." [12]

Now hear the same court in 1954. The unanimous opinion, written by Chief Justice Earl Warren, quoted approvingly a Kansas lower-court finding:

> "segregation of white and colored children in public school has a detrimental effect upon the colored children. The impact is greater when it has the sanction of the law; for the policy of separating the races is usually interpreted as denoting the inferiority of the negro group. A sense of inferiority affects the motivation of a child to learn." [13]

Justice Warren also stated:

---

[11] *Plessy* v. *Ferguson, op. cit.,* p. 544.
[12] *Ibid.,* p. 551.
[13] *Brown* v. *Board of Education, op. cit.* p. 691.

> ... To separate them (Negro students) from others of similar age and qualifications solely because of their race generates a feeling of inferiority as to their status in the community that may affect their hearts and minds in a way unlikely ever to be undone.[14]

While finding segregation with or without the sanction of law detrimental to Negroes, the court did not call for desegregation across the board and across the country but only in those states where the pupils were mandatorily separated by race.

SUBSEQUENT LITIGATION

In the ten years since then, the High Court has never said what, if anything, school boards must do to break up the segregation that exists because of housing patterns rather than laws. In May of this year, the justices left standing a decision that school boards have no constitutional duty to end racial imbalance resulting from housing. The case came from Gary, Indiana. Complainants charged that Gary's school board had no right to "acquiesce" in de facto segregation which found 97 per cent of the Negro children attending predominantly Negro schools. A lower federal court, ruling in favor of the school board, had said that racial balance in our public schools is not constitutionally mandated. The U. S. Supreme Court did not pass judgment on the merits of the case; it simply refused to review the lower-court ruling.[15]

However, those who oppose such integration steps by northern school boards as busing and school pairings have taken comfort from the Supreme Court's non-decision. They argue that school boards may accept the racial status quo found in neighborhoods without trying to foster integration. And with the Supreme Court refusing to speak out, they cite the interpretation of the 1954 decision given by the late U. S. Circuit Court Judge John J. Parker. When one of the original school segregation decisions came to him for implementation in 1955, Judge Parker sought to spell out exactly what the high court had decided and what it had not decided:

---

[14] *Ibid.*
[15] *New York Times,* May 5, 1964, pp. 1, 27.

Analysis of Approaches to School Desegragation

"[The Supreme Court] has not decided that the states must mix persons of different races in the schools or must deprive them of the right of choosing the schools they attend. What it has decided, and all that it has decided, is that a state may not deny to any person on account of race the right to attend any school that it maintains." [16]

School Plans to Effect Integration

IN NEW YORK CITY

In any event, many Northern school boards are not waiting for the Supreme Court to tell them what they must do. New York City started the fall term by experimenting with the so-called Princeton Plan of pairing elementary schools to effect integration. Under this arrangement, which was first tried in Princeton, New Jersey, the boundaries of a predominantly white elementary school and a predominantly Negro one nearby are joined. Instead of continuing as six-year schools, however, they become three-year schools. All the children, white and Negro, in the enlarged attendance area, go to one school for the first three years and switch to the other for the second three.

New York paired eight schools. Only about 3,000 of New York's one million public school children were involved, and bus transportation was needed for only about 300. The rest of the children lived close enough to walk to their school.[17] Modest as the program was, it provoked bitter protests from organizations of white parents. They staged a boycott which kept tens of thousands of children out of school for the first days of the term. The boycott was not as massive as the one staged last winter by Negro groups protesting the New York school board's alleged failure to move fast enough on integration. But it showed how high feelings run when the schools are used as instruments of social change.

For a number of years, New York has sought to desegregate its schools through a policy of open enrolment. The school board pays for the transportation of pupils taking part in this program. Hun-

[16] J. W. Peltason, *58 Lonely Men* (New York: Harcourt, Brace and World, Inc., 1961), p. 22.
[17] *New York Times,* September 8, 1964, p. 1; September 10, 1964. p. 26.

dreds avoid ghetto schools in this way, but in a city the size of New York, the impact of open enrolment is almost negligible. New York also has set up a central zoning unit, headed by an assistant superintendent whose approval is required for all new school construction. His job is to see that schools are built in integrated areas whenever possible. But since Negroes and Puerto Ricans comprise about 75 per cent of the public school enrolment in Manhattan, the most densely populated of the five boroughs of New York, site selection does not help in fostering integration much of the time.

THE PHILADELPHIA SITUATION

Despite all the criticism of New York's desegregation effort and despite the boycott troubles its school board has encountered, the nation's largest city has clearly led the way in tackling the problem of de facto segregation. In all candor, Philadelphia had done very little about this until late in 1963. Then it became apparent that Federal Judge Harold K. Wood would require action, and much more than token action, from the board. Judge Wood has jurisdiction over a suit filed by the Philadelphia chapter of the National Association for the Advancement of Colored People, accusing the school system of discriminating against Negro pupils and teachers.

Last fall the two sides reached an agreement which kept the suit from going to trial then and may have avoided trial of the case permanently, although Judge Wood still has jurisdiction and the NAACP has said it may yet go to trial if it is not satisfied with the progress of desegregation here.[18] Under the agreement, the board ordered a freeze of teachers to prevent transfers from slum schools. It now limits the choice of new teachers coming into the school system. And special rules apply to schools where the teacher vacancy rate exceeds 10 per cent, that is, in schools where more than one-tenth of the teachers lack full certification.

This fall, in another major step prompted by the NAACP suit, the school administration changed boundaries and ordered bus transfers of pupils on a record scale. A total of 110 schools was affected. Some 3,000 pupils are now being transported by bus from their

[18] *Philadelphia Inquirer,* October 1, 1964, p. 20.

overcrowded neighborhood schools to others, sometimes miles away, with vacant space.[19]

A long, bitter controversy erupted over the busing program. Initially, it was billed as a move both to ease crowding and foster integration. The school board in January adopted new policies committing itself, for the first time, to work for integration. Previously, it had always declared that it was "color-blind" on race matters and would neither work for nor against integration. As part of its new policy, it endorsed busing as an integration tool, placing a 30-minute limit on the rides and going on record against the "compulsory interchange" of pupils. By this, it meant that it would not take white children from their neighborhood schools to predominantly Negro schools just for the sake of desegregation.

As the Parents and Taxpayers Association was formed to combat busing, as Mayor Tate, Council President Paul D'Ortona, and others spoke against the program, the school board soft-pedaled the integration aspects and stressed that its major purpose was to relieve overcrowding in Negro areas. This was true. It was interesting to observe, however, that when the civil rights groups were pressing the board for action last winter, the busing program was described one way, and when the "white backlash" became apparent over the summer, it was described another way. Finally, strong civic support built up for the program; D'Ortona, who had been perhaps the most vocal critic, withdrew his opposition, and the busing began on September 11 without incident. However, PAT, as the insurgent parents call their group, has filed a court suit seeking to stop the busing, have the school board fired, and force the board members to pay the estimated cost of the busing—some $260,000—out of their own pockets.[20]

By this time, busing has become a bad word in education. It has come to mean the compulsory transfer of white children from their perfectly adequate neighborhood schools to other buildings, perhaps many miles away, solely for the purpose of fostering desegregation. Obviously, this does not describe the Philadelphia program. The only white children being bused here are going from

[19] *Evening Bulletin*, September 11, 1964, pp. 1, 9.
[20] *Ibid.*, September 4, 1964, pp. 1, 8.

white schools to white schools, solely because of overcrowding. Negro pupils are helping to desegregate some 15 predominantly white schools, but as a general rule they are being shipped to the nearest schools with space available—and the white schools just happen to fit that description.

As indicated, the opposition to desegregation efforts in Philadelphia, New York, and elsewhere has been strong. And this could have an important effect on the pace of school integration outside the South.

IN BOSTON

In Boston, for example, the top vote-getter at the school committee election last year was the incumbent who had been most outspoken in her opposition to civil rights groups. She actually drew 50,000 votes more than Boston's Mayor John F. Collins, who won re-election at the same time.[21]

THE IMMEDIATE GOALS

Although both Philadelphia and New York have expressed interest in possible switching to a new 4-4-4 school organization, which would cut two years from often segregated neighborhood schooling, and although both cities are talking about experimenting with educational parks and campuses, these are long-range goals requiring vast outlays of money. What are the short-range prospects?

EQUALITY OF EDUCATION

It seems possible, at least, that instead of attempting massive desegregation, many Northern cities will strive to provide the best possible education for Negroes in their own ghetto schools without pushing for artificially induced desegregation. To some, this approach will sound suspiciously like "separate but equal" education of the races. *Plessy* v. *Ferguson* upheld this concept and *Brown* v. *Board of Education* struck it down. Of course, the South never provided equal

[21] Peter H. Binzen, "How to Pick a School Board," (Unpublished article, n.d.).

education for Negroes in the half century that separation under those terms was lawful. And its failure to do so doubtless was a factor in the 1954 decision.

It is also clear, however, that the North has not had equal education, either. A study in New York City, just after the 1954 decision, found predominantly Negro schools woefully inferior to predominantly white schools on every count. In Philadelphia, school authorities for years put up a brave front in denying inequalities. But this year, the school board's special committee on nondiscrimination, including representatives of civic and educational groups as well as school officials, set the record straight. It confessed that "in every major category" Negro schools in Philadelphia are inferior to white schools. It drafted a crash program to attempt to equalize education and put the first-year price tag at eleven million dollars.[22] The program is aimed at providing Negro schools with small classes, good teachers, and as many instructional extras as can be afforded. Enough kindergartens would be built to accommodate every child wanting to go. As it is, hundreds are turned away every year. And there also would be preschool training for disadvantaged three- and four-year-olds. Many cities are interested in this early school idea. It is seen as the one and possibly only hope of helping the poor youngsters who normally come to first grade with meager family backgrounds, often unable to speak English properly, and who fall behind their mates on the first day of classes and never catch up. In the worst slums, schools might stay open longer during the regular school day, and they might operate on an 11-month year. All of these steps and others like them that educators hope to take will cost money, big money. But the recently enacted Economic Opportunities Act, or antipoverty bill, will give money to the urban school systems for just such efforts.[23] And as the appalling plight of the cities becomes increasingly manifest, the chances of their getting more federal and even state money would seem to be improved.

It is such experiments rather than dramatic attempts at desegregation which appear to interest educators and schoolminded citizens

[22] *Evening Bulletin*, September 30, 1964, p. 12.
[23] *Ibid.*, September 29, 1964, p. 7.

and civic groups at the present time. Indeed, a new spirit may be growing.

James B. Conant was taken to task by civil rights leaders when he suggested in his 1961 book, *Slums and Suburbs,* that the schools should not try to correct the consequences of voluntary segregated housing. Conant wrote that, in his view, satisfactory education can be provided in an all-Negro school through the expenditure of more money for needed staff and facilities.[24] He said schoolmen were "on the wrong track" in yielding to political pressures to have Negro pupils shifted to essentially white schools.

One of the sharpest attacks on Conant came from Kenneth B. Clark, a City College, City University of New York psychologist whose findings on race were cited by the Supreme Court in support of its 1954 decision. Clark accused Conant of advancing "moribund, early 19th Century educational snobbery." Clark, who grew up in Harlem, still favors strong action for desegregation. Just recently, he told a gathering of New York state educators that it would be just as wrong to let the people decide school integration policies as it would to let them prescribe medical treatment in a hospital. Asking that the schools be used as instruments of social change, Clark said: "'When one asks a community North or South to vote on any status change, the majority tend to vote to express their opinion in terms of the past . . . rather than in terms of the imperatives of the future.'"[25]

He said the key decisions on desegregation should be made by professional educators with the background and training "'to face squarely their professional responsibilities.'"[26] But Clark served on a special advisory committee (the Allen committee) that examined the New York City situation this year and then reported: "'Total desegregation of all schools . . . is simply not attainable in the foreseeable future and neither planning nor pressure can change that fact.'"[27] The report also appeared to take the position that schools

---

[24] James B. Conant, *Slums and Suburbs* (New York: McGraw-Hill Book Company, 1961), p. 29.
[25] *New York Times,* September 29, 1964, p. 24. © 1964 by The New York Times Company. Reprinted by permission.
[26] *Ibid.*
[27] Barbara Carter, "New York's Jim Crow' Schools: Bleak Facts and Bright Vision," *Reporter,* XXXI (July 2, 1964), 24.

can be good even if segregated. " 'To argue that no classroom can be good without a white child in it,' " said Clark and his fellow committee members, 'is inaccurate and cruel.' " [28]

Did this put the committee on the side of separate but equal schools?

STAGES IN DESEGREGATION

Clark has written that improving Harlem schools

> "cannot be delayed or obscured by ideological controversies such as 'separate but equal.' These are important and difficult issues, but they cannot be given precedence over the fact that the present generation of Negro children have only one life within which they can be prepared to take their places in the mainstream of American society. . . . The upgrading of the quality of education in predominantly Negro and Puerto Rican schools to a level of educational excellence is an unavoidable first step in any realistic program for the desegregation of these schools." [29]

In suggesting that desegregation be thus carried out in stages, Clark himself has been criticized by some civil rights advocates who want, "Desegregation Now." But his approach seems to have widespread support throughout the North. It is a fact that in the analogous situation down South, the Supreme Court required an end to segregation "with all deliberate speed." It said nothing about allowing time for Negro schools to reach a level of educational excellence that might make possible a smooth transition to desegregation. The court probably felt that time had run out for the South, since it had had almost 60 years—from the time of *Plessy* v. *Ferguson*—to equalize education.

Of course, the North has also had all these years to improve Negro education without ever getting around to it. But the Northern problem was newer, since Negroes did not start moving up in large numbers until World War I, and bigger, since the nonwhite populations of Northern cities have increased tremendously while their numbers have decreased in the South.

[28] *Ibid.*, p. 25.
[29] *Ibid.*

PUBLIC SUPPORT

Indeed, it is the arithmetic of integration that makes it appear likely that future emphasis in the North will be more on improving the quality of Negro schools than in physically shifting pupils from place to place to end segregation. As indicated, there is very little support for busing as an integration ploy, either among the people, the politicians, or the educators. It was no accident that both the Republican and Democratic candidates for U. S. Senator in New York went out of their way to oppose this kind of busing. Recently, another *Bulletin* reporter and I spent several days asking the parents of Philadelphia school children what they thought of the school board's special busing program. We found most parents supporting the program, simply because it was helping relieve the overcrowding. But among white and Negro parents alike, we encountered virtually no one who wanted it to be made permanent. The strongest impression I received from these interviews was that, regardless of race, parents prefer to have their small children attend schools near their homes, if this can be arranged. While I talked to some white women who made no secret of their anti-Negro prejudices and who clearly opposed the board's bus program for this reason, I also became convinced that many of those who support neighborhood schools are neither opposed to progress nor to Negroes.[30]

John H. Fischer, president of Teachers College, Columbia University and a member with Kenneth Clark of the committee that studied New York schools, has warned that busing may cause more problems than it solves. He sees no justification for busing white children into Negro neighborhoods and does not think it would work anyway. If this were tried on a mass scale in New York, he thinks, the white children and their parents "would simply do what thousands of them have done before—move out of New York City, or move out of the public schools." [31]

[30] Peter H. Binzen and J. William Jones, "The Classroom Crisis: Part One," *Evening Bulletin,* September 8,1964, pp. 1, 80; "Part Two," September 9, 1964, pp. 1, 31; "'Part Three," September 10, 1964, p. 28.
[31] "Scholastic Teacher Interviews: Dr. John H. Fischer," *Scholastic Teacher,* LXXXV (September 23, 1964), 10-T.

Conclusion

This is the arithmetic of integration. In Philadelphia, Negroes comprise over 54 per cent of the total public school enrolment, and the percentage has been rising about two points a year. It is expected to reach 75 per cent before levelling off.[32] Already, there are more white children attending Catholic schools in the city than public schools. And if something is not done to reverse the trend or slow it down, there will be no white children with whom the Negro children can be integrated. Growing awareness of this arithmetic will, it seems to me, militate against drastic desegregation moves in the big cities.

[32] *Evening Bulletin,* September 25, 1964, p. 3.

Education for the Socially Disadvantaged Youth

N. NEUBERT JAFFA [*]

INTRODUCTION

THIS TOPIC is an encompassing one, even though there is a limiting modifier for the word *disadvantaged*. Because a child is socially disadvantaged, it follows that he must be disadvantaged or deprived in other areas, for it is through social interaction that most of his learning takes place.

DEFINITIONS

The descriptive term "socially disadvantaged" could mean, in its narrowest sense, deprivation of social contacts, but this is not realistic when applied to children living in today's world in urban surroundings. It could mean lack of social contact with those of middle-class social status and, therefore, lack of opportunity to acquire those skills, habits, and attitudes which have high value for the bulk of Americans. It is this description which has significance here. It means that speech patterns, vocabulary, values of all kinds, aspirational levels, concept of self, and many other learnings will, in varying degrees, be different for those who do not have social contact with middle-class people.

"Disadvantaged" as applied to children is not a universally accepted descriptive term, because some will argue that it is actually a misnomer, or that its usual application is restricted only to one part of a larger group. Typically, the term is applied to those chil-

[*] Supervisor of Special Projects, Baltimore City Public School System, Baltimore, Maryland.

dren who live in the "inner city," usually in slum areas, and whose families are on a low socio-economic level.

It also can be shown that children living under conditions diametrically opposed to those already mentioned are also disadvantaged. These are the boys and girls whose parents have no financial problems, who can, and do, purchase many services which they should be rendering personally for their children. These parents want the best for their sons and daughters and are willing to provide them by proxy: nursery schools during the day, baby sitters and live-in maids at night and on the weekend, and boarding camp experiences during the summer. These children are deprived of the real love, understanding, and family relationships that parents alone can supply. Thus, the usual and popular concept of disadvantaged youth leaves out a large segment of our young people who might well be included in the group. Children of affluent parents have problems, too, but theirs typically are quite different from those of children whose parents have more limited means.

Because the scope of this total problem is so great, this discussion will be limited to children of low-income families living in the inner city—those usually termed "disadvantaged." What happens to them, what help they get, and what educators do for them depends upon where they live. For the last few years, this group has been the focus of attention for local, state, and national endeavors. Programs that have been put in force vary with the perception of the professional staffs of school systems in metropolitan centers where the problems exist. Very often, the scope and depth of the efforts are governed by the presence, absence, or size of the grants obtained from foundations or individual philanthropists.

Funded Progress in Urban Areas

Studies have shown the chances for success in school which disadvantaged children have in some selected urban areas. It has been demonstrated that children enter first grade or kindergarten with varying amounts of the preschool experiences which serve as background for in-school learning. For some children, communication skills are lacking or are on a very low level. Desirable social habits and acceptable group living patterns are all but non-existent for others. Health and dental problems are legion. All of this is in contrast to children who have none of these handicaps, and who may attend the same school and perhaps be assigned to the same classroom. The less fortunate children must catch up, and they cannot do so if schools use only the old, so-called "tried and true" methods, techniques, instructional materials, and aims and objectives applicable to specific age groups.

TYPES OF PROGRAMS

Preschool education.—Now let us examine a few of the forward-looking steps already planned or under way in some selected school systems. For the child who lives in certain parts of Baltimore, Bucks County (Pennsylvania), New Haven, Englewood, and Ypsilanti, among other places, a pre-kindergarten or early admissions program is available to him. He is indeed a lucky child. The Ford Foundation funds some of these programs for four-year-olds where they accumulate those experiences recognized to be assets, and indeed basic requisites, for in-school learning. Most middle-class children, although not all of them, get this preschool background from the home and community. In families where this does not happen, some agency must help the child fill the gap. Since the problem has implications for education, it is appropriate for the schools to be involved.

Where preschool programs are not included in the public school system, provisions for help to disadvantaged youth should start in the kindergarten and reach as high into the grades as necessary. For some, this will be through high school, because catching up for them is not an easy task. Such programs must also include opportunities for parents and other members of the community to participate.

The New York Higher Horizons Project.—If he lives in certain parts of New York City, the disadvantaged child may be included in the Higher Horizons Project, where an expanded guidance and teaching staff for each school provides individual and group counseling, remedial work, pre-school and post-school homework clinics, special trips on an intensive basis, plus closer school co-operation with parents and community.

Boston's ABCD Program.—Should this child be a Bostonian, he could possibly be part of the proposed Action for Boston Community Development Program, which is "Dedicated to Enriching the Lives of Boston Residents and to Providing New Opportunities for the City's Youth." This ABCD Program, privately sponsored and non-profit (it is funded by the Ford Foundation), has set up as part of its goal: (1) to help design new programs in education, employment, social services, and similar fields, and (2) to assist public and private agencies to put the programs into action.

A four-year-old might be enroled in one of the pre-kindergarten classes. His older brother or sister at the elementary or secondary level could get help from the School Adjustment Counseling Program, designed to deal with serious emotional, behavioral, or environmental problems. At these older age levels, the child may also have help from guidance advisors who will aid him in seeing the connection between present school experience and the world of work. An elementary school child in the program who needs help in reading could have a teacher who has the services of a reading consultant as a resource, a reinforcement, or a demonstration agent. A child who is one of the more able pupils may work in a group of ten to twenty students in an enrichment program. This is the projected plan in a most abbreviated form; how much of it has been put into operation at this moment, I do not know.

The Pasadena Program.—Let us now look at the West Coast—at Pasadena, California. Here, if a child is in one pilot project and adjudged as being disadvantaged, he could be in a class of no more than thirty pupils, including up to twenty disadvantaged children who are there for intensive work in reading and language skills. If he were enroled in another school, he might be in an ungraded primary class during his first two years of school (exclusive of kindergarten). If he were in attendance at still another school, he might be included in a special reading program using an audio-visual centered approach which employs a basic set of readers and accompanying filmstrips.

Programs developed for the disadvantaged child on the secondary level include a plan of grouping for each subject, by ability and need, which is designed to help him. The child could be assigned to the reading clinic which is part of every junior high school. In one junior high school, the disadvantaged youngster might be assigned to a smaller class. In one senior high school, if he were one of those screened as a potential dropout, he would have instruction by teachers who have formed a teaching team and who employ both large- and small-group techniques. The four-member teams each handle one hundred students.

The Higher Horizons Program in Pasadena has involved citizens in addition to the professional staff, and the superintendent, authorized by the Board of Education, has appointed a Citizens-Staff Advisory Committee to facilitate maximum use of community resources.

CHARACTERISTICS OF THESE PROGRAMS

There are some common threads running through all of the programs mentioned, as well as unique approaches in specific instances. For example: (1) Educators have recognized needs at all of the traditional levels of public schools—kindergarten, elementary, and both levels of secondary education—and have added, or perhaps prefixed, the four-year-old level. (2) Experimentation with new approaches in each of the areas has brought out promising practices. (3) Answers appear to be coming from school people of all levels who wish, and sometimes dare, to be inventive and who take the time to implement their ingenuity. (4) Contributions are coming from educators who make use of resources from all of those disciplines which are now recognized as contributing to success in school. Teaching is no longer a one-man job. Such knowledge as exists in the arts, the sciences, and the humanities is being used by the professional educator. Particularly helpful are the contributions which can be made from the fields of anthropology, sociology, medicine, and psychology. These sources are helpful, not only for background material in content, but also for guidance in understanding people. (5) Parents and other members of the community have been included in the programs, both as co-learners with their children and as resources in the on-going planning and presentation of educational programs. (6) Just more of the same, the old "tried and true" curriculum, materials of instruction, teaching procedures, and school organization, is not usually the answer to the problem.

Education for the Socially Disadvantaged Youth

It is impossible here to give a full discussion of the details of the programs which have been mentioned. All of these activities are well documented, and descriptive data as well as evaluations are available. It is well worth the time of the classroom teacher, the supervisor, and the administrator to become acquainted with the details surrounding these proposals and active programs which are designed to help meet the needs of the disadvantaged child.

LESS-EXPENSIVE, CO-OPERATIVE PROGRAMS

There are, of course, many other programs operating all over these United States which are equally well-planned as those already mentioned. These are not funded and have not been publicized in media having nationwide circulation. For this reason, the discussion here will be somewhat more specific, because such programs may have implications for those who wish to operate their own programs to fit the unique needs of each situation.

AMONG SCHOOLS

The School Interchange Program.—A promising practice which has overtones of intercultural activity is a program entitled "The School Interchange." Classes are matched in two schools of diverse cultural and socio-economic backgrounds, and these schools operate an on-going program which spans the entire school year. Typically, intervisitation between schools occurs about once every two weeks; therefore, each school has an opportunity to travel to the other school once a month. Teachers plan together, in advance, the activities which are based upon their normal programs. The interchange serves to enhance the programing and planning done by the individual teachers. It affords the opportunity for functional use of communication skills, and thus fills one of the greatest needs of the disadvantaged child.

For example, the two teachers may plan around a similar center of interest, such as: community study, science, arithmetic, language arts, literature, or any other content or skill. After pre-planning has occurred in each of the schools, a common learning situation occurs when the classes meet. The pupils operate in a large group situation, for which techniques are being developed, and become involved in making contributions in the common interest area. The use of communication skills, no matter what specific center of interest has been chosen, has high priority.

Such interchange also puts the resources of the two schools at the disposal of the two classes, including professional personnel such as supervisors and building principals as well as teachers. Material resources in the two school buildings and in the communities which they serve thus become available to the children of both classes. There is no added expense to parents, since the children are transported to the other school by the school buses.

The evaluation at the end of the first year has indicated that much of a productive nature has happened in changing the attitudes of the parents and children towards those of a diverse cultural background. Teachers have expressed continuing interest in the program and, in many cases, have stated that they would like to start very early in the new year to continue their participation. Leadership roles for teachers in carrying on the program and in providing for its needs have also made it a very commendable, in-service education activity.

FOR INDIVIDUAL SCHOOLS

An interdisciplinary approach to meet learning problems.—In one school, a team approach has been used to meet the needs of the children who have a-typical behavior patterns. The membership of the team includes the school principal, vice-principal, guidance counselor, school nurse, social worker, and classroom teacher, and the group has the service of a psychologist on call. In this approach, a meeting time is set where all of the personnel except the psychologist meet together and listen to a description of a child, then examine all of his records. The contributions made by each member of the team reflect his training in the diverse fields. Recommendations are made, and these are followed through in the hope that remediation will take place without involving other than in-school resources. The counselor, as a follow-up procedure, engages in individual counseling with the child and in group counseling when other pupils share the same problem. A record is kept of the proceedings and the remedial steps. Should there be no significant growth in the desired direction, the record is then forwarded to the psychologist, who, at this point, will either make recommendations from the record or will meet with the team to discuss further steps. This procedure is not intended to supplant the services of a psychologist or a psychiatrist in a one-to-one relationship with the child; it is rather a useful technique for constructively utilizing the limited time of the specialists. It is further productive in that all of the members of the team may get further insights and increased competencies from these in-service activities.

Operation Understanding.—In one elementary-school neighborhood, there had been much evidence of unrest among the children—broken window panes in the school building and fighting, even on the school ground. The principal and his staff surveyed the situation and, along with the parents, set up an organization designed to channel the energies of children in other directions. Eventually, the clergy, social and community agents, and principals of neighboring schools were also involved. The news media were instrumental in publicizing the activities so that there was greater understanding of the aims and objectives of the project.

Tutorial programs.—The use of high school students as tutors has had varying degrees of success. Where pupil growth has been the greatest, it can usually be traced to the preparation and supervision of the tutors by the professional staff of the schools. Volunteers for tutorial roles have come from Future Teachers of America members and from high school honor students. Problems of differing nature have arisen when the service has been offered to children on the elementary as compared with the secondary level. One big stumbling block is the approach used in teaching reading and arithmetic to elementary children. For the slow learner, conflict and frustration often result when the tutor attempts to use different methods and materials from those used by the child's teacher.

While problems do exist in this area, it is still worth a try. Perhaps some situations do not have the problems resident in other places. It might be that someone soon will discover how to overcome problems thought to be insolvable by others.

Homework Centers.—This program has been a highly successful venture in some schools. The Homework Center is designed to provide a quiet place for students to study or do their homework every day, for about an hour after school. Many children have no such facility at home. Parents are used to supervise the rooms where the pupils are at work. One teacher is on duty and is only called upon when serious problems arise. This faculty member is in a nearby room and uses this time to do his own work. In a sense, this teacher does not give any extra time to the program.

In order that the program operate successfully, teachers must be careful in assigning homework. Programs will only work when assignments are based upon the kinds of work children can do independently in order to get needed practice that is not always available in the school day. Under these conditions, the academic ability of the parent is of no consequence; any parent able to manage the group can participate.

This last group of projects or activities has included those which have required no extra staffing, no extra funds, and no extra facilities. All of these have been dependent upon volunteer services of high school students, members of the community, and teachers from the school faculties. These programs offer an opportunity for those who want to do so to serve. Sometimes, the example set by the pioneers in a project serves as a catalyst to motivate others to volunteer their services.

Conclusion

There is much to be done; the total reservoir of potential help has not yet been fully tapped. Many of us are, to coin another word, *advantaged;* it is up to us to use our skills and knowledge to help all disadvantaged children.

III

Elementary Education

The Methods Controversy in Reading

LEO C. FAY [*]

SPEAKING ON a controversial topic has its dangers, especially when one expresses a point of view in regard to the issues. To have the opportunity to discuss the reading controversy in Pennsylvania is most appropriate, however, for it is to this state that eyes are turning to watch the Fries experimentation in Philadelphia and the i/t/a project in Bethlehem. It is through such endeavors which provide for the testing of ideas in typical classroom settings that we can hope for further progress in teaching our children to read. Both the experimenters and the school systems should be sincerely thanked by all of us for what they are doing.

Unfortunately, in some quarters of the land a strident barrage of verbiage fills the air as proponents of this or that point of view battle their opponents—real or imagined. Dichotomies are forced with no choices but the extremes. "If you can't be for us, you must be against" is the attitude that too often prevails. A casual, but insightful, observer would find much of what is being said at least amusing, if not ridiculous.

Nevertheless, there is a real controversy in reading with emotions running high. As one starts studying this scene, he finds that the current controversy relates almost entirely to beginning reading. Such questions as, "How should reading be defined?" and "What should the approach to the child be?" are being raised. Nor is the questioning simply a matter of challenging the devil in the form of the "Establishment." The major issues are:

(1) Should reading be approached as first building a mastery of

[*] Professor of Education, Indiana University, Bloomington, Indiana.

the word through the initial teaching and synthesis of word elements? (The Phonics Method.)

(2) Should reading be approached on a whole-word basis, with word attack skills taught through the analysis of words the child knows by sight? (The Whole-Word Method.)

(3) Should reading be approached as breaking the code used to transcribe the oral language into written form through a study of word patterns? (The Linguistic Method.)

(4) Should reading be approached as an extension of the oral language experience of children? (The Language-Experience Approach.)

(5) Should reading be based upon materials that are presented in an alphabet that maintains a consistent, one-to-one correspondence between the sound and written symbols? (The Phonetic Alphabet Approach, as represented by the Augmented Roman [i/t/a], the World English, and the New Single Sound Alphabets.)

(6) Should reading instruction be based upon a diagnostic, and hence individual, approach? (Individualized Reading.)

One immediately recognizes that these six questions, while reflecting major points of controversy, range beyond a strict definition of methods—a term that has a long history of being battered, bruised, and belittled.

Phonics versus Whole-Word

According to the accounts of Nila B. Smith [1] and of Charles Fries,[2] the controversy in regard to these two methods has been raging for generations. First one position enjoys public favor and then the other. The result of all this "see-sawing" has been a continuing refinement of both approaches and a typical school practice today that is highly eclectic.

During the last several years, much emotion has been engendered around a point of view that can be expressed in the battle cry—

---

[1] Nila B. Smith, *Reading Instruction for Today's Children* (Englewood Cliffs, N.J.: Prentice-Hall, Inc., 1963), pp. 187-253.
[2] Charles C. Fries, *Linguistics and Reading* (New York: Holt, Rinehart and Winston, Inc., 1963), Chapter Two.

The Methods Controversy in Reading

"Phonics, *si*—look and say, no!" As late as 1962, Mortimer Smith, a spokesman for the Council on Basic Education, writing to the editor of the *Saturday Review* said that there was a war in American reading instruction between phonics on one hand and look-and-say on the other.

This war continues to the present moment, although it represents an extreme point of view and forces a dichotomy that does not really exist in school practice. Unfortunately, the real issue—and there is one—becomes obscured to the disservice of our children and our schools.

The simplest way to react to the extreme position in regard to this controversy is to quote Mrs. Louise B. Scott, the author of a phonics textbook and a lecturer on phonics, who in an interview reported in the Louisville *Courier Journal* of August 19, 1963 said, "I have never talked to a primary teacher in my life who wasn't using phonics in some degree . . . I just don't believe the whole-word method per-se exists and I ought to know. I'm an old war horse. I have been at this for years and I have taught at every level."

This same general point of view was expressed in the Conant report on reading. The simple fact is that all one must do to see that the real issue is not "Phonics, yes—look and say, no" is to follow Mrs. Scott's example and visit primary classrooms to talk to teachers and to observe what they do.

The real issue in the phonics-whole-word controversy is concerned with how phonics are to be taught, when they should be introduced, and the sequence and rate to be followed to develop an independent reader.

THE PHONICS POSITION

The rationale of the phonics method is built upon a logical analysis of the language. Words are built from letters that represent sounds. It is logical, therefore, to start reading instruction with the letter-sound elements, building individual elements into phonograms, then into monosyllabic forms, and eventually into polysyllabic words.

The process involved is one of synthesis. Meaning is de-emphasized in beginning reading. Drill is provided on lists of words, and where material is presented in context, the purpose is to review the particular phonics facts being taught. Hence reading is defined, at least at the beginning level, as mastering the word form. Although there are some differences among phonics programs, typically 70 to 80 per cent of the phonics facts and generalizations are presented in the first year of school. Many sub-questions revolve about the phonics position which result in some marked variations in practice. For example, "Should all phonics generalizations be taught?" "Should vowels be taught before consonants?" "How should exceptions to rules be treated?" are all questions that are treated differently in different phonics materials.

THE WHOLE-WORD POSITION

The rationale of the whole-word method is built upon a definition of beginning reading that emphasizes meaning and the function of reading as one of the communication arts. It recognizes the importance of the mastery of the word form, but emphasizes the importance of both form and context in developing this mastery. Phonics are approached first through an analysis of how sounds are represented by letters in words that have previously been learned as sight words. As the phonics facts are presented, they may be used in unknown words through substitution. For example, work with seeing and hearing the use of *f* in *father, family, fun,* may lead to such exercises as *car—far, bat—fat*. Now the unit of instruction is the total word and the elements within the word are approached through analysis. Somewhat confusing in this picture is the fact that synthesis and analysis skills are both needed by the mature reader. Hence, regardless of how the child is introduced to phonics, he must use his skill both through synthesis and analysis.

With whole-word methods as with phonics programs, variations in rate of introduction may be observed. In some programs, work with phonics facts is started almost immediately following the introduction of sight words; in other programs, such work is delayed until 50 to 75 sight words have been introduced. In any event, the rate at which phonics facts and generalizations are introduced in whole-word methods is substantially slower than with the phonics method

The Methods Controversy in Reading

during the first grade. In the meantime, however, the child does substantially more context reading, with an increasing emphasis upon comprehension as he progresses in his ability to read.

During the first grade program, the typical whole-word approach as represented in widely used basal reading programs introduces approximately 25 to 35 per cent of the phonics facts and generalizations. Agreement is virtually unanimous that consonants be presented before vowels and that work with the vowels is best delayed until the end of the first year or the beginning of the second. The number of phonics generalizations that are taught varies widely among the different whole-word programs.

Before attempting a judgment as to the relative merits of the two approaches, it should be recognized that proficiency in word recognition is one of the most basic of reading skills. The goals in this area, stated in terms of the tasks the child faces, are:

(1) A child must learn to recognize known words at a glance. Sight vocabulary is important.

(2) Partially known words should be recognized with a minimum of study. The child should be able to take advantage of what he knows.

(3) New words must be recognized through the use of various word attack skills used in combination. This involves using visual and sound clues as well as context clues.

COMPARISONS

Recognizing these goals and the differences in approach between the phonics method and the whole-word method, it is natural to ask, "Which is better?" The lines are tightly drawn on this issue, but let us try to approach it as dispassionately as possible. So much of what has appeared supporting both sides of this question is more propaganda than research that selection is necessary. If we restrict our judgment to the evidence from controlled comparative studies, the following conclusions become apparent:

(1) The product of today's reading program, which while eclectic is based upon a whole-word approach, is superior to the product of the 1920's when phonics programs were in extensive use. Let us

not lose sight of the quality of today's youth. Our young people are performing better than any previous generation. College freshman classes this year again provide eloquent testimony to this fact. This is true in spite of the much higher proportion of our youth continuing their education. It is ridiculous to consider the suggestion that we simply go back to school practices of a generation or two ago as some critics suggest.

Yes, there are serious reading problems in our schools, but these problems to a large extent relate to other difficulties facing our children and our society for which a method may not be the solution at all.

(2) Recent studies show no clear cut overall advantage for either approach for all children.

(3) Recent studies do show advantages of one approach over the other for particular groups of children. But even in these studies, we must be cautious, as extenuating circumstances must be carefully considered.

One of the outcomes of this controversy has been a significant improvement in the word attack programs of basal readers.

CONCLUSION

After reviewing a vast quantity of material that has appeared in the popular press as well as the professional literature on this controversy and weighing it against the best knowledge we now have of children and of the reading process, I have come to the painful conclusion that this argument is one of the great tragedies in American education. Somewhere along the line, the child and his problems have become lost. The forced dichotomy of "phonics" and "look-say," with the resulting need to defend one's position and to save face, has led to thinking of *a method* as *a panacea* and of positions from which there is no retreat. Unfortunately, this controversy has become a disservice to children, to teachers, to education.

The question we should concern ourselves with is "What is best for a particular Jimmy, Bill, or Mary?" When this is done, we find there is no panacea in *a* method. We find the good teacher fits method to the particular learner. And as a consequence, we find that the teacher is more important than any particular method.

The Methods Controversy in Reading

Recently, together with colleagues at Indiana University, I have become interested in the problems of children suffering from constitutional language disability resulting from injury or other neurological involvement sufficiently severe to result in difficulty in learning to read. Specialists at our Medical Center estimate that the proportion of children so handicapped is at least 7 per cent, which in terms of today's elementary school enrolment means that two and a half million of these children are in school. These children are characterized by perceptual difficulties and other physiological problems that have implications for method. For example, in spite of adequate vision they tend to have great difficulty in distinguishing between letters such as *b* and *d* or *n* and *u*. They may also twist the order of letters both in reading and in writing.

These children typically are confused by a complex grouping of symbols, such as all the letters in a word, and need small learning units. They usually benefit from multisensory activities, and typically, in learning to read, a synthetic approach tends to work better than a whole-word approach. But even with severely disabled children, it should be emphasized that a relationship between child and teacher based upon trust and understanding is critically important. It seems there is more than method involved in learning, even within a specialized population.

Other groups of children bring still other problems. Vernon Simula,[3] in a doctoral dissertation completed at Indiana University this summer, was able to show differences in learning patterns among children divided into groups on the basis of the two personality factors of "rigidity" and "anxiety." Simula's findings, when related to other studies of learning and personality, indicate that a child's personality structure may be quite important in the choice of the most effective methods for him. For some, the whole-word approach would be most efficient. For others, a more restricted learning unit would be more effective.

Other studies suggest that children with limited language backgrounds may benefit from one kind of treatment, whereas children with a richer background would best be served by another approach.

---

[3] Vernon Simula, *An Investigation of the Effects of Test Anxiety and Perceptual Rigidity Upon Word Recognition Skill of Second Grade Children* (Doctoral Thesis, Indiana University, Bloomington, August, 1964).

The purpose of these examples is to emphasize that the first concern in regard to choice of method is the learner. This is not to deny the importance of what is to be learned and the effective methods of teaching it, but is merely to indicate my view of what should come first—the learner. This, in turn, is why the teacher must be considered of greater importance than a method.

The Linguistic Approach

The question of what is to be learned and how best to present it has caught the fancy of linguists in recent years. While these students of language do not agree among themselves as to a linguistic method, several are currently working at the problem of applying the results of their studies of language to the problems of teaching children to read.

The linguist is critical of both the phonics and whole-word approaches. He points out that phonics programs tend to distort speech sounds and are often built upon erroneous understandings of the language. The whole-word approach as represented by basal readers, in turn, is criticized for a lack of phonetic consistency in the words introduced in beginning reading. The nature of the sentence patterns of basal readers is also criticized as being unnatural and hence a hindrance to learning.

While at this time the linguist is not able to provide much specific help based upon extensive classroom experience, his entrance into reading comes as a breath of fresh air. His stress upon the oral base of language, the importance of the alphabetic principle, and the advantage of using the patterns of language both within words and sentences are valuable contributions regardless of what approach to reading is followed.

The importance of the learner must again be stressed, however, as many linguists, while undoubtedly excellent students of language, are naïve in regard to children and how they learn. This is not too serious *if* their ideas can be put to the test and tempered by master teachers working with children. It is serious, on the other hand, if the linguist goes no further than theorizing. Consequently, the Philadelphia program testing the Fries materials is highly significant.

A thoughtful review of the linguistic approach, including contributions and limitations, is to be found in Spache's new book, *Reading in the Elementary Echool*.[4] At this stage, linguistics must be looked upon as an aid to understanding language better and not as the foundation of a new panacea in reading instruction.

THE LANGUAGE-EXPERIENCE APPROACH

Other specialists looking at reading see the picture quite differently. The student of child development tends to see reading as but one facet of the child's total language development. As language ability develops, the child is able to think about and then to talk about his experiences. Reading is but a logical extension of the child's communication skills and is taught in relation to the other language skills. Following the language-experience approach, reading stems from the oral and written expression of children. Reading, then, is an outgrowth of a child's experiential background, thinking, and oral expression. The importance of these factors is recognized in several experimental programs in culturally deprived environments. The publications of the San Diego Reading Study Project describe this approach in detail.

While this approach has its limitations, its significance in this discussion is that it emphasizes that reading must be concerned with more than skill development or the breaking of a code. Reading must be viewed in relation to the total language development of the child.

PHONETIC ALPHABETS

Another facet of the current controversy suggests that the major difficulty of teaching reading is to be found in the way our language is written. Some innovators say that there is too little consistency between written symbol and sound in spelling English. Ralph D. Owen, formerly of Temple University, developed a quantitative rating of the relative difficulties of learning different languages. Italian and Turkish, which both use 27 letters to represent 27 basic sounds, are rated as 100 per cent. German with 38 symbols and 36 sounds and Russian with 36 symbols for 34 sounds are rated at 90 per cent.

---

[4] George Spache, *Reading in the Elementary School* (Boston: Allyn and Bacon, 1964)).

Far down the scale is English with 379 symbols (letters or combinations of letters) representing 40 to 44 basic sounds for a rating of 20 per cent.

As a result of this type of analysis, various phonetic alphabets have been developed over the years, three of which are being discussed in the literature at the present time—the Augmented Roman or initial teaching alphabet, the World English Alphabet, and the New Single Sound Alphabet. The i/t/a materials and programs in the United States and England are attracting much attention. Again the experimentation, such as that in Bethlehem, Pennsylvania, and now in many other communities across the country, is exactly what is needed to determine the value of this approach to a more consistent application of the alphabetic principle to the spelling of English.

Here, as with all innovations, one can find a great deal of skepticism. In discussing alphabet change with participants at the Linguistic Institute which was held at Indiana University last summer, I received a consistent reaction of doubt whether in the long run phonetic alphabets would really solve the problem because of the marked dialect differences in oral English. The impression given was that the goal of an absolute one-to-one correspondence of sound and symbol was impossible to attain.

I do not think we should write off the idea of a phonetic alphabet as an aid to beginning reading so fast. Granted it may not be a panacea, but let us be willing to test the idea. It may prove highly significant for children who have difficulty understanding how the alphabetic principle operates and who have little insight into how words are structured.

Much more information is needed before a real evaluation of programs such as the i/t/a experiments can be made. While the idea should not be rejected, we also have the responsibility of maintaining a healthy skepticism and of avoiding a stampede to a bandwagon until longitudinal testings have been completed.

Individualized Reading

To review current issues there is one more direction to look—individualized reading. This concept is rooted in the work of Willard Olson and is based upon his three principles of self-seeking, self-selection, and self-pacing. So much has appeared in print on this approach that only a few comments will be made about it here.

Essentially, the argument of the individualized approach is that while children may be put into groups to be taught, learning is an individual matter. Therefore, at any given time, instruction should be determined on the basis of each individual and his development. The effective teacher is a diagnostician who knows well both the learner and what he is to learn. The fundamental ideas of individualized reading have often been obscured in the literature and in practice where even the simple permission to select what one wants to read parades under this label.

However, individualized reading is significant in the total picture of the reading controversy for two reasons. First, the individual nature of learning is stressed, and secondly, the teacher has the role not of a manipulator of the materials of a particular method but as a diagnostician guiding the development of children using whatever materials or methods are needed to do the job.

Conclusion

We have looked at the current reading controversy and have seen that it is not a simple one. Complexities are found in the language, the reading process, and the learner. We are beyond the point where we should even consider the simple replacing of one method with another as the way of finding the treasure at the end of the rainbow.

Rather, we need to encourage the continued study of the teaching of reading by scholars of many disciplines—linguists, psychologists, neurologists, sociologists, educationists. Ideas need continually to be tested in classrooms by master teachers, and this testing needs to be done systematically over fairly long periods of time.

The very complexity we face suggests, furthermore, that the teacher must be eclectic in approach, selecting that which seems most promising for children in a particular situation. This implies that the teacher must possess strong professional understanding and competence in regard to children, the reading process, methods, and materials.

Rather than expend our time on the debate of "Should children be taught by this or that method," we should seriously raise the question of how our teachers can be better prepared to do a truly professional job of teaching them. For as different approaches are developed, the importance of the able teacher evolves as the most important ingredient in teaching children to read. It may just be that the weakest link in reading instruction is not methods or materials but the education of our teachers.

Off the Beaten Track in Spelling

MARY ELISABETH COLEMAN [*]

FOR MANY YEARS, teachers have been disturbed at the discrepancies between the high scores of children in spelling tests and the accuracy of the spelling of these same words in composition. Perhaps we have been teaching spelling in a way that makes the test more important to the child than the correct spelling of the words in written expression. He may verbally agree that the purpose of spelling instruction in school is to learn to spell words correctly whenever he is writing. If the focus of the instruction, however, *seems to him* to be the test which comes at the end of the week, he will continue to show less concern about the spelling in composition than he does about the weekly test. Giving a test that uses the word in a sentence rather than merely presenting words in a list will not eliminate this imbalance. To him it is still a test.

Actually, what are major concerns in the teaching of spelling? We have one goal, that is, that the child be able automatically to spell correctly in his composition (and by "correctly" is meant conventionally) so that he may communicate more effectively with others.

REQUISITES FOR SUCCESS IN SPELLING

What leads to successful reaching of the goal? Some of the requisite abilities, knowledges, and skills, will first be listed, then a few of the ways in which the child can be helped to develop these will be discussed. This list is not all-inclusive, and a more extensive list might well be set up.

[*] Associate Professor of Education, University of Pennsylvania, Philadelphia, Pennsylvania.

PERCEPTUAL ABILITIES

Two factors in learning to spell are abilities which are limited in part by the child's neurological structure and by his rate of maturing. One is the ability to grasp a clear visual image, detailed enough to reproduce the image completely and in the correct left-to-right order. The second is the ability to associate sounds and letters or combinations of letters with which the sound is commonly associated. Many children have difficulty with spelling, not because they lack will or industry in study, but because they are slow in maturing or are permanently deficient in these areas. However, they may be helped in developing their abilities in the school program. For such children, the number of words as well as the difficulty of words might well be varied. Some of them can retain a few words correctly but get hopelessly muddled when the number is too large.

KNOWLEDGE

There are also areas of *knowledge* which assist in successful conventional spelling. These are: (1) knowledge of roots and affixes and their consistencies in spelling; (2) knowledge of the spelling of crucial words that have unique spellings; (3) the ability to identify appropriate meanings and spellings of homonyms; and (4) how to use the dictionary to find the spelling of words.

ATTITUDE

Thus far the discussion has pointed out that the child needs perceptual ability and some areas of knowledge to aid him in spelling. Now, what does he need to feel? He is not likely to be a good speller unless he has a concern about spelling, a need to spell conventionally, and a satisfaction when he has achieved this.

Spelling Instruction

How may we promote these learnings? We can begin by doing two things: declare a moratorium on spelling tests and declare a mora-

Off the Beaten Track in Spelling

torium on the use of graded word lists. Now we are already freer in our teaching! We are free to plan our spelling instruction, setting up one specific learning which we are going to develop in a lesson or sequence of lessons and then planning our activities to achieve this learning. You may call it a spelling unit if you like.

USING THE SOUNDS OF WORDS

For example, we may work on sounds and letters in words. So the teacher may say to her seven-year-olds (and I hope there is no formal spelling program before that), "We know enough about sounds and the way we write letters to use those sounds to help us work out new words in reading. Now let us see what sounds we need to work on to help us *spell* words when we want to *write* them. I will say some words, and you write the consonant that stands for the sound at the beginning of the word—'mother,' 'mine,' 'pet,' 'big,' 'more,' etc." Using two or three initial consonants in a list of ten or fifteen words, the teacher can find which children are not able to record the consonant associated with the initial sound of the words. These children may then be grouped for special work with that particular consonant. We can move on from consonants to consonant blends, and then to the much more difficult short vowels and the easier long vowels. In each case, the child would write the letter or letters associated with the sound. The vowels and consonants may appear anywhere in the word.

As in the general pattern of phonics in reading instruction, it is customary to start spelling with the initial consonant, since this seems to be easiest for children to hear, followed by monosyllables with a medial long vowel or a final long vowel sound, followed by final consonants and by medial short vowels. Consonant blends and consonant digraphs are more difficult. The teacher will have to judge the progress of the pupils to determine whether these should come in second grade or in third. An older group of children may develop a class list of all the different ways they come across for writing a given sound, with illustrative words.

Not all words, of course, are spelled as one would expect from their sounds. Hall points out, ". . . we must recognize that there are different degrees of 'wrongness' in mis-spellings, and that not all errors are to be condemned or marked down with equal severity."[1] When a child spells a new word by ear, he must be assured that his association of sound and letters is well thought out. The commendation comes first; then we can tell him that, contrary to expectation, the word is spelled another way. If we can tell him *why* the spelling seems irregular, it helps him remember the conventional spelling. He spells *know,* "n-o," a logical pattern. If he learns that this word once was spoken with a sound at the back of the throat, he has less difficulty in remembering the initial *k*. Spelling words by ear is an important skill, but the child learns early that there are other aspects to be considered.

FORMING PLURALS

Every spelling series which I have looked at gives definite instruction on the forming of derivatives of root words. In order to get spaced practice, however, many of the series scatter the applications of a rule through an entire book, without ever helping the child focus his attention on this particular generalization and this one alone. Spaced practice is excellent if the child is aware of his goal, but in some of the books there is nothing to give him a cue as to what the specific goal is. It would seem more effective to develop units, such as the ways in which one can form plurals of words ending in *y*. Observation of words in their reading and words that the teacher gives them as they write will lead children to see that some of these plurals require a change in the ending of the singular form while others do not. The question may be raised: Are these endings haphazard? If this is the case, each plural form must be learned separately. Is there a *pattern* which will allow us to figure out a possible plural form without study of each specific word?

The procedure would be to collect a number of words ending in *y* and then determine the plural of each. (Here is an obvious need for use of the dictionary.) The words would next be put in two categories: those which form the plural by adding *s* without changing

[1] Robert A. Hall, Jr., *Sound and Spelling in English* (Philadelphia: Chilton Books, 1961), p. 33.

Off the Beaten Track in Spelling

the root, and those which change the final *y* of the root word to *i* and add *es*. Inspecting the root words in each category should lead to formulating some hypotheses as to ways in which one can tell whether or not the plural form involves changing the final *y*. Some of these hypotheses may be wrong, perhaps even all of those initially stated.

Children may work in pairs or larger groups selecting one of the hypotheses, making a list of singular nouns, and then checking the dictionary to see if the plurals are formed as the hypothesis would indicate. They will find that some of their hypotheses are not correct. If none is correct, then they must search further. Each subgroup should report to the total class their success or failure. If there are *no* hypotheses which hold true, then the class must look further. Teacher guidance certainly will be a factor here. If one or more of the hypotheses does seem to operate, then the class will continue to test it by examining words in the dictionary and in their reading materials. When they have eliminated all those generalizations which do not work, they should be left with their final rule, "That when the final *y* is preceded by a consonant, the *y* usually is changed to *i;* if the final *y* is preceded by a vowel, it is not." Pupils thus arrive at the answer to a question which they have been pursuing over a number of days. The evaluation of the learning comes, not in a test of specific words, but in the ability to form plurals of words ending in *y* as they occur in required compositions and in free writing.

Did the children waste a great deal of time in pursuing false hypotheses? In the long run, no, because every word they looked up to check whether or not an hypothesis would hold gave them an opportunity to focus their attention on the current spelling of the plural of that particular word.

ADDING SUFFIXES

Similarly, a spelling unit may be set up to answer the question, "When does one change a root word when adding *ing* as a suffix?" First the possible changes would have to be investigated. Sometimes the root word is not changed at all, as in *singing*. Sometimes a final *e* is dropped, as in *hoping*. Sometimes a final consonant is doubled, as in *hopping*. Children have already learned all this as part of their program in identifying words in reading. They have learned that some words do not change, that some words are changed by dropping the final *e,* and some by doubling the final consonant. They do not know, nor do they need to know in reading, how one can tell which of these three patterns will be followed. It is only when one is writing that it becomes necessary for him to distinguish the characteristics of words which indicate which of the patterns will be used.

ADDING PREFIXES

There may be a unit on prefixes, emphasizing the way in which a prefix can give the word a negative meaning. An investigation can be made to determine whether or not the prefix is changed with different roots. For example, does *disappear* have one *s* or two? How do we know? What about *disappoint?* What about *dissatisfy?* Why does *misuse* have one *s* and *misspell* have two? We may set up the hypothesis that the negative prefixes *un, mis,* and *dis* remain unchanged regardless of the initial letter of the root word. Here again we will need to collect a number of words which can be used to test this generalization and then turn to the dictionary to check the validity.

We can also examine the meanings of the prefixes. Are they all ways of simply indicating the same negative idea? Let children examine the meanings of *uninformed* and *misinformed, unused* and *misused,* and *unsatisfied* and *dissatisfied.* Such study leads to precision in speech and writing.

LOCATING DERIVATIVES

We may have a unit dealing with common root words, and then look for as many derivatives as we can find. English books for junior high school often list common roots and affixes. Some of these might well be brought down to the fourth and fifth grade levels. When children are interested in code language and in communicating with each other in "pig Latin," we may point out the

Off the Beaten Track in Spelling

code of our conventional speech and how it can be varied to meet our needs of expression.

Sixth graders who are beginning work on parts of speech may be alerted to the change in our language (which seems to be very rapid now) in which nouns become verbs. "Let me 'cue' you in on how you may 'contact' this prospect," says the sales manager. A cigarette "travels" the smoke further. We "jet" to San Francisco and "bus" to New York. The whole matter of the history of words and their changes is a fascinating study and one to which children should be introduced in the elementary school.

LEARNING TO SPELL THE "DEMONS"

There are some words which do not follow patterns and which are important words. Some words are troublesome to many members of a class. These may well be posted on the bulletin board, where anyone can see them at a glance, or kept by each child on a card for ready reference. In addition, individual children may have particular "demons"—words on which they once were confused and now cannot remember the right spelling, or words which for some reason or another they confuse with other words. Each child should feel free to have his particular word demons also written on a card for ready reference.

One can *learn* to be confused, and this some children do. Recently, an English teacher said that after he had read a word misspelled a certain number of times, he began to be unsure himself and needed to resort to the dictionary. You may have discovered this yourself in reading recurring misspellings. We have learned to be confused and words which we once knew for sure now have to be looked up. Rather than foster this situation in school, we should make readily available for the child his particular problem words so that he may glance at them whenever he has to write them and so may write them correctly. An occasional fourth or fifth grader will still reverse the *r* and *i* in *girl*, but this would be an individual demon. Fourth and fifth graders may have posted before the class the correct spelling of the word *receive,* for it is more commonly misspelled than *girl* by the time children reach the age of ten.

DIFFERENTIATING HOMONYMS

We have discussed the appeal to the ear in the association of sound and letters and groups of letters. Much less commonly used, and one which can be explored, is the use of the ear in helping children determine which form of a homonym is appropriate. We have commonly stressed meaning, and this should not be given *less* attention, but we can add an awareness of the intonation of words which help in distinguishing the appropriate form of some homonyms. When *too* is used to mean "also," it tends to come at the end of a sentence and is used with a falling intonation. "She plans to come, too." "Please hand me the book, too." Even in the middle of a sentence, the voice falls. "She, too, will come." "We plan to visit Independence Hall, too, if we have time." *Too,* when it is used to intensify, is usually pitched lower than the adjective which follows it. "This hat is too big." "She went too fast for me to follow." *Two* used as an adjective is usually spoken with a rising sound. "I have two apples." "There are two children who have offered to decorate the bulletin board." *To* is really not pronounced like *too* and *two,* but is more likely to be pronounced as "tuh." "She is on her way to school." "I want you to stop at the store on your way home." Children have both the pronunciation and the intonation to help them hear.

Let us look at a pair of homonyms which seems to offer difficulty even to graduate students. We may make an association with meaning by pictorial or graphic devices. We may also listen to the differences. The abbreviation for *it is* seems to stand alone in a sentence. "It's not likely that all children will be able to hear differences in sound." "It's not likely." Whereas the possessive form of the pronoun *it* always leads into the noun which follows. "The storm lost its fury as it passed over the mountains." "The dog misses its master." "The dog chases its tail." Listen to the sound of the abbreviation. "It's going to be a good day." "It's a new recipe." There is a force behind the use of the abbreviation that we do not have in the possessive. "Its fury," "its master," "its tail"—each of these is really said as a unit, just as we say "the storm," "the dog." In ordinary use, *its* is unemphasized.

Utilizing Sensory Appeal

Another aspect of the language program which can contribute to our goal of good spelling in composition is the attention which is given to words in the composition program. In the fall, many teachers ask their pupils to think of words which suggest the sounds of leaves. Suppose these words are suggested: *rustle, whisper, swish*. As the teacher writes them on the board, the group may look for common sounds and note the recurring of the *s's*. They will find clear *s* sounds, the consonant blend *sw,* and the consonant digraph *sh*. Or, in the upper grades as children hear poetry, they may note how some words resemble sounds. Eleanor Farjeon, in "The Sounds in the Evening" shows it clearly.[2] And Walter de la Mare uses alliteration which we hear in "Quack": "The duck is whiter than whey is,/His tail tips up over his back."[3]

Conclusion

In the teaching of spelling, we must always be aware that spelling is only a tool, an aid to effective communication of ideas. When words themselves become important to children, when children see how words have grown in our language and how powerful they are, when children see the patterns which allow them to predict letter sequence, then spelling comes alive.

Mary Ellen Chase has said about the teaching of literature, "I like to teach my students to see a word in terms of light and color, whether it is clear and shining, heavy and dark, black or white or yellow. . . ."[4] We are well on the way toward our goal if, at the end of the elementary school program, our children see words not just as a sequence of letters but as marvelous conveyers of meaning.

---

[2] *Eleanor Farjeon's Poems for Children* (Philadelphia: J. B. Lippincott Company, 1951), pp. 94-95.
[3] From *Bells and Grass,* by Walter de la Mare. Copyright 1942 by Walter de la Mare. Reprinted by permission of The Viking Press, Inc., New York.
[4] Mary Ellen Chase, *A Goodly Fellowship* (New York: The Macmillan Company, Paperbacks Edition, 1960), p. 275.

Children's Language, Literature, and Composition

RUTH G. STRICKLAND [*]

ENGLISH AS a discipline at the college level is said to consist of three components: language, literature, and composition. In the elementary school, teachers consider themselves responsible for teaching the language arts whose components are listening, speaking, reading, and writing, with spelling, handwriting, grammar, and children's literature as part of the constellation. Elementary teachers have come to call the area the "language arts," not English; yet it is English, and the beginning of every aspect of the program found in a good college English department is there in some measure.

LANGUAGE

Scholars in linguistics tell us that the more one knows about language the more readily one can learn any language, his own or a foreign one. Study of language as a human phenomenon, what it is, how it operates, and how it grows and changes, warrants increasing attention from kindergarten to graduate school. The reasons are plentiful. They range from the fact that language fascinates children to the fact that nations and governments all around the world are concerned about language. In newly emerging nations whose people

---

[*] Professor of Education, Indiana University, Bloomington, Indiana.

speak a variety of languages and dialects, the diversity of languages is a barrier to the co-operative interaction and homogeneity of culture and values which are a necessary attribute of any society that must function as a unit in world affairs. The government of the United States is expending money appropriated by the Congress for teaching foreign languages under the National Defense Education Act and for research on the teaching of English through the Co-operative Research Division of the United States Office of Education. Individual Americans are becoming keenly aware of the need for proficiency in the use of their own language. Many of them are noting the increasingly higher educational qualifications being set for jobs at home and the need for foreign languages on the part of all those who go abroad to represent the government, business and industry, or the religious or welfare interests of the United States in other countries.

CHILDREN'S KNOWLEDGE

The interest in language which children continuously express can be utilized to teach them a great deal about language. They have learned an amazing amount about it before coming to school. Practically all normally developing children master the sound system of their language at an early age and are in control of its grammar scheme by the time they enter first grade at approximately six years of age. It is interesting to note that the same is true of children everywhere, that all languages seem to be fairly well mastered at the age of six by the children whose mother tongues they are. Once the sound and grammar systems are learned, vocabulary can be added indefinitely as it is needed.

Certainly, this does not mean that no work needs to be done with language. In some geographic areas and in some sections of almost any community, children need an immense amount of help, over many years, with refining and improving their language. This is true, in most instances, because they were unfortunate in the language they first learned—unfortunate because its usage differed from the standard English usage that is required for participation in many vocational and social enterprises.

CONCEPTS TO BE LEARNED

There are a number of concepts about language that elementary school children can be helped to learn. Seeds can be sown as early as kindergarten or first grade, and the concepts continuously expanded, deepened, and sharpened. Among these are certainly the following: (1) Language is a system of sounds. (2) The sounds convey meaning only when put together in patterns of words and sentences. (3) The patterns of sound convey meaning to the initiated—those who know the language. (4) Pitch, stress, and juncture are a part of the sound system of the language and help to convey meaning. (5) The sounds and their connection with the things they represent is purely arbitrary. (6) The sounds are put together in characteristic designs; these designs can be composed of a great variety of appropriate fillers. (7) A language changes; old words may be given new meanings and new uses. (8) Likewise, old words are dropped and new words are coined of old parts to represent new meanings or modifications of old ones.

Teachers have opportunities almost daily to introduce or to reinforce these concepts. A teacher who has a clear understanding of language finds many points at which the concepts function and many ways of calling attention to them.

Sound patterns.—The fact that words are arbitrary patterns of sound can be brought out in a number of ways. The children are intrigued to learn that the *thank you* they are trying to remember to say would be *danke schön* or *merci* in another language and carry the same meaning, or that the dog they are discussing would be called *el perro, le chien,* or *der Hund* in Spanish, French, or German instead of *the dog* as they label it in English. Learning to count in another language delights many children. Even an elementary knowledge of a foreign language can be put to use to develop the concept of language as an arbitrary patterning of sounds. American dialects interest children also. Most of them call the stream near the school a *creek* but one or two may call it a *crick* or a *run.* Some bring their lunch to school in a paper *bag* or *sack,* but some may carry a *poke.*

In their work in the social studies, children continually encounter place names which were borrowed from other languages. Many of these came from American Indian languages, though there are names borrowed from French, Spanish, Latin, Greek and other sources as well. Interesting words found in literature and troublesome words with irregular spellings are often borrowed words or words adapted to specific purposes.

Graphic patterns.—Two other basic concepts that children need are (1) the concept that the sounds of a language are put together in characteristic designs and (2) the recognition that the sounds are represented in writing by the graphic symbols of the English alphabet. The systematic analysis of English spelling presented in Fries' book on *Linguistics and Reading*,[1] the study being carried on by Boord,[2] and the massive study of English spelling being completed by the Hannas[3] all call attention to the fact that English spelling is alphabetic and that much of it is amazingly regular.

The most common pattern of English spelling, of course, is the consonant-vowel-consonant pattern of monosyllabic words like *cut, pin,* and *hat* and the many syllables in polysyllabic words such as the two syllables in *velvet* and the first two syllables in *continue* and *committee.* Add to the pattern the double consonant of *bell* and the two-for-one consonants *ck* in *back,* then add two or more consonants at beginning and/or end as in *bend, blend* and *scrap* or even *scratch,* and a large number of words are added to the list which follow the C-V-C pattern. One can go on to the silent *e* which signals a change in vowel sound and to the "far-out" words such as those which begin with the silent *k,* and the regularity of vast amounts of English spelling shines forth with unmistakable clarity.

Syntax.—Speakers of English arrange their words in sentences which follow patterns that are clearly characteristic of English. Children enjoy taking a basic sentence core or kernel such as "John ate," "Mother bought," or "The boy made," noting the fact that

---

[1] Charles C. Fries, *Linguistics and Reading* (New York: Holt, Rinehart and Winston, Inc., 1963).
[2] Robert O. Boord, *Application of the Alphabetic Principle of the English Language in the Presentation of Spelling Vocabularies of Five Widely Used Spelling Series* (Doctor's thesis in progress, Indiana University).
[3] Jean S. Hanna and Paul R. Hanna, *Phoneme-Grapheme Relationships Basic to Cues for Improvement of Spelling* (Study in progress, Stanford University).

the order of these words cannot be transposed if they are to make sense, then expanding the sentences to answer one or all of the questions, *what, when, where, why* and *how*. Children's sentences might become as simple as, "Mother bought John a new sweater yesterday because his old one was worn out," or as complex as, "Last week, because John's old sweater was worn out, Mother bought a new sweater at the mid-summer sale at Penney's." As they experiment with sentences and fit a variety of fillers into the slots, children can be introduced to the names of the various parts of speech, entirely in functional situations and certainly without abstraction and without definition. Words and patterns can be recognized in such manner that children see clearly how each functions. They can find real interest and enjoyment in constructing, generating, if you please, vivid, interesting sentences in which the meaning is clear and the purpose well achieved.

Pitch, stress, and juncture.—The part played in English by pitch, stress, and pauses or juncture can be made clear to even primary grade children. They can see quite readily that one can ask several questions with the four words, "What are you doing?" depending upon which words are stressed most vigorously and pitched at the highest level in the flow of tone. They can recognize that in the sentence, "When my grandmother came in from the country to visit us last week, we had a birthday party for her," the clause in the sentence is a long tone that must not be broken into segments but kept as a unit. All such attention to the intonation patterns and the "suprasegmentals" of the language, as the linguist calls them, aid children with generating good sentences. It affords them equal help with the task of turning the stimulus of the marks on a page back into flowing speech, both in their oral and in their silent reading.

Changes.—It is not necessary to dwell on ways to help children see that a language grows and changes. They enjoy the Mother Goose rhymes, even though they probably do not "fetch" a pail of water as Jack and Jill did or sit on a "tuffet" as Miss Muffet did. Neither do they ask, "Prithee sir, whither goest thou?" as Robin Hood might have asked it. They see new words in the current newspapers and hear them on television and take in their stride words that are as new to the adults of the family as to them. To watch for and call attention to the new words and note how they are made up of old parts makes clear to children the way the language expands and changes.

Literature

Literature is the source to which the teacher must turn to show children the possibilities of their language. Science and mathematics show them how precise the language can be in its presentation of facts and processes. Literature introduces them to the heights that language can attain in its expression of beauty and in appeal to the emotions and spiritual aspirations. It alone of all written material attempts to portray human beings as they are, to show why they behave as they do, how they interact, what experience does to them, and the whole picture of the interwoven mesh of interrelationships that make the human being what he is.

Most of the language children encounter is either of the free, informal sort used in their homes and among their friends or the common work-a-day language of most of what appears in the newspapers or on television. Even their textbooks in social studies and science, adequate as the language may be, are in most instances uninspired writing. Children need to experience language that serves the humanizing purpose which literature aspires to serve.

RESEARCH PROJECTS

Two of the Curriculum Center projects being developed under Project English of the United States Office of Education utilize children's literature as the springboard for composition and for creative writing. The Nebraska Project is in its third year, and the one at Wisconsin in its second year of development. In Nebraska, a core program of literature includes at each grade level examples of a number of literary genre, folk tales, fanciful, animal, and adventure stories, myths, fables, stories of other lands and people, historical stories, and biography. Folk tales range from "The Billy Goats Gruff" and "The Gingerbread Boy" for first grade to *Arabian Nights* for sixth grade, and biography from *They Were Strong and Good* for first grade to *Cartier Sails the St. Lawrence* for the sixth grade. The stories are read to the children in all instances. The activities which follow may include dramatization, illustration, the writing of a group-composed story based on a similar pattern, and the like in the primary grades. Among older children there may be discussion of the development of characters, the ethics or logic of action, or the differences between the English of the story and modern English in the interpretation of a story like "Robin Hood." The aim in both the Nebraska and the Wisconsin projects is to improve the quality of children's writing through immersing them in good literature. Both projects recognize the fact that children can enjoy, appreciate, and understand literature that they cannot yet read for themselves with equal understanding, and that with skillful guidance, they can delve beneath the surface of language to search for hidden meanings, overtones, and the psychological as well as the literary effect the author sought to create.

CHILDREN'S CHOICES

Literature is a part of children's cultural inheritance which they need for complete and wholesome growth. In his precious little book, entitled, *Books Children and Men,* Paul Hazard says, children reject for their own intimate experience, ". . . books which teach them only what they can learn at school, books which put them to sleep but not to dream." [4] But once they have found books they like, they take them to live with. They like, says Hazard, books that offer them ". . . an intuitive and direct way of knowledge, a simple beauty capable of being perceived immediately, arousing in their souls a vibration which will endure all their lives." [5] They like books ". . . which respect the valor and eminent dignity of play; which understand that the training of intelligence and of reason cannot, and must not, always have the immediately useful and practical as its goal." [6] And he tells us that nowhere in the world is

---

[4] Paul Hazard, *Books Children and Men* (Boston: The Horn Book, Inc., 1947), p. 51.
[5] *Ibid.,* p. 42.
[6] *Ibid.,* p. 43.

there such a wealth of good books for children as in America. One hopes that no child will be deprived of his inheritance by any short-sightedness on the part of those who plan his school experience.

Composition

The poorest results in the language arts field are generally conceded to be in the teaching of composition and writing. In the topic for this lecture, language, literature, and composition were linked together because it seems logical to believe that the way to the last, writing, is through the first two, language and literature. To be sure, a child needs experience of many sorts to furnish content for writing, but writing represents language. The child who has a fairly clear concept of language, what it is and how it operates, can more readily put the part he wishes to express of his experience and the workings of his inner mind into graphic representation than he could if he lacked these fundamental understandings.

THE CONCEPT OF WRITING

Above all, a child must learn what writing is—that the ideas he expresses in speech through patterns of sound are put on paper and preserved through the use of graphic symbols which represent speech. He must learn that there is system in writing that must be learned and followed if his symbols are to mean anything to anyone else. Whereas in talk, one may invent as he goes along because he can to some extent revise and edit as he talks, in writing he must come to terms with the plan of a sentence before he starts to write it. In speaking, even experts change the direction of a sentence or revise the wording of it as it is produced, and children do a great deal of this. Probably it is because seven-year-olds are still unable to plan each sentence in advance of writing that Gesell, in his studies of children, has called this age "the eraser age." Experience in clear thinking and in noting how others have, in their writing, caused him to paint mental pictures, to reach out in empathy, or to resolve to act help him learn how to represent his own purposes and ideas so that he, too, creates the responses he would like to create.

In learning the system of representing ideas on paper, the child learns the reasons for placing certain elements in a letter in certain positions on the paper, because people become conditioned to look there for them and nowhere else. He learns that paragraph indentation and punctuation marks are not just arbitrary items demanded by exacting adults but signals to the reader that help him turn the stimulus of the marks back into speech, with as nearly as possible the same groupings of words, the same pitch, stress, and pauses that would make the material carry its message in face-to-face talk. He must learn the value of organization and compression which differ from the less structured form of his informal talk.

LEVELS OF WRITING

All of this is important and must gradually be learned. But often the poor writing in our schools does not result from the lack of this but from the failure on our part to put first things first in teaching writing. An English headmaster's ranking of levels of writing is worth quoting. Bell says there are four levels: (1) writing that is just plain bad, (2) writing that is correct but dead, (3) writing that is incorrect but good, and (4) writing that is just plain good.[7]

Too often teachers are far better satisfied with the correct-but-dead level than with the level above it, but Bell feels that this level gives the teacher nothing with which to work, whereas writing that is incorrect but good proves that the child is becoming a writer. He has something to say and can say it in a style that is his own. Now he needs help in order to learn how to clean it up and put it into shape, but this must not be done at the expense of style.

THE DEVELOPMENT OF SKILL

If one were to ask any adult audience how many of them truly enjoy writing, it is a fair guess that few hands would be raised. Somewhere along the line, most adults have come to think of writing

[7] Vicars Bell, *On Learning the English Tongue* (London: Faber & Faber, 1953).

as work, not pleasure—drudgery, not fulfillment. How and when did this occur? In all probability, it began to happen as early as the primary grades when children were asked to write with too little guidance and too little help with the essential steps in thinking and action that lead to a good production.

It is for this reason that the first steps in writing must, just in common sense, be graded so that not too much of responsibility is heaped onto the shoulders of little children before they are ready to carry it. The first step, logically, is the thinking step. Children are encouraged to tell the teacher what they want to write. More often than not, this is not yet in the form for writing; so the teacher helps the child turn his often rambling and unorganized talk into clear-cut sentences for writing, without doing violence either to his style of expression or the ideas. Then the child dictates and the teacher writes. He does the important job of thinking and composing and she the mechanical one of pencil-pushing and setting up the form on paper. Gradually, the child takes over the actual writing as he is ready. He is not in any way forced to make his ideas conform to the strength of his muscles, his level of fatigue, or his ability to remember many points of mechanics all at once.

It seems ironic how long it is taking us to learn where the weight of emphasis and effort are needed in teaching writing. Some school systems are hiring lay readers (well-trained mothers who are college graduates, usually) to help with composition at the high school level and to confer with students about their papers and give them individual help. It was somewhat startling to hear a famous physicist from the Massachusetts Institute of Technology say with conviction in a recent committee meeting, "Everyone knows that writing has to be taught individually." There is nationwide effort to cut the size of the load of high school English teachers so that they can do a better job of teaching composition. But the primary grade teacher and the teacher of upper elementary grades still works with from twenty-five young children in the most critical stages of learning to write and does so with no help from any source. Perhaps some day, some school may try inviting interested mothers or retired teachers in the neighborhood to come in for a few hours, from time to time, to sit down with one or two children and help them see how to clarify, organize, compose, and transfer to graphic form the nebulous ideas that are in their heads.

Conclusion

There still is a long way to go to find best ways to improve our teaching of speech and writing, but the importance of the task should spur us on. So much of the work of the world is being done nowadays through face-to-face talk that all teachers need constantly to be reminded of the importance of speaking and listening. Writing is graphic representation of that speech. Unquestionably, the fate of the world hangs on man's ability to solve the world's problems through sounds made with the mouth and marks made with the fist rather than through missiles made of metals and chemicals. All that we do with language in the elementary school can be pointed toward this end.

An Integrated Program of Instruction in Descriptive Grammars

V. LOUISE HIGGINS *

"IT IS UP to the people primarily concerned with the curriculum to build an integrated system out of the (grammar) materials available," says Gleason.[1] With this brief statement, he throws the torch to the classroom teachers. In Westport, we are attempting to implement Gleason's suggestion—to build an integrated system of grammar instruction out of the materials available.

It would be fine to claim that we understood exactly what we were committed to in 1956, the year we started to work in descriptive grammars, that we outlined the whole endeavor in one glorious convocation, and that we have been systematically producing books and worksheets ever since. Truthfully, it has not been like that at all. We did fashion and do operate from a plan, but it is a plan that is evolving slowly.

The two aspects of our work that will be discussed here are: (1) the nature of our instructional program in grammar, and (2) the method by which we developed and are developing this program. Because grammar instruction must cohere, this discussion will include not only grammar in the secondary schools and structural linguistics but also what is taught in the elementary schools, for secondary grammar is based upon it. The terms "descriptive grammars" or "grammar," are used to mean generative as well as struc-

---
* Director of English, Westport Public Schools, Westport, Connecticut.
[1] H. A. Gleason, Jr., "What Grammar?" *Harvard Educational Review,* XXXIV (Spring, 1964), 275.

133

tural grammar. At present there is little articulation between grade levels; cumulative examples will be used to suggest how one might build a grammar sequence from grade five to the senior high school years.

THE INSTRUCTIONAL PROGRAM

Westport Public Schools
Descriptive Grammar Curriculum
1964–1965

Concepts — *Texts and Materials*

Grades Three and Four

Sentence
  purpose—tell,
    ask,
      command

No commercial text
Westport "Composition Syllabus," Grades 3–6
Teacher-prepared material

Grade Five

Subject and predicate
Simple subject and predicate
Five types of subjects

No commercial text
Westport "Manual of Language Instruction," Grade 5
Westport "Composition Syllabus," Grades 3–6
Teacher-prepared material

Grade Six

All of above reviewed
Form classes
Structure words:
  determiners
  auxiliaries
  intensifiers
  prepositions
Concepts as indicated in text

Westport "Manual of Language Instruction," Grade 6
Westport "Composition Syllabus," Grades 3–6
Discovering Your Language, Holt, Rinehart, Winston, 1963 [2]
Teacher-prepared material

Grade Seven

Concepts as indicated in text

Completion of *Discovering Your Language*
Roberts, *Patterns,*[3] approximately one-half of text

---

[2] Neil Postman et al., *Discovering Your Language* (New York: Holt, Rinehart, & Winston, 1963).

[3] Paul Roberts, *Patterns of English* (New York: Harcourt, Brace, & World, 1956).

Concepts as indicated in text	Grade Eight Roberts, *Patterns,* text completed
Concepts as indicated in text	Grade Nine Roberts, *English Sentences* [4]
Dialects of spoken English Dialect in literature Language history Style	Grades Seven to Nine Westport "Composition Supplement," Grades 9–10 Teacher-prepared material
Review of all previous concepts Application of concepts to style	Grades Ten to Twelve Roberts' texts as references Roberts, *English Sentences* may be completed in some sections Teacher-prepared material Roberts, *English Syntax,*[5] grade level to be decided

NOTES

Usage grammar (e.g., punctuation rules) is taught each year; references are standard commercial handbooks. Details of MS writing are taught throughout, culminating in a grade eleven research paper. Where applicable, language concepts are used in the composition program.

The above schedule would vary according to type of section; it shows the work for average students. Grades three to six and seven to nine have three-level grouping; grade ten has four levels; grades eleven and twelve have five levels.

Most of the texts that are available in descriptive grammars are used. At present the work in kindergarten to grade four is very sketchy, not even minimal by our standards. The work in grades five and six is becoming more focused than at present, for we have completed a teachers' manual of instruction in language for these grades. In grades seven to nine, work in grammar is much more extensive, with the use of at least two texts plus much special work

[4] Paul Roberts, *English Sentences* (New York: Harcourt, Brace, & World, 1962).
[5] Paul Roberts, *English Syntax* (New York: Harcourt, Brace, & World, 1964).

in language history and dialects. Grade ten is in the "clean-up" position. We are presently examining Roberts' new text *English Syntax* for use at the senior high level. That this new text is based on generative or transformational grammar seems to us no serious problem, since we have been using generative concepts for at least two years in our classes.

From grade five on, the descriptive grammars are the base of instruction. The new manual carries the statement, "The Westport Schools will not allow any teacher of language arts to work solely from usage grammar." Our program consists of teaching several grammars, and appropriate usage grammar is taught at each grade level. Taken as a whole, our grammar program is underway, although still full of peaks and valleys. Some valleys are attributable to the turnover in personnel, some to the lack of certain technical information in the field of grammar itself. We anticipate an additional ten to fifteen years of work, hoping that this time may be telescoped as more people than now address themselves to the task.

Although we have recently seen our program cited as a "daring experiment," there is little that is startling. If anything, we are more determined than daring.

THE CUMULATIVE NATURE OF CONCEPTS

The first example consists of five worksheets taken from the manual for grades five and six, references to the Roberts texts, and a transparency used in teaching grade ten students.

We begin, in the primary years, talking about "telling," "asking," "commanding," or "requesting" kinds of sentences, largely for purposes of understanding of punctuation in reading and for proper intonation contour. In grade four, we have students construct sentences by developing a noun phrase and a verb phrase and putting them together. In grade five, we start to abstract the concept of the constituents of a sentence, the subject and predicate or the noun phrase and verb phrase. There is quite a bit of difference between using sentences, i.e. producing them in speech or in writing, and abstracting about the sentence.

Abstracting sentences constituents.—Students are given a set of sentences; each sentence is on a separate strip of paper, and there are fifteen items in the first set.[6]

Worksheet #5
        Subject and Predicate—Exercise 1
1. JILL'S BROTHER WILL START SCHOOL NEXT YEAR.
2. FARMER BROWN'S COW CAN SAY "MOO."
3. The black and white cat was lapping milk from a saucer.
—
—
13. Sue's big sister is wearing lipstick.
    (Sentences 1 and 2 represent primary type that should be used throughout.)

    Students are asked to divide the sentences into their two parts. The parts are referred to as "Part I" and "Part II" until the initial abstraction is achieved. The manual offers three different sets of sentences: Exercise 1 uses animate subjects and active verbs; Exercise 2 uses plural subjects and passive verbs; Exercise 3 uses a variety of subject types with verbs in the non-passive. By using the fifteen sentences in any one set, the children can make up new sentences by putting together a different Part I and Part II.

    At this point, the concept of grammatical meaning as opposed to lexical meaning can be introduced. Although the sentences are rigged syntactically, they are designed to produce combinations which would be nonsensical in the world of experience, or at least unexpected. For example, the student might produce a sentence such as "The black and white cat is wearing lipstick." By combining the different parts, we can demonstrate that not just any subject can go with any predicate. It is in this way that we lay the foundation for the very important concept of noun and verb sub-classes—a concept taken up on higher grade levels. Incidentally, the manual details not only the nature of the concept, but it also specifies the immediate and ultimate use of each concept so that each teacher knows exactly why a particular concept is being taught.

    By using this method, we are able to begin the abstracting process

[6] Editor's note—Only parts of the total exercises on the worksheets have been included for illustration, and unfortunately not all exercises described could be included.

by relying on the native speaker's feel for the language. We expand this initial concept and go on to teach five different types of subjects in grade five. We also teach simple subject and simple predicate, which involves some initial work on nouns and verbs, but it is only initial. Throughout, we emphasize the difference between grammatical form and lexical or referential meaning.

A sample of sixth grade work emphasizes the verb as a form class, a concept already started in grade five, where pupils started to distinguish between form changes.

Worksheet #7
Verb Exercise—Exercise 3
1. The bird sings.
   The birds sing.
2. He washed the car.
   We wash the car.

Questions:

1. Go back and circle the simple predicate in each sentence.
2. In which pair of sentences did the lexical verb form change to agree with the subject? What was the change?
3. In which pairs of sentences did you find the name form of the verb? Write the name forms.
4. In which pairs of sentences did the lexical verb show the action was completed? What was the change that showed this? Write the past form of those words.

The following excerpt shows some of the work on verb functions:

Worksheet #10
Verb Functions—Exercise 1
A. 1. Examine the following sentences.
      a. The water was glistening in the sunlight.
      b. The glistening water attracted the thirsty travelers.
   2. Underline the predicate in each sentence and circle the simple predicate.

3. Notice that the word "glistening" is used in each sentence.
   a. What is it in sentence "a"?
   b. Is it the same thing in sentence "b"?
   c. You already know that in sentence "a" *glistening* is what part of speech?
   d. What function does "glistening" perform in sentence "b"?
B. In the next group of sentences you are to write the correct form of the verb in parentheses.
   1. The (*bark*) dog ran to the gate.
   2. The (*drift*) snow blocked the road.

The verb phrase functions as a predicate, but this is just one function, and the concept is expanded with such worksheets.

The worksheets are the basis for lessons, not the lessons in their entirety. A lesson such as this will be followed by one in which the child is asked to identify the various signals that produce certain meanings. He will be able to distinguish between the lexical element, the tense carrier, the modal signal, and the aspect—even though not all of these terms will be used.

In grades seven to nine, students are introduced to sentence patterns as detailed in Roberts' *English Sentences* and *Patterns of English*. The idea of sub-class is presented and expanded as it becomes evident that certain sub-classes of verbs appear in certain "kernel" sentences—or it might be better to say that a particular noun sub-class plus a particular verb sub-class trigger a certain pattern. The rest of the structure words are taught, and there is increasing emphasis on structure within sentences, clauses and the like, as well as variations on the kernel sentences, the so-called transforms. It is not hard to see how all of this is an outgrowth of the concepts beneath.

By grade ten, most of the students have been exposed to subject and predicate, form classes, structure words, function groups, and sentence patterns, both kernel and transform. Very early, also, work in the relation of syntax to style is started. Because the teaching of literature is so much a part of their work, senior high teachers are understandably concerned with style. Style is probably the worst taught item in the senior high curriculum, more because there exists no adequate vocabulary with which to discuss it than for want of interest.

One can say that George Eliot uses long sentences and that sentence length tends to slow down reading rate or to make her prose difficult to read. Yet, this is not a particularly helpful statement, since other authors use lengthy sentences and reading rate is not necessarily impeded.[7] Reading difficulty seems to be affected by complexity of syntax, not so much by length of sentence. How does a teacher demonstrate complexity of syntax so that it is meaningful to students? If the teacher would talk of style, he has to show the confluence of various concepts—the sentence pattern, the isolates, such as the prepositional phrase, the subordinate clause, and the participial phrase.

For illustration, a series of transparencies using *Silas Marner* demonstrates the following: (1) the basic sentence pattern on which the sentence is constructed, and (2) the way in which the basic pattern is expanded and the nature of the constructions used for the expansion. The items will not be taken in this order, but instruction will probably start with the examination of certain constructs. At the conclusion, the pattern will be clear, as will the expansion techniques.

The basic transparency which gives the entire sequence—8 lines long, about 65 words, is as follows:

> Dunstan Cass, setting off in the raw morning, at the judiciously quiet pace of a man who is obliged to ride to cover on his hunter, had to take his way along the lane which, at its farther extremity, passed by the piece of unenclosed ground called the Stone-pit, where stood the cottage, once a stone-cutter's shed, now for fifteen years inhabited by Silas Marner.[8]

The first overlay shows the prepositional phrases, of which there are several.

The second overlay shows the subordinate clauses. As might be expected, these are fewer in number but longer than most of the prepositional phrases. In some cases, the phrase will be subsumed

---

[7] See Francis Christensen, "Notes Toward a New Rhetoric," *College English*, XXV (October, 1963), 7-18.
[8] George Eliot, *Silas Marner* (New York: The Macmillan Company, 1899), p. 35.

in the clause, as is common in English. The prepositional phrase is both an expansion device of the structure as a whole and of parts within that overall structure.

When the two overlays are put together, much of the sentence is blocked out in color.

The third overlay shows the participles. These may function as modifiers (as for example, *unenclosed*), but these may also function as phrase formers, that is, items which trigger larger grammatical constructions.

When the sentence has the prepositional phrases, the subordinate clauses, and participles blocked out, the bare bones of the structure are apparent. This is sentence pattern #4—subject, verb, object—according to the numbering used in *English Sentences*. "Dunstan Cass had to take his way" is the basic sentence.

In using this transparency in the classroom, the teacher would have the students identify the various constructs. As prerequisites, the students must know form classes, structure words, and function units, as well as kernel and transform sentence patterns. Our experience with the inductive method has shown that it is necessary to direct the attention of students, and the transparency does this very well. Syntactic analysis has to be taught slowly, and students do not profit by being given a sentence and simply being told to analyze it.

The sentence is expanded in the subject by a participial modifier (omitting determiners and other items), four prepositional phrases, and a fifth which is an expansion of the object in one of the phrases ("pace of a man"), and one relative subordinate clause. This is basically the subject expansion, and all other words included in the subject appear in these constructs somewhere.

The predicate expansion consists of five prepositional phrases, with a sixth that is part of one of the five, of two subordinate clauses (one a relative), of two participial constructions ("called the Stone-pit" and "inhabited by Silas Marner"). All other words belong in these larger patterns. The predicate expansion is greater than the subject expansion, a very common phenomenon of English sentences. This is so common that the "there" transform, as in "There is a man in the blue car," is available so that we can move the longer part after the verb. (Sentence monotony often derives more from an incessant repetition of this common arrangement than from lack of variety of complex or compound sentences. One reason for starting a sentence with an adverb or a clause is to get more expansion in the front part of the sentence and so to break the deadly rhythm set up by the "workhorse" arrangement.) The "front-heavy" sentence is more common in poetry, and it is one of the reasons why students have so much trouble with poetic syntax. The student needs syntactic training to read Shakespearean drama, although he rarely receives such training.

Length is not achieved by compounding elements—by using compound subjects, or having a string of independent or dependent clauses, or by any real amount of parallel structure. Nor is length attributable to direct modification of the simple subject and simple predicate; the modifiers of these basic elements are expanded. For example, "along the *lane* which at its farther extremity passed by the *piece* of unenclosed *ground* called the Stone-pit where stood the cottage."

In this one transparency there is ample material for several class sessions. Verbs may be studied in this context, or nouns, or phrase structure. This example also gives a glimpse of what is meant by "cumulative instruction."

Style analysis.—The second example deals with style analysis. The exercise shows one approach used in grade six. As children read an excerpt from one of the stories, the following directions are given:

> Worksheet #5
>
> Determiners—Exercise 5
>
> Following is a paragraph taken from the reading book *Aboard the Story Rocket*. Read the selection carefully and consider the role (function) of the determiners in this selection. Then do the exercises below.
>
> Chip heard the snapping report and saw the transformation it wrought in Glare. Left alone, the lynx was merely curious. But stung on the nose by a BB pellet, Glare became a mad thing. He was a volatile creature, anyhow, and his always uncertain temperament was further unsettled by hunger. For a second he crouched

at the edge of the thicket while he wavered between running and rending the thing that had hurt him.[9]

1. Identify each determiner and label it "D."
2. Next, remove all determiners and rewrite the paragraph without the determiners.

For good thinkers:

1. As you listened to the rewritten paragraph read aloud, did it sound to you like any English that you have ever heard?* If so, where? If not, why not?
2. Bring to school directions on how to assemble a model airplane (anything that needs to be assembled) or a cooking recipe. Rewrite the directions, adding the determiners.
3. The name of the story from which this paragraph was taken is "Chip, the Beaver." What would happen if the "the" were omitted? Did you know that many surnames had "the" in them?

* Directions on how to assemble, recipes, and the like often contain "telegraph" English.

In the junior high years, style is discussed in a number of ways, none very complicated. Material may be taken from one of the literary works being read. A passage may be examined and the student asked to produce an imitation of the model in the novel—the familiar technique of model writing. Emphasis is not so much on precise definition or labels but on the ability to reproduce structure. Structure is of course discussed, for model writing by accident is not of much help.

Another transparency shows a paragraph from Bryher's *The Fourteenth of October*. It is one of about ten such samples.

It was not only Laurel whom I had lost, but Rafe too. Even Cornwall. I looked up at the sky that spread from faint blue to

[9] Jim Kjelgaard, *Chip, the Dam Builder* (New York: Holiday House, Inc. 1950), p. 215.

dark and saw, instead of ropes and canvas, only the speedwell on that rock, the bird-wing blue, the white, the amethyst her cloak had brushed as she came over the stile. Everything reminded me of Laurel, and yet—if she were to come again, down the same path at the same hour of the morning, there would be a rift, an insecurity, a knowledge deeper than love itself, that a stone once cracked cannot be mended with words, that there is finality, that on that July evening something between us had forever ended.[10]

A companion transparency shows a paragraph written by a student in the ninth grade. The emphasis is not on identical number of words or modifiers but on similar grammatical constructions.

It was not just the house that I had lost, but a part of me. Even a way of life. I looked down the path into the garden and saw, instead of the weeds and overgrowth which were there now, a beautiful array of roses in bloom, the fresh, pale, yellow, the delicate, fragrant pink, the fresh, spicy white which had bloomed as summer came to my childhood home. Everything I saw reminded me of this old life, and yet—if I were to live it again, on the same ground, in the same house, there would be a change, a crack, a recognition that a life once lived cannot be lived again, that a time past cannot become the present, that with my departure from this home, a tie had been broken forever.

A transparency can be used to show how language concepts may be applied to poetic syntax. The teacher, Jane Hastings Silver, explains a lesson, using "Sunset" by e. e. cummings,[11] this way:

To begin with, the slide has only the poem on it. As the class identifies the words in the poem (Roberts' symbols from *Patterns* are used), the teacher pencils them onto the transparent slide. As the class discusses line two, an excellent opportunity for pointing out intentional poetic ambiguity will arise. Instead of being dogmatic about a 'correct interpretation,' it is best to suggest that you are looking for an interpretation that will satisfactorily account for every word in the poem. . . . If it seems plausible to the students that there is a missing subject and predicate in the mid-section of the poem, here is a fine place to talk about ellipsis. The students

[10] Winifred Bryher, *The Fourteenth of October* (New York: Pantheon Books, 1952), pp. 93-94.
[11] e. e. cummings, "Sunset," *Modern American Poetry,* Louis Untermeyer (ed.) (6th rev. ed.: New York: Harcourt, Brace, & Co., 1942).

Integrated Program of Instruction in Descriptive Grammars

should be able to discover the general movement in the poem from 'stinging' awareness to near-oblivion. The separation of the morpheme [z] at the end should be a key to this movement; the reader is forced to extend his pronunciation of the last word—'dream-s'.

In grade ten, there is an emphasis on many grammatical concepts as they affect style. A transparency can be used with average and above average sections near the end of the year's training in syntax to show how transition is achieved. Transition is too often relegated merely to a study of lexical connectives, and the student remains unaware of the complex ways by which the writer (or translator) provides transition. The excerpt is from "The Twelfth Oration of Isocrates: called the Panathenaicus; or Panegyric of Athens." [12]

The first overlay shows the gross connectives of the "first," "next," "besides," "fourthly," "most important of all" type. The second overlay shows also gross connectives, this time within sentences, the *and, but, or;* the *no more, than.* The next overlay shows the repetition and connective function of the determiners, *all, their, our.* These are references to previously expressed items. The fourth overlay shows the pronouns, and its accompanying overlay shows how these are cross-referenced. The first *those* is the referrent of the summation pronouns, *these, them, these* in the concluding paragraph. Within this overall structure are numerous cross-references. The next overlay picks up the relative pronouns, and the last overlay shows their antecedents.

The final picture may look like a jumble, and indeed we do want the student to understand the complexity of the connective structure in this excerpt. The lesson shows how transition is achieved by various means—through actual transition words such as *first, next,* with basic connectives such as *and, but,* with determiner signals, and with pronoun connectives of various kinds, personal, general, relative. This material can also be used for other types of structural analysis, but its main purpose is to demonstrate the intricacy of relationships, how relationship is achieved not just by vocabulary but also through syntactic arrangements.

In order to encourage teachers to create their own materials, it

[12] *The Orations and Epistles of Isocrates,* trans. Joshua Dinsdale and rev. the Rev. Mr. Young (London: T. Waller, 1752), p. 253.

should be pointed out that this transparency was created by an instructor of only five to six years' teaching experience and only about three years' experience in working with descriptive grammars. The example using the cumming's poem was created by a teacher of only two years' teaching experience. The material on *The Fourteenth of October* was created by a teacher of considerable experience; it is but one of her many creations.

These examples should point up what we mean by an "integrated" program of grammar instruction, showing how one level feeds into another.

THE DEVELOPMENT OF THE PROGRAM

The second major topic relates to the way in which we developed and are developing our language program. Material such as has been included here cannot be created by people who have merely "looked over" *Patterns of English* or *English Sentences*. Some of the teachers do not have twenty years' teaching experience, but all of them have had at least two courses in descriptive grammars.

The sequence of activities.—A brief history of our program development includes in-service courses, seminars, curriculum workshops, and one foray into the field of basic research done under the aegis of the United States Department of Health, Education, and Welfare.[13]

While no single activity is unique to Westport, I shall not pretend that this is what most school systems are doing, for it patently is not. Nor is all you have to do to build an integrated curriculum to buy some books, arrange for a course here and there, and when you get some budget money, dash off a manual or two. In seven years, we have written one manual and two halves. There is some information on language in the Grades 3–6 "Composition Syllabus," and some in the Grades 9–10 "Composition Supplement." The one manual wholly devoted to language instruction was completed just this summer. We do base much of our work on the mammoth "Curricu-

[13] Some curriculum materials are available and may be obtained by writing directly to Dr. George Ingham, Administrative Assistant, Town School Office, Westport, Connecticut. Copies of Project #1826 are not available except through libraries co-operating with U.S. Department of Health, Education, and Welfare.

Integrated Program of Instruction in Descriptive Grammars

lum Guide," published in 1959, but this is not so detailed as are the manuals and to some extent is now out of date. To start work in descriptive grammar, it is necessary to buy books and arrange for courses.

Our new manual, more than anything else, may be representative of the tone of our development. The manual discusses theory at length and makes no compromise with the reader who does not want to have to learn theory. It includes sample lessons and discusses very practical classroom matters, but everything is focused on concepts of grammar. The manual does not sell, exhort, placate, or cajole. It is a document to be "weighed and considered, chewed and digested, to be read wholly and with diligence and attention." So that it will receive such attention, it is the text for the in-service course for teachers in grades four to six now in progress. This elementary school syllabus stands in sharp contrast to the program in those schools that are still wondering whether they dare to introduce form classes in grade ten, and it does contradict the long-standing assumption that the last thing in the world a teacher will read is theory. In any event, the manual is a result not a cause.

While we did not start with a preconceived plan, some of us shared an attitude which can only be termed as a sort of Jamesian tough-mindedness, and we had a respect for "elegance," as the term is commonly used in mathematics. Perhaps we were just simple-minded. Whatever we were or are, we learned early and fast to turn to no one for consolation; we learned to assess our situation candidly, no matter how discouraging the findings. Our first blunt assessment told us that whatever was going to be done was going to have to be done by professional teachers who had relevant information about grammar. This enabled us to forswear some very wasteful motion. We never once solicited the support of the public; in the beginning, the program had the aura of a bootlegging operation. After some initial disappointment, we gave up on help from the universities. Early days were not all dark, for we found that we had the constant support of many linguists. They gave us not sympathy but the thing we needed most—information. The National Council of Teachers of English and other organizations provided a forum for the discussion of grammar; the College Entrance Examination

Board included grammar in its English institutes; and we read various articles or pamphlets as well as books on grammar. In our individual circumstance, we were blessed with an administration that encouraged inquiry. While such a situation was reasonably satisfactory for a few, it would not do for an entire school system.

Creating the climate.—The real dilemma was to get the bulk of the teachers to shift to a new orbit of somewhat frightening dimensions without cajolery, without exploiting their weaknesses—a dangerous game which in the long run has a boomerang action. Common sense told us that a program handed down from "the Mount" was of little value; experience told us that success favors those who do.

How did we resolve this dilemma? We approached the staff at their strongest point, their professionalism. This was not some kind of plot but the natural solution of people who were teachers and who rightly or wrongly believed that teachers could both teach and do. Slowly but surely, it became unprofessional not to inquire. We took teachers at their best. They were searchers after truth? All right, they could start searching. They were objective critics. Fine, we knew how they felt about the gerund, now we tried to get them to *think* about it. The *sine qua non* of any new development is the desire for information, for validity. Such desire cannot be legislated; it only appears when the climate of opinion is such that a teacher is expected to *know*.

Climate is not generated overnight; it has to evolve. In our system, the strongest teachers were the ones who first inquired into descriptive grammars and started teaching them. Little by little, whether by imitation or otherwise, more teachers started to ask questions. Teachers using descriptive grammars gave information only if asked; there was no proselytizing. Those who asked questions were also told that there were few texts (at first, there was only one), that there was no help to be had, and that the whole business was grueling work. Talk about the "hard sell!" This was positively like flint. There were teachers who felt that the new grammars were not for them and who were assured that they probably were not. No one said that this is *the* grammar, only that it seemed professional to inquire. Perhaps out of embarrassment and, not knowing, perhaps out of curiosity, hopefully out of professional integrity, the climate was developed.

It may sound as if such a climate has all the charm of the Massachusetts Bay Colony with Cotton Mather at the helm. This is not so, for actually the introduction of a new program is really fun. It has challenge, unexpected rewards, and humor by the bucketful, especially if you have a taste for irony. You cannot help but be invigorated by watching students discover the wonders of their native language, by presiding over a spirited class discussion on points grammatical. You cannot help but enjoy the frantic notes from teachers asking help on some two-headed grammatical calf that the students have found, and the students just do find some "crunchers." It is hard not to chuckle when you have one of your eighth or ninth graders address a university class on Shakespearean syntax. Inquiry has a playful side to it, for it is the playful mind that can toy good-humoredly with an idea. Yet, one must have not only a playful mind but also a tough mind, for there are mighty opposites with which to contend. Truth has to be found by digging deeply, and there are many obstacles before you can ever start to excavate.

Providing the information.—Once the desire for information was nurtured, it was necessary to provide the information itself. It was mostly curiosity which brought people to the first in-service course in language, but it was healthy curiosity. The course was open to all staff members on a voluntary basis. In this course and in the many that followed, the members of the administration have set a good example. Principals, as well as the superintendent, sit in at one time or another. Except for the advanced theory courses, all in-service courses are taught by a qualified member of the Westport staff; so there never is any feeling that the instructor does not understand Westport problems. The main orientation course in language is an all-lecture course (usually with one demonstration session), and theory is laid on with a trowel. No questions are allowed until late in the course on the premise that it is impossible to ask "useful" questions until one has heard the hypotheses. While this is a risky procedure, it does work for us, possibly because we promise nothing but information to be examined. Advanced theory courses are open only to those who have had some prior training, on the supposition that an expert linguist should not be brought in to explain the phoneme.

A general course in language could not produce a curriculum; it could only acquaint teachers with basic concepts and only a few concepts at that. Orientation of the whole staff meant waiting patiently while people got off on tangents, did some backsliding, charged off with renewed vigor, gave up—and cautiously edged their way back into the main stream. Because there are always new teachers, orientation is at this time a constant.

Course work and sporadic classroom experimentation enabled us to identify problems. By 1962, we were ready to essay some research and one of our junior high schools applied for a federal grant. In 1962–63, we carried on research into the language of junior high students. We learned very few answers from this research, but we were able to refine our questions tremendously and this is very important in a new discipline. While many instructors participated in the research project, the bulk of the work was done by a project investigator appointed from our staff. The results involved rather high level theory that we knew most of the staff would not understand, but we had some people who did understand, enough of them.

One item we clearly saw from the research and from numerous class observations was that the inductive method was a real stumbling block. We found an infinite deal of talk about problem solving and very little palpable evidence. Consequently, in 1963–64, we held a seminar in which we discussed the inductive method. The seminar met every two weeks for three hours and in the seminar we probed, fought, despaired. The directors of mathematics, science, and foreign language sat with us now and then, for they too had this problem in their disciplines. No report was ever issued from this seminar (one reason why the seminar is so useful—it encourages free, tough-minded discussion free of term papers), but its fruits are contained in our manual just published. There we have set down what we know so far—not at all enough.

This year, our courses shift into another gear. The general orientation course is not being offered, because the available instructors are all involved in another large project. We do need a course, and fortunately there is one being given in the Adult Education Program. While this course is not designed specifically for teachers, it will serve us well. It is being taught by one of our staff members. The course we are offering is open only to teachers in grades four through six, Westport staff only. (One junior high principal will sit in and no doubt the elementary principals will drop in when they can.) Originally our courses are open only to Westport staff, then gradually we open them up to any teachers from surrounding towns who wish to attend. There is no charge for any of these courses, and they all carry Westport in-service credit. (The public of course is never admitted, except in the Adult Education Program.)

Simultaneously, we shall conduct a seminar at the junior high level with an eye to writing a manual of instruction for grades seven through nine. This seminar will be in charge of Mrs. Ella Demers, the English Department Chairman at Long Lots Junior High School, a teacher well-known for her work in descriptive grammars. One of the most experienced and highly trained teachers, who was also the project investigator for our research, Ruby Kelley, has been made available to the senior high, where she will act as a resource person for the staff there in addition to her regular teaching duties.

Fortunately, in the past few years, more courses have become available in colleges in the area. We do like our staff to study with various linguists, for they all have something of interest to us.

You can see how much of our development is dependent on two things: having staff members who know the discipline of grammar, or are at least sufficiently grounded to spearhead the inquiry, and working unremittingly on the central problem of building a grammar curriculum. We may not be the ones who will produce this needed curriculum, but if and when it appears, at least we shall recognize it and be able to use it.

This knowledgeable staff all arrived upon the scene knowing nothing about descriptive grammars. The teachers with the most university training received that training after they worked in the Westport System and were there introduced to the new grammars. Lately, we have been able to employ some teachers with prior training, but this is still the exception rather than the rule.

Conclusion

When teachers are committed to inquiry, then the new grammars will gain momentum. These grammars will not be accepted at face value, but in the finest tradition, they will be studied closely, weighed, and considered. It is very possible that the new grammars will soon become a fad, and if this fate should overtake an essentially solid discipline, then teachers have only themselves to blame. They will condemn their schools to a reign of alchemy when chemistry is already known. To teach is to inquire.

My purpose has been to commend inquiry to you and to offer living proof that one *can* inquire into the new grammars. "It is up to the people primarily concerned with curriculum to build an integrated system out of the (grammar) materials available." I suggest that we catch that torch and hold it high; otherwise, we may find that it will set our house on fire.

Techniques of Evaluation in Arithmetic

BEN A. SUELTZ [*]

LET US CONSIDER evaluation very broadly to include the whole range from a casual impression to a careful assessment that uses a sophisticated statistical procedure. The teacher, both consciously and subconsciously, is constantly appraising and judging her pupils and storing impressions of their behavior in respect to learning as well as to the many other facets of school life. These are evaluations, even though they may not enter into a school mark or be reported to parents. For example, the teacher notes that Susie counts on her fingers, Jane clicks her tongue on her teeth in counting, and Sam looks at Joe's paper for a correct answer. It is worth noting that Susie, Jane, Sam, and Joe all have succeeded in an addition exercise, but the fact of success is a different evaluation from noting the avenue by which the success was reached.

On the other hand, a school may use a most carefully prepared standardized test which has established norms. The use of such an instrument, the way in which this is used, and the interpretation of the results indicate how a school views the role and importance of evaluation.

THE CURRENT CONCEPT

By "arithmetic" is now meant much more than the old concept of computation and solving written problems. The ideas included in the term "mathematics in the elementary school" are accepted as being more applicable than the term "arithmetic." Arithmetic or

[*] Professor of Education, State University College, Cortland, New York.

mathematics at this level includes information, concepts, principles, understandings, judgments, computation, and problems. And principally, the concern is with the ability to think and to work with all the facets of arithmetic. The individual pupil must be held above the machine. His role in life should not be restricted to that of an automaton.

THE PUPILS

The pupils in any given class or school are never a homogeneous group. They range in mental ability, in experience backgrounds, in social and emotional development, and in attitude and maturity toward school and learning. The family circumstances are a strong affecting factor in many cases. It is desirable for a teacher to have some knowledge of these factors as they pertain to learning and to evaluation of arithmetic.

Normally one expects to find approximately two-thirds of a group in the middle one-third of a class range. Evaluation should substantially cover the complete range, and hence it usually is desirable to employ several types of assessments. The insight expected of a really bright child is different from the rote learning of the less able.

THE FUNCTIONS OF EVALUATION

What functions may evaluation serve? Primarily, we think of evaluating the learning of a particular pupil, not only in terms of our best appraisal thereof but also as this relates to other pupils within his class, pupils within our school and city, and in relation to national standards of achievement. These evaluations also are related to the expectations that have been set down in curricula.

In a broader sense, we consider evaluation as an essential in instruction. The pupil must move ahead, but in arithmetic, many new learnings are dependent upon previous learnings. Every difficulty that is encountered by pupil and teacher calls for an evaluation of the present status and of how best to proceed from there.

Many schools are experimenting with what they call the "new arithmetic." This calls for careful evaluation, not only for the sake of knowing what and how much is being accomplished, but also in providing a record that may be useful in intelligent public relations with the clientele of the school.

The results of evaluation form the raw material for research in learning and in appraising experimental procedures and new curricula, as well as forming the foundation for pupil reporting.

But basically, evaluation is important for its service to the teacher and the pupil in enhancing the learning of arithmetic.

Modes of Evaluation in Arithmetic

PUPIL SELF-DIAGNOSIS

One aspect of evaluation that is often neglected and one that is particularly useful in diagnosis is that of pupil self-diagnosis. By a little adroit questioning on the part of the teacher, a pupil often can locate his own difficulty, and he is already on the road to improvement. Perhaps you recall the story of the boy in kindergarten who always used a black crayon. His teacher became concerned by the blackness of his drawings, and since she had studied psychology, she became disturbed. She consulted the principal and the school psychologist, who immediately arranged for the parents to visit in an attempt to locate the sinister influence behind the black crayon. After some probing and discussion, the boy's father, who took this rather lightly, suggested that the boy be brought in. When the father asked why he always used a black crayon, the boy said simply that this was the only color left in the box when it came to him. Yes, we can learn much if we will deal honestly with pupils.

Many teachers have developed procedures for pupil self-appraisal. In my own experience, pupils have been very honest and remarkably acute. I recall using a "Pupil Record Booklet" which was made by folding, cutting, and stapling blank paper into a size 4¼ by 5½ in. On the left hand side, each pupil kept his record of items he really knew, and on the right side, he recorded his trouble spots. Such a booklet is not only a useful record but also a good stimulus. Likewise, a check list may be employed periodically.

OBSERVATION AND INTERVIEW

The technique of careful observation coupled with interview is most fruitful. The good teacher is like the good physician. She knows what questions to ask, how to evaluate answers and how to draw valid conclusions from what she sees and hears. Then the remedy, the service to learning, is intelligently prescribed.

Let me cite two examples:

In a rather well-known private school, grade seven, a boy was working on his contract of arithmetic problems. The teacher sat at the desk, because the school felt that learning was individual and that a pupil should work and learn independently. After obtaining permission to speak to the pupil, I asked him to read a problem to me, because I had noted that all his answers were wrong. Then, using an old-fashioned-teacher technique, I asked him some questions including the reasonableness of his answer in terms of the information given. The boy sensed that something must be wrong and said, "I'll ask Miss——— (the teacher)." I heard her say, "Do this and that and you will get the correct answer." Here was an opportunity to diagnose, to evaluate, and genuinely to serve learning, but it was missed.

In the second school, also in a grade seven that was working with problems, the teacher had previously worked with the whole class on careful reading and, through discussion and by illustration, had led them to an understanding of the basic problem pattern. Then, while pupils were individually at work, she observed, stopped and asked questions to redirect their thinking and understanding of the relationships in a problem, asked one boy to draw items to represent the problem situation, and generally was continually assessing, appraising, and guiding the learning of each pupil.

TEST SITUATIONS

How valid is the careful assessment of a pupil by a teacher? Can it be used as the basis of a school mark and of a report to a parent independent of performance on a written test? Several years ago a group of teachers tentatively accepted the idea that they should be as competent to judge and evaluate as any medical practitioner. As a first step, they established five levels of pupil understanding and achievement and then placed their pupils in these five categories. (The five levels were chosen so that later they could be compared with the typical A,B,C,D,E marking pattern.) After the personal appraisals were made, the pupils were given school class-tests and also standardized tests. It was most revealing to note the several teachers' feelings and behavior. Some were sure that their appraisals were more valid than the results of the written tests, but a few of them were unwilling to use their own judgments instead of test scores in determining the pupil's mark. Others just were so worshipfully steeped in testing that they immediately rejected the personal appraisal. A compromise was reached by using the test scores as a basis with only slight modifications based upon judgment. I still think we ought to have such well trained and experienced teachers that there can be no doubt of the validity of their personal appraisal of pupil work.

Certainly, in the area of appraisal of such factors in arithmetic as insight, discovery, and judgment, we have not been able to design tests in which we have great confidence, and hence we must rely upon our own, hopefully valid appraisals.

PRACTICAL PROBLEMS

The *dictum* that arithmetic shall be socially and economically useful to the citizen is still accepted. To serve thus, the individual must be able to sense a mathematical situation and to know what to do about it. In other words, arithmetic consists of many items of information and processes that should be useful in one's life. Knowledge of common measures and their uses and interrelationships is an example. Consider the "quart." It is a quarter of a gallon, holds two pints, and the dry quart is a little larger than the liquid quart. The sensing of the concept of a quart and the various uses thereof, such as a quart of ice cream will serve eight persons generously, has value. Basic information is easily tested by a written measure, but the sensing of quart and its relationships is oft best appraised through casual discussion. Likewise, a good technique for appraising the ability to associate a process with a situation may be evaluated by exercises such as the following:

(1) Present a descriptive situation, such as preparing for a party, to a class and ask the pupils to write problems in terms of the given information.

(2) Ask pupils to state problems, using one or more processes, such as addition and subtraction, or multiplication and addition.

(3) Make a list of typical problems that use division. From such procedures it is amazing how pupils reveal their abilities.

EXERCISES

The ability to sense and to discover a mathematical relationship may be measured by presenting items such as the following:

(1) How many different numbers can you find to satisfy an equation that asks for two components to equal 12? Can you change the equation?

(2)
3	8	1
6	12	2
9	16	3
12	20	—
15	24	—
18	28	—
—	32	98
—	—	99
—	—	100

Can you discover a way to find the sum of these figures without adding all of them?

(3)
1				
1	2	1		
1	3	3	1	
1	4	6	4	1

What would be the next row of figures across? Can you discover the pattern?

(4) Consider a rectangle as flexible, with pegs in each corner. Suppose we change the shape to a parallelogram. Have we altered the perimeter? the area?

Exercises such as these enable the teacher to judge the pupil's ability to sense relationships. This is of genuine importance in mathe-

Techniques of Evaluation in Arithmetic

matics, for it helps locate those pupils who may become the mathematicians of the future.

CHECK LISTS

Check lists are also useful in evaluation. Usually, the list used by a teacher should be different from that used by pupils. In order to be most fruitful, especially for analysis and diagnosis, a check list must be fairly detailed.

Since a considerable portion of mathematics is encountered orally and pictorially, some attention should be given to evaluation by these approaches. For example, the child hears "10 cents a piece" or "three for 27 cents," and the adult is told that "It pays $2.40 and is quoted at $60 per share." The child sees by the clock that it is now 10:10 in the morning and reasons that it lacks only ten minutes from being two hours until noon. The young housewife sees a piece of sirloin and visualizes that 3½ lb. will serve four people, because it is nearly half bone and fat. Then if she is really mathematically intelligent, she will know that the posted price of 89 cents per pound means about $1.75 per pound for the meat.

WRITTEN TESTS

Written tests, both those constructed by a teacher for her class or by a local school group and those that presumably have been carefully constructed and standardized, will continue to be our most respected instruments of evaluation. It must always be remembered that a child is being evaluated in terms of the content of the particular test that he is taking.

Curriculum Validity.—If a test is intended for more than one school grade, it should follow the curriculum sequence. For example, a certain test was standardized on performance of a "normal group" in grades four, five, and six. It so happened that a typical item for grade six had a high percentage of correct responses, and because of this was placed early in the test sequence. But when Joe, who was in grade four, took the test, he was puzzled and spent several minutes on the item. On the other hand, some pupils looked at the item and immediately went on to the next. With the time thus saved, they scored 4 points higher than Joe, which gave them a grade score of 6 months higher.

The test content should approximate the curriculum in the proportion allocated to the major segments of learning. Children have a right to be evaluated on the things they are expected to learn. I recall two grades six. One was a few days ahead of the other in the textbook and had done a little extra work. Both grades were given a standardized test that had a number of items based upon a simple understanding of percentage. The one grade rated a year higher than the other because of a basic weakness in the test. Likewise, if the basic work of grade four is based upon advances in addition and subtraction and multiplication, these should form the rubric for testing. If, on the other hand, a class has been working on sets and structures, these should be the basis for evaluation.

Scope.—A test should cover a wide range of abilities, including such features as insight, understanding, and judgment as well as the usual computations and problems. For example, the ability to follow the reasoning and calculations of another may involve no actual calculation, but his conclusion can be tested. Likewise, there are many "either-or" situations, such as: "Shall I take Route 87 or 32?" "Shall I buy item A or item B?"

Administration.—The make-up and presentation of the test should be such that it is easily administered and scored and that the directions and procedures are clear. You can identify one test in which certain pupils fail to note that computation items are mixed and that a pupil who proceeds rapidly and does his work correctly, but adds when he is supposed to subtract, rates a year lower than his less able but cautious colleague. When testing in mathematics, it is important not to give too much attention to reading or to following specialized directions. A test in mathematics should be a test in mathematics and not intelligence or some other related area.

If we believe that mathematics should become functional to the individual, we should test in functional settings. It is not valid to assume that a pupil who responds well on isolated skills and concepts will automatically have the ability to apply these to socio-economic situations or to synthesize these into a pattern of thinking.

Techniques of Evaluation in Arithmetic

Norms.—Test norms should be sensibly related to the number of exercises on the test. That is, a mean norm of 10 on a test of 50 items suggests that the pupils' time is not being well used. Several years ago, I recall seeing a test on which the norm for grade two was 3. We should be wary of extrapolated norms and of tests that aim to cover a wide range of school grades. Likewise, we look with alarm at a test for which the norm for grade five is but three or four points above that for grade four. When one realizes the probable error in such a test, one should be careful in interpretation, especially in applying a norm to an individual pupil.

Interpretation.—Teachers should also be wary of drawing unwarranted conclusions from standardized tests results. Recall that on any test, pupils are being appraised in terms of the content of that particular test. In general, from a good test it is valid to compare groups, but it is dangerous to make claims such as, "Susie has made a gain of 1½ years in the past 4 months," and "Sally is doing eighth-grade level work, but she is only a sixth grader." When my own daughter was in grade four, she reached the eighth grade norm. She was not doing anything beyond the normal grade four, but she was doing this exceedingly well.

It is important to consider expectations in terms of ability. For example, a child with an I.Q. of 121, which is one standard deviation above the mean, should be achieving at the 84th percentile. Some years ago when we were surveying a school with pupils of high ability in which the teachers and principal were happy with the achievement of pupils because they were one year above standard norms, we found the pupils actually to be underachievers in terms of their abilities.

In my own work in the development of tests, it was necessary to interview pupils in order to establish the validity of a number of test items. Some pupils were giving correct responses for the wrong reasons. It is like the pupil who makes two compensating errors in addition and gets the right answer. From this experimental work, a test was constructed in which the norm for grade eight is lower than for grade seven, and yet by normal statistical procedures, it is a perfectly good test. Let us be most careful in the construction and selection of tests and then be sensible in interpreting the results.

Summary

Evaluation has been viewed very broadly in terms of all the aspects of a modern program in arithmetic or elementary school mathematics. Evaluation should be concerned with information, concepts, principles, understandings, and computations, problems, and drawing conclusions.

Evaluation is considered primarily an aid to the teaching and learning of mathematics, recognizing that it has other uses, such as in reporting pupil progress and as a basis for research.

There are many modes of evaluation which range from casual impressions to sophisticated statistical procedures. The teacher is regarded as a competent diagnostician and appraiser who should be able to make valid assessments of her pupils.

Mathematics is important in the social, economic, and cultural lives of intelligent citizens. Much of this mathematics does not involve complex computation but is concerned with reasoning and thinking, which is not presented via written words and need not be accomplished via paper and pencil.

Written tests continue to be a major mode of evaluation. Such tests should be carefully constructed to measure all of the aspects of the arithmetic curriculum. Likewise, it must be remembered that many unwarranted conclusions are frequently made from the results of standardized tests.

Schools developing programs in what is called the "new mathematics" must develop evaluations in terms of the basic aims and structures of these programs. Evaluation can serve to measure, but it should not attempt to establish or to defend goals.

Finally, it should be restated that evaluation is a most important aspect of the school's function in guiding the learning of the individual pupils. In the United States, we expect each pupil to achieve those learnings which will enable him to fulfill his best role in our society.

IV

Secondary Education

Major Concepts in History: Implications for the Secondary Social Studies Program

RUSSELL F. WEIGLEY *

"HAPPY IS THE people that is without a history, and thrice happy the people without a sociology." So goes an observation of Christopher Dawson, himself a distinguished historian and philosopher of history. Whether a people without a sociology is thrice happy is questionable. Most historians probably suspect that Dawson's observation is correct as far as sociology is concerned, but that question is for the sociologists to deal with. The teaching of history has enough problems of its own, and it is with those problems that this paper deals.

THE TYRANNY OF HISTORY

The teaching of history does involve many problems, even to the point that there is a great deal to be said for the observation, "Happy is the people that is without a history." For history is a kind of tyrant, and the principal purpose of the teaching of history is, paradoxically, to liberate us from history. For in a number of ways history is a thing that imprisons us and tyrannizes over us, limiting our possibilities for constructive action, both as a society and as individuals. This tyranny is exercised by history in both senses of the word, that is, by the past as it really was and by our writing about, teaching about, and understanding of it. And the only way to set ourselves free as much as possible from the limitations imposed upon

* Professor of History, Temple University, Philadelphia, Pennsylvania.

us by the past is to understand it as thoroughly and as clearly as we can.

The past tyrannizes over us in various ways. In the first place, the past is difficult to understand. We can never recapture it altogether; we must rely on fragmentary evidence for our knowledge of it. It is therefore an elusive thing, and it is readily misunderstood. And because we misunderstand and misconstrue the past, we try to draw lessons from it that are not really there, and we turn out to be misguided.

Very few men in our day still argue that history is "bunk" and claim to be so "practical" that they have no use for history. Instead, we are surrounded by appeals to history and the past as sources of guidance for the present. Our political leaders endlessly exhort us to look to the wisdom of the founding fathers, to return to the true spirit and letter of the Constitution, to read the Constitution as its writers intended it to be read, and then, they say, we shall save our country and the world.

THE PAST AS IT HAS BEEN INTERPRETED

But how often are the appeals of political, business, and labor leaders to the past appeals to the real past? How often do appeals to the wisdom of the founding fathers of the Republic base themselves upon what the founding fathers actually thought and said? How often are such appeals pleas to a specious rather than a real past? Too often, I think.

Isolationism.—For example, as the United States has made its difficult and reluctant way out of the hemispheric isolation in which it was encased through most of its history and into increasing entanglement in the affairs of the whole world, how often have the opponents of American involvement in a League of Nations or United Nations organization and the like cited George Washington, especially his Farewell Address, as warnings against the abandonment of our isolation? [1] This sort of thing is of course no longer heard so often as it was in Woodrow Wilson's day, or even Franklin D. Roosevelt's or Harry S. Truman's, but most of us can remember hearing

[1] See Washington Irving, *The Life of George Washington,* Vol. V, Limited Centennial Edition (New York: G. P. Putnam's Sons, 1889), p. 279f.

at least echoes of it. Washington's Farewell Address is so often cited as an indictment of entangling alliances that almost everyone now unquestioningly accepts it as such.

But it is by no means a blanket indictment of foreign alliances. Instead, Washington specifically approved such alliances in extraordinary circumstances, and most people would agree that the circumstances which have threatened the United States since the second world war might be considered extraordinary. Furthermore, to the very real extent that the Farewell Address does warn against alliances, it makes clear that the warning is against alliances at a specific time and under specific circumstances. Washington warned against foreign alliances for a weak nation in a world of incomparably stronger predatory powers, and he said specifically that it was to such a situation that he was referring. We should wait until we were stronger, he said; once we became a strong power, we could choose our course of action more freely as our interests might dictate. Furthermore, the premise upon which Washington based his reasoning was that "Europe has a set of primary interests which to us have none or a very remote relation." Few informed people can believe that this premise is true today. To allow ourselves to be guided by the kind of history that appeals to Washington's Farewell Address while ignoring the historical setting of Washington's advice and the qualifications which he attached to that advice is to allow ourselves to be tyrannized by a history that is not even true history.

The civil rights movement.—But we submit to such tyranny again and again. One of the most effective arguments of those who oppose the civil rights movement in the South is that legislation to impose civil rights is futile, because segregation and discrimination are deeply rooted in the whole long history of the South. Many thoughtful people who might otherwise favor pushing forward with the civil rights movement pause in the face of this argument, wondering how we can change a whole way of life that has developed over centuries. But C. Vann Woodward has shown in his book *The Strange Career of Jim Crow* that much Southern racial segregation is not rooted in centuries of Southern history but dates only from the relatively recent 1890's.[2] There is much evidence that as late as

[2] C. Vann Woodward, *The Strange Career of Jim Crow* (New York: Oxford University Press, 1955).

the 1880's Negroes and whites in the South ate at the same restaurants, traveled side by side on the same public conveyances, marched together in processions, sometimes worshipped in the same churches (with Negroes appearing in white churches), and generally mingled much more freely than they do today. Complex historical circumstances having to do with the political role of the Negro in the Populist movement brought about a harsher segregation during the 1890's and at the turn of the century. But whatever the wisdom or lack of it in civil rights legislation, such legislation cannot rightly be called unwise on the ground that segregation of the races as we have come to know it existed in the South from time immemorial; it did not.

Spurious histories.—Appeals for guidance from a past that never existed are so frequent that sometimes it seems the chief function of historians and teachers of history must be a rather gloomy negative one, that of constantly doing battle against historical misconceptions. Great though the difficulties of knowing the past are, nevertheless I am continually amazed as well as appalled by the ease with which false history wins public acceptance. In recent weeks considerable publicity has been given to a new popular history, aimed at the general public, of the Mollie Maguires, the secret organization which is supposed to have terrorized the anthracite fields of Schuylkill and Luzerne Counties during the late nineteenth century. The new history of the Mollies has been widely reviewed in the press and in magazines, and it has been almost uniformly praised by the reviewers as a readable history of a fascinating incident. Only one popular review that has come to my attention, the one in the *New York Times Book Review*,[3] has failed to recommend the book and has pointed out the truth about it: that it is based almost entirely on the accounts of James McParlan, the Pinkerton agent who allegedly infiltrated the Mollie Maguires, and that McParlan is now known to have been an incorrigible liar. His uncorroborated testimony is worth almost nothing. Even then, the book fails to distinguish between what McParlan said at the trial of the alleged leaders of the Mollies at the time

[3] William A. P. White, "Miners and Murder," *New York Times Book Review*, August 30, 1964, Sec. 7, pp. 10, 12. A review of A. H. Lewis, *Lament for the Molly Maguires* (New York: Harcourt, Brace, and World, 1964).

Implications for the Secondary Social Studies Program 169

of the incident and what he wrote thirty years afterward. In fact, most historians who have made reasonably thorough studies of the anthracite area now believe that the Mollie Maguires never existed, that there was no such secret organization, and that the whole myth of the Mollie Maguires was contrived by Franklin B. Gowen, the president of the Reading Railroad, with McParlan's help, to discredit labor unionization in the coal fields. Historians have been skeptical about the existence of the Mollies for years; yet a book devoted to their dubious history is pawned off upon the public with hardly a protest from the reviewers. Surely one of the first duties of teachers of history must be to stress the need for caution in appraising historical evidence, and at least to keep well enough informed that we ourselves can distinguish the true from the specious in history and guide our students accordingly.

Of course, a specious history of the Mollie Maguires is no longer likely to do much harm; the Mollies do not have much relevance to present day labor problems. But other distortions of the past can affect policy today and can do real harm, can in effect tyrannize over us. No doubt there is often an element of deliberate deception in the kind of appeals to history that oversimplify Washington's Farewell Address, but we can misunderstand history and be misled by it for much more subtle reasons and in more subtle ways. For one thing, history itself causes us to distort history. That is, because of our own particular historical circumstances, we tend to notice some aspects of the past and to overlook others. We see the past through the mirror of our own minds, and that unfortunately is often a distorting mirror.

Subjective interpretations.—There exists a fascinating book by Merrill D. Peterson called *The Jefferson Image in the American Mind*.[4] This book is not a biography of Jefferson but a history of the different aspects in which Jefferson has appeared to his countrymen from his own time to ours. It shows that each era since Jefferson's own has constructed its own Thomas Jefferson, has seen Thomas Jefferson by its own lights, and, in a sense, has seen the Jefferson it wanted to see. During the slavery controversy before the

[4] Merrill D. Peterson, *The Jefferson Image in the American Mind* (New York: Oxford University Press, 1960).

Civil War, abolitionists saw the Jefferson who had written the Declaration of Independence and had inserted the provision outlawing slavery into the Northwest Ordinance. Southerners saw the Jefferson who himself owned slaves and the Jefferson who enunciated the doctrines of states' rights. In the twentieth century, the New Deal took Jefferson as a symbol and erected the great memorial to him in Washington. But opponents of the New Deal made much use of his conviction that the best government is the one that governs least.

Our interpretations of the Civil War also have followed a wandering course which reflects the people and the age doing the interpreting almost as much as it reflects the Civil War itself. For example, about the beginning of the twentieth century, there was more agreement between Northern and Southern historians about the causes of the Civil War than there ever was before—or ever has been since. North and South, historians emphasized the constitutional issues of the war, theories of a strong central government versus states rights or perhaps economic issues, and generally agreed as to what were the main causes. Significantly, at that time, the turn of the century, Northerners were not much interested in the race question, and they tended to entrust the fate of the Southern Negro to the hands of the Southern whites. With no live dispute "heating" racial issues, Southern and Northern whites were able to agree on what had caused the Civil War.

But with the growing Northern interest in civil rights that developed through the twentieth century and especially from the New Deal period onward, Northern and Southern attitudes diverged not only on the place of the Negro in America today but on the place of the Negro a century and more ago. While the interpretations of the causes of the Civil War that were advanced around the turn of the century had tended to downgrade the importance of the slavery issue per se, Northern historians observing the force of the civil rights movement recognized the similar nature of the antislavery movement a hundred years before and re-emphasized its importance in bringing on the Civil War. Indeed, it is probable that more Northern historians today cite the slavery issue as the single most important cause of the Civil War than any other issue. Not only has the slavery issue been re-emphasized among the causes of the Civil War,

Implications for the Secondary Social Studies Program 171

however, but Northern historians have also viewed the antislavery movement with increasing sympathy. In the South, on the other hand, the rise of the civil rights issue has created a new Southern hostility toward the antislavery men of a century ago who seem, in Southern eyes, so much like the civil rights leaders of today. Northern and Southern views on the causes of the Civil War, therefore, have again diverged under the influence, not so much of a new knowledge of the Civil War era, as of events in our own times.

To Northern historians, the Civil War now often appears as a conflict caused by the failure of the South to keep in step with the nineteenth century. Slavery was an anomaly in the liberal nineteenth-century world, especially in the United States, and as such it was bound to find itself in difficulty. In fact, it was not only an anomaly; it was intolerable in its violation of all the principles upon which the United States otherwise was founded. The antislavery leaders were morally right in attacking it and in refusing to compromise with it; but more than that, it was so great an anomaly that conflict over its existence was truly irrepressible. Southern historians of today, on the other hand, argue that the South if left alone could have adjusted its own institutions to changing values in the long run and that a needless conflict was stirred up by Northern antislavery fanatics, much as, in the Southern view, a needless conflict is being stirred up by civil rights fanatics today. So greatly have Northern and Southern views of the coming of the Civil War diverged under the influence of the modern civil rights controversy that some writers speak with good reason of a "new civil war" among the historians.

Distortions from contemporary perspectives.—This new civil war of the historians is another example of history tyrannizing over us: in this case, the history of our own times so imprisons us as to distort our vision of the past, for Northern and Southern views have come to be so different that surely at least one group must be seeing the past through a distorting mirror.

Of course, history ought to be relevant to issues that remain alive, and to the extent that it is, we are bound to see history in the light of those issues. But history must not become simply a servant of opinions regarding current controversy. If teachers of history are to liberate us from the possible tyranny of history, they must especially guard themselves against the very great temptations to make history subservient to their own values and opinions; they must seek with special care to dedicate themselves to the truth of history and to discovering it to the best of their ability. We can never see the past wholly as it was, independent of our own concerns, but we must try to see the real past as clearly as we can, for only then can history help liberate us rather than tyrannize over us.

THE PAST AS IT REALLY WAS

And yet, it is not only the past as we picture it that can be a tyrant over us. Even more disturbingly, the past as it really was can also be a tyrant; in this sense, too, we might say, "Happy is the people that is without a history." Yet even here, teachers of history can do something to liberate us from tyranny, to minimize the extent to which history imprisons us.

The frontier in American history.—Let us examine an outstanding example of our being imprisoned, not merely by a misunderstood past, but even by the past as it really was. A consideration of the Turner frontier thesis of American history gives us a good example of our imprisonment by the past.

No interpretation of the nature of American history has more thoroughly influenced writing and teaching in the twentieth century than the old, now time-worn frontier interpretation announced by Frederick Jackson Turner of the University of Wisconsin in 1893.[5] Even those teachers of history who remember only dimly ever having heard about the Turner theory in their college days can scarcely help but teach under its spell. The theory argues, of course, that the principal element that shaped American civilization was the frontier experience. Every part of the United States at one time or another stood on the frontier of civilization, on the very dividing line between civilization, on the one hand, and barbarism and the unknown on the other. The experience of thus serving as the cutting edge of civilization drastically modified old institutions and old ways of life, so much so as to create in America a new civilization that was no

[5] Frederick Jackson Turner, *The Frontier in American History* (New York: H. Holt and Company, 1920).

longer a European civilization but one that had become distinctively American. America is a unique civilization, according to Turner, because of the frontier experience.

The Turner thesis has come under a great deal of attack through the years, and it is true that its sway over the writing and teaching of American history is no longer so great as it once was. Its influence diminished somewhat during the Great Depression of the 1930's, when the Depression reminded us that, as an industrial and urban society, we now had much in common with industrial and urban societies everywhere, especially in Europe. Our participation in World War II, in defense not only of our own ideals but of those of Western civilization in general, reminded us that, if we had undergone the frontier experience, it was like the frontier of western Europe; our civilization, however modified, was basically a European civilization. The continued involvement of the United States in the world-at-large since World War II has continued to remind us how much we have in common with other societies, how much our values especially have been inherited from elsewhere, and how much their survival in our country depends upon their survival elsewhere.

Yet, despite all the criticism which the Turner frontier thesis has undergone in the past thirty years, the thesis still has much validity; historians today still generally recognize that the thesis does much to explain the American past, and, indeed, the pendulum of historical opinion has swung away from criticism of the Turner thesis toward a renewed respect for it. Some historians in the past decade have attempted to enhance the usefulness of the Turner thesis as an explanation of the nature of American life by embellishing it so as to make it more clearly applicable to twentieth-century America. A good example of this approach is a recent essay which holds that the key element of the frontier experience was the mobility of the American population, and that in continuing mobility the essence of Turner's frontier experience still remains and continues to shape American life. This attempt to adjust the Turner thesis to the twentieth century may well be over-sophisticated to the point of severe distortion of the original frontier thesis. Other recent historians have been content simply to argue that, since the 1930's, we have overreacted against Turner, and that it is time to restore our appreciation for the virtues of his thesis.

Many of those virtues seem almost self-evident. Turner argued that the frontier experience made America more democratic than Europe. On the edge of European settlement in America, European social and economic distinctions, indeed, did seem to have little meaning, and the individual's own ability to carve out a farm or a trading business or to participate in defense against the Indians became much more important than inherited family distinctions. A rough social and economic equality marked frontier America, and when political institutions developed in frontier communities, political democracy developed naturally as a reflection of that social and economic democracy. Similarly, the frontier nourished egalitarianism, especially an emphasis on equality of opportunity. America did precede Europe in the development of an egalitarian democracy and, in many ways, continues in advance of Europe in many of the social aspects of democracy. The frontier appears to offer one of the most important explanations of this situation.

Beyond democracy and egalitarianism, the frontier may well have nourished American individualism and also the notably pragmatic bent of American thought, for the frontier was nothing, if not hostile, to abstract thought and demanded practical approaches. The frontier may well have nourished the optimism of American thought as well, for the frontier offered great untapped riches, and the problems it presented were practical problems which, because they were practical, could be solved.

In sum, the Turner frontier thesis remains a widely influential interpretation of American history and may even be gaining in influence after a period of partial eclipse. Its influence rests on the fact that it has genuine, even self-evident, relevance to an understanding of American society.

The Turner thesis, however, presents some important insights into the imprisoning qualities of a country's history. Because it does explain much about the nature of American society, the Turner thesis also points to some of the difficulties which have attended our national history during the twentieth century. The Turner thesis holds that because of the frontier experience, which no other country underwent in quite the same way, American civilization is unique. To say that the Turner thesis still seems to hold a considerable validity is to argue, then, that American society is unique; that while related to European society, it is sufficiently different to be judged a distinct civilization. In the nineteenth century, it was easy for the United States to live its own life as a distinct civilization, standing apart from the rest of the world. Certainly during the nineteenth century, the United States was completely secure against any military threat from elsewhere in the world; nineteenth-century military technology gave no foreign power any reasonable possibility of crossing the oceans and imposing its will upon the United States. Woodward has suggested in recent years that the concept of security, complete security from external danger, is as important to an understanding of nineteenth-century America as the frontier concept. But in the twentieth century, technology has so shrunk the world that other societies cannot help but impinge upon ours, and ours upon theirs. And to the extent that American society is genuinely different from other societies, it seems inevitable that there should be friction and difficulties of adjustment in our encounters with the rest of the world.

What is surprising is not that there should be resistance among Americans to the increasingly close involvement of their country in the affairs of all the rest of the world, but that so far, at least, the resistance has been so slight. Those Americans who cry out against the growing entanglement of America's destiny with the destinies of distant peoples cry with a voice that proceeds naturally out of the American past, for in the past we developed a distinctive society and a distinctive national character and were secure to go our own distinctive way. In the past, in short, American isolation from the rest of the world was not a policy but a simple reality. That we should feel a national nostalgia for the days when we could live a national life completely our own is surely inevitable, and that such nostalgia should take political expression is hardly surprising.

Conclusion

Our own national past, then, does tyrannize over us, does limit our ability to respond to the pressures of the twentieth century. We might in some ways be a happier people without a history—without our particular history which makes so difficult our involvement in events beyond our own shores. But at least to understand our past and the effects it has upon us is to be less at its mercy. Any people so unfortunate as to be living under the government of a tyrant are careful to learn the ways of the tyrant so as to find the maximum area of liberty for themselves, and so we must adjust to the tyrant "history."

The duty of teachers of history remains, then, a gloomy one. Perhaps the best we can do is to try to teach our students that we must not attempt to learn too much from the past. Perhaps the chief goal of understanding the past ought to be to liberate ourselves as much as possible from the past. Though this view of the reason for teaching history is a gloomy one, nevertheless, the teaching of history is important. It is the man who is uninformed about Thomas Jefferson's relation to the time in which he lived, for example, who seeks too literal a guidance from Jefferson. He is likely to neglect the clear dependence of Jefferson's political thought upon the existence of a rural, agrarian America; Jefferson himself would be the first to urge that his thought would not apply to an urban industrial society such as ours. It is the man who is relatively uninformed about Jefferson and his time who is likely to overlook Jefferson's single most important precept for us: "Nothing then is unchangeable but the inherent and unalienable rights of man."

It is only by knowing history and to the best of our ability understanding the past that we can fully appreciate the force of Abraham Lincoln's observation in his Annual Message to Congress on December 1, 1862: "The dogmas of the quiet past are inadequate to the stormy present. The occasion is piled high with difficulty, and we must rise with the occasion. As our case is new, so we must think anew and act anew. We must disenthrall ourselves, and then we shall save our country." [6]

[6] John G. Nicolay and John Hay (eds.), *Complete Works of Abraham Lincoln*, VIII (New York: Francis D. Tandy Company, 1905), p. 131.

Teaching Economics in High School

HELEN RAFFEL *

ECONOMICS is the study of how a society decides what goods and services it will produce, how much of each kind of good or service will emerge from the production process every day, and how the output will be divided up among the members of the society. It is the study of how people earn their daily bread, what the larger forces are that determine both how big the whole loaf will be, and what kind of a slicing job is done. Certainly "man lives not by bread alone," but the bread must arrive very regularly if the less materialistic fruits of civilization are to arrive at all.

High school students are very sharply aware of the fact that very soon they are going to be thrown on their own into the economic arena. They know that the acceptable way to get a share of America's very large output is to contribute to the production of that output. And they also know that mere willingness to contribute does not automatically spell success in finding one's own niche in the production process. Very likely they also know that young people nowadays are generally having a rather hard time finding jobs, and despite youth's proverbial optimism, some high school students are probably deeply concerned about how they are going to fit into the work world.

REASONS FOR STUDYING ECONOMICS

Now there are several reasons why young people might come to be very interested in learning about a subject like economics. One

* Assistant Professor of Economics, University of Pennsylvania, Philadelphia, Pennsylvania.

reason is the pure joy of discovering how an intricate mechanism works, how the parts mesh together and influence each other, so that the whole apparatus takes shape in the mind's eye and is no longer an overwhelming collection of seemingly incoherent activities. A second reason stems from social concern. If something impinges in a painful, dangerous, or possibly disastrous way on human experience—disease, poverty, war—one can be moved to study the relevant subject matter in order to ameliorate and control the threatening situation. A third reason is a purely personal one. A student may think that learning about the subject can help him avoid inconvenience, pain, or disaster in his own life. Unfortunately, although the student may know abstractly that he will feel inconvenience later on if he does not force himself through the study grind right now, he is not likely to feel the future inconvenience in his imagination so strongly as he may feel the present inconvenience of studying. Of course, if the student has a marvelous teacher, there will be no present inconvenience, and the problem evaporates! But the best policy to follow in order to stimulate an interest in economics in the student who is tempted to give up the whole educational experiment is to suggest the deplorable situation in which he may find himself if he remains economically illiterate.

Some students will see the wonder of the fact that, day after day, a multitude of complicated commodities becomes part of his family's possessions—commodities that his own family could never create for themselves if they were isolated from the rest of the world—and all in return for about 40 hours a week of not too onerous exertion. These students can appreciate economics as the study of an intricate mechanism that continually causes goods and services to be created out of raw materials and labor and to be distributed all over the world in a cornucopian flow.

Some students may be made aware of the fact that the flow of production and distribution is not always ideal; that in the United States perhaps an uncomfortable number of people are on unemployment or welfare relief; that without an informed citizenry Congress will not necessarily be moved to take steps to banish the specter of the 1930's; and worse still, that in other parts of the world periodic famine still occurs. For these students, economics can be seen as a field of social challenge.

Those that do not respond to these abstract statements should be confronted with a few economic facts that illustrate the kind of guidance they can get for their own direction in life. Consider the following items:

(1) Approximately one-fifth of the families whose head dropped out of high school before graduation are living in poverty, according to the 1964 *Economic Report of the President*. More than one-third of the families whose head had no more than 8 years of schooling are poverty-stricken. This fraction drops to one-eighth for high school graduate family heads and to one-twelfth for those who have gone beyond a high school education.[1] (High school teachers take note: one-fifth of the children of our country belong to families that are classified as living in poverty.) The fraction of the U. S. population that may be called poverty-stricken has been dropping rapidly since World War II, but at the same time, the educational level of the labor force has been rising rapidly.[2] Since the beginning of World War II, the median level of education of the male labor force aged eighteen to sixty-four has risen by more than 50 per cent.[3]

The moral here is to go on studying, but why study economics? The answer is that economics tries to explain why it is that the demand for brains is outrunning the demand for brawn. Economics explores the ways in which consumer demand filters down through the productive system and is transformed into demand for different types of labor skill, as well as demand for other types of productive inputs. The study of economic trends can indicate what type of further education will be valuable to the breadwinner.

(2) In the United States between 1950 and 1960, the number of farmers and farm workers *decreased* by 40 per cent; between 1953 and 1963, total employment in manufacturing, mining, and the construction industries *decreased* by 2 per cent. Meanwhile, population *increased* during the fifties by 20 per cent. Does this mean that unemployment increased disastrously? No. Unemployment in 1950 was 5.3 per cent of the civilian labor force, and in 1960 it was 5.6 per cent. Where were the workers absorbed? Briefly: in trade,

[1] Council of Economic Advisers, *Economic Report of the President and Annual Report of the Council of Economic Advisers* (Washington, D.C.: Government Printing Office, 1964), pp. 66, 83.
[2] *Ibid.*, p. 71.
[3] *Ibid.*, pp. 101, 182.

finance, services, and government.⁴ Economics copes with the reasons why certain large fields of endeavor stagnate in employment opportunities, while others expand.

(3) The unemployment rate fluctuates. It was 2.9 per cent in 1953, 6.8 per cent in 1958, and has remained above 5 per cent since 1958. (In 1933, it was 24.9 per cent.)⁵ What can be done to keep the unemployment rate low? The study of economics offers a number of answers. To underscore the importance of this question, let us add the following facts. The unemployment rate for the non-white population is about twice that for the white population. For example, the white unemployment rate in 1953 was 2.3 per cent, while the non-white rate was 4.1 per cent; the white unemployment rate in 1958 was 6.1 per cent, while the non-white rate was 12.6 per cent.⁶ Only part of this difference can be accounted for by the difference in educational level: equal opportunity for education by itself will not eliminate the disadvantaged position of the Negro. The greatest opportunities for permanent social and economic advancement by the non-white segment of the population stem from a booming job market. This was well illustrated during the World War II and Korean War periods.

A SEMESTER'S COURSE IN ECONOMICS

The following presents what I think might be covered in a semester of high school economics. It does not attempt to present the material in the way in which it ought to be presented to the students, but does try to supply some of the building blocks. The bare framework consists of questions, which shall first be named and then elaborated upon one by one. (1) What is economics? (2) What are the advantages of being dependent upon others for one's livelihood? (3) How do prices act as an "invisible hand," causing those goods to be produced that are most desired by the community? (4) How does the economy change and grow? (5) What can go wrong with our

⁴ *Ibid.,* p. 99.
⁵ *Ibid.,* p. 230.
⁶ U.S. Department of Labor, *Manpower Report of the President and Report on Manpower Requirements, Resources, Utilization, and Training* (Washington, D.C.: U.S. Government Printing Office, 1963), p. 145.

economic system and what can be done to keep the economy prosperous?

1. WHAT IS ECONOMICS?

Economics is the study of how men direct their efforts to producing the things they desire. If we lived in the Garden of Eden, where our material wants were small and easily satisfied by simply reaching out our hands and plucking fruit from the trees, there would be no economic problem and no study of economics. Economics deals with how people economize the use of resources that are available in smaller quantities than they would like.

In a simple economy.—The simplest kind of economy one could imagine would be Robinson Crusoe on his island. In addition to the limited supplies of materials retrieved from the ship or available on the island, Crusoe has only a limited amount of time and energy each day, and a limited amount of eighteenth century "know-how." With these resources, he must decide in what order he will produce the things he needs. We must bear in mind that if he produces more of something higher on the list, he will have less time, energy and material left for producing the things lower down. One very important decision he must make and about which more will be said under Question 4, is whether he ought to sacrifice some of the goods that he might have produced to satisfy his current needs in order to devote his resources to producing tools and implements instead. Once he has made certain tools, he will be able to produce, with their help, much more goods for his daily consumption than he could have done without them. He must decide whether the current belt-tightening is a reasonable price to pay. For example, if he can catch four fish a day with a sharp stick picked up on the beach, he must decide whether he can survive on two or three fish a day for a while, in order to give up a few hours each day to collecting thin willow branches and weaving them into a fishnet. The rewards will be great if the temporary sacrifice is not the ultimate one! In oversimplified and perhaps exaggerated form, this is the problem of economic growth—the problem faced by the underdeveloped nations today.

In a complex society.—Robinson Crusoe's economic problems are the essential economic problems faced by any society. But his method of solving them certainly does not give a clear picture of the way a modern industrial nation like the United States proceeds in making production decisions and supplying its citizens with consumption goods. Let us see what changes must be made in order to change from a one-man economic system to a society of 180 million members—a society which has economic dealings beyond its own borders, in addition to a complicated network of internal economic inter-connections.

Once even one more person is added to relieve Robinson Crusoe of his solitude, new types of economic organization are introduced, for it is highly unlikely that each person will continue to produce alone, entirely for himself. The reasons for this will be discussed under Question 2, but let us point out here the fact that co-operation in production—what has been called, since Adam Smith's day, "division of labor"—necessitates some mechanism for sharing out the work to be done and some mechanism for sharing out the jointly-produced goods. Even if each workman is his own employer, say a farmer or a craftsman, some means must be found for informing each farmer and each craftsman which crops or which handicrafts he ought to specialize in and how much of each product he ought to turn out. In our society, this is the function of the market place, more specifically of the going market prices, as will be shown in the discussion of Question 3.

The existence of a market for the purchase of goods or for the purchase of labor services almost invariably gives rise to the use of money. The value of money is more than the value of the goods that money can buy, for money performs a very important service in its own right. The value of the things that money can buy actually depends upon when and where they are delivered to the purchaser. If a farmer goes to market with a truckload of tomatoes, he may not want to accept in exchange exactly what the others are offering at this particular time. He may want to make purchases at the county fair next month, but his tomatoes will not keep till then, and besides, there are people who are eager to eat his tomatoes this week even though they have nothing to offer in return that he is interested in purchasing right now. The great service that money performs is to break the barter exchange of goods or services into two parts—the exchange of money against other goods and services there and later.

No description of what economics is would be complete without mentioning the fact that money is a produced good (produced by banks), that it is sold in the market at a price (the interest rate), and that it is one of the man-made resources (like a machine) which helps in the production of goods and services and their delivery to the consumer.

One further feature of the description of a modern economic system is the fact that most production takes place outside the home. The family farm and the domestic production system (like the small store at the front of the house) are still around, but a very small percentage of the gross national product, something like 4 per cent, originates there. Most people leave their homes to go to work, either selling their services to their employers or themselves employing others. This means that the study of the markets for buying and selling such productive resources as labor services is just as important as study of the markets in which consumers' commodities are bought and sold.

The study of economics describes how households sell the services of the resources they own (labor, land and buildings, money) to businesses, in return for payments (wages and salaries, rent, interest and profits). With these payments, they in turn purchase from businesses the consumer commodities that they need or desire. In these two sets of markets, the productive input markets and the product markets, the prices of the goods and services bought and sold affect the amounts purchased and the amounts brought to market for sale. The markets thus determine what the businesses will produce and what the households will consume. This is the basic subject matter of economics.

2. WHAT ARE THE ADVANTAGES OF BEING DEPENDENT UPON OTHERS FOR ONE'S LIVELIHOOD?

Suppose there are two completely independent individuals, say two back-woodsmen, each producing all the items he needs, spending his mornings in his garden plot, afternoons hunting in the woods, and evenings taking care of chores around the house. Suppose that one man is a good farmer but a poor hunter, while the other man is much better at hunting than the first but equally as good a farmer. If the two men could arrange to have the better huntsman spend all his time at hunting, with the first man tending his own garden half a day and the hunter's garden during the rest of the day when he would otherwise have gone hunting, then the total amount of garden food will be the same as when each worked for himself alone, while the total amount of game caught will be a good bit larger.

In this situation, the advantage of dividing the work is evidently that more can be produced in total. It is efficient to have people specialize according to their talents. In fact, the arrangement is even more efficient than would appear at first sight, because when a person specializes, he tends to become even better at his specialty than when he only devotes a small part of his time, and a small part of his mind, to a number of trades. Furthermore, the time it takes to clean up and change over from one job to another is time saved that can be used in actual production rather than in mere preparation for the job.

But if the same total amount of garden food is produced as before and the total amount of meat is greater, why would the hunter be willing to let the farmer share in the surplus? The hunter might reason that if he takes half the total crop, he is only receiving from the farmer what he could have produced for himself anyway. It might seem to the hunter that the total surplus of meat was achieved by his own efforts alone, and that the farmer therefore deserves only that amount of meat that he, the farmer, had previously bagged when he was on his own.

It is true that the hunter could have produced half the combined co-operative crop on his own time by spending half a day at farming and half a day at hunting. But then his total hunting catch each day would be, on the average, just half the amount he bags by hunting all day long. Thus, if the arrangement between the two men were to allow the hunter half the crop and half the catch, he would be no better off than when on his own, but if the arrangement were to allow the hunter half the crop and slightly more than half the catch, it would pay the hunter to co-operate.

The farmer, on his own, could produce half the combined co-operative crop, but less than half the co-operative catch, since he is not so good at hunting. Suppose the farmer can catch only two-thirds as much as the hunter during the same period of time. This means that half a day's catch for the farmer would amount only to one-third of the co-operative catch. Then, if the arrangement were to allow the farmer half the co-operative crop, plus anything more than one-third of the co-operative catch, *both* men are simultaneously better off than on their own.

Either of the two men can convince the other that it pays to share the co-operative surplus, because neither one on his own can achieve as much. The hunter is simply wrong if he thinks that the surplus was achieved by himself alone. There would have been no hunting surplus if the farmer were not there to relieve the hunter of his farming duties. Even if the farmer had been worse at both farming and hunting than the hunter, they would still both be better off by a degree of specialization and sharing of the co-operative surplus.

Just so you do not have to take my word for this claim, let us run through the arithmetic again. Suppose the farmer is still two-thirds as good as the hunter at hunting, but now only three-fourths as good as the hunter at farming. Since the farmer can produce 3 crop units in half a day, he will produce 6 units in a full day, while the hunter could produce 4 and 8, respectively. Thus the pre-co-operative farm total would be 7 units of crop. Since the hunter can produce 4 farm crop units in half a day, it will, therefore, take him one-fourth of half a day, or one-eighth of a day, to produce the seventh farm crop unit under the co-operative system to equal the previous production. This leaves seven-eighths of his day for hunting, and since he bags 3 game units in half a day, at the same rate he will bag 5¼ units in seven-eighths of a day. The pre-co-operative game total would be 5 units, 2 for the farmer and 3 for the hunter; therefore, the surplus is one-quarter of a unit of hunter's game.

This constitutes the very essence of any modern economic system. Adam Smith begins *The Wealth of Nations* with the sentence, "The greatest improvement in the productive powers of labour, and the greater part of the skill, dexterity, and judgment with which it is anywhere directed, or applied, seem to have been the effects of the division of labour." [7] Smith adds, in reciting the advantages of division of labor, that further subdivision of productive processes into simple repetitive steps inspires the invention of mechanical machinery, with its remarkable augmentation of the output of a day's labor. (It would be well to read—and perhaps to have students read —at least the first few chapters of *The Wealth of Nations*.)

But enumerating the advantages of the division of labor conjures up the possibilities of malfunctioning. My use of the words "dependent upon others for one's livelihood" in the heading of this section was meant to convey a vague uneasiness about what might happen if the flow of goods were somehow blocked or misdirected, or if one's services were somehow not continually valued and remunerated. The joyful salute to the machine by Adam Smith has been darkened by other writers with the word *automation*. The sharing of the co-operative surplus may not be easily accomplished by threatening non-co-operation, if such an act would do more harm to the threatener than to the threatened. But these matters will be dealt with under Question 5.

3. HOW DO PRICES ACT AS AN "INVISIBLE HAND," CAUSING THOSE GOODS TO BE PRODUCED THAT ARE MOST DESIRED BY THE COMMUNITY?

Specialization.—When the hunter-farmer example is expanded from a society of two men to a society of many millions, the productive advantages of division of labor are amplified. But the difficulties in the way of drawing up an agreement about how the tasks and the outputs are to be divided would be simply staggering if the agreement had to be simultaneously haggled over and approved by everyone in the manner described. As a matter of fact, in a free market economy like ours, all the minute economic agreements are haggled over and approved by everyone. But all the arrangements that affect the economic outcome for each individual are not simultaneously

[7] Adam Smith, *The Wealth of Nations*, Vol. I. *Everyman's Library*, No. 412 (New York: E. P. Dutton & Co., Inc., 1910), p. 4.

decided upon and are not decided upon with full knowledge, by each individual, of all the details that may turn out to be crucially important for the success of his own venture. When a businessman decides to specialize in a certain type of commodity, he does not know in advance whether or not other people will choose complementary specializations (in the manner of the farmer and the hunter) so that everyone will be an eager buyer of everyone else's product. It may turn out that no one wants his specialty enough to remunerate him adequately. This might happen because too many people were specializing in the same commodity, or because he had simply guessed wrong about other people's tastes. Such misguided specialization is also possible by substituting specialization in a certain type of labor skill on the part of a worker for specialization in a certain type of product on the part of a businessman.

If mistakes by one individual are not quickly communicated to society at large, others are very apt to make the same mistakes. But a wrong choice involves a painful transition to another choice, and during this transition period, the individual will be unemployed and unproductive. If information about which choices have been proven wrong and which have been successful is not rapidly disseminated, the whole situation will degenerate into confusion, unemployment, and poverty. All the potential efficiency to be derived from the division of labor will be lost.

Supply and demand.—In a market economy, the price system constitutes the necessary vast communication network. If a product or a skill is already in large supply relative to the community's demand for it, its price will be lower than if it is in short supply. This is because the most eager buyers will be willing to pay a higher price than those whose demand for other things only permits them to buy the item in question when its price comes down. Hence, when supply is short, the total supply can be disposed of at a higher price than when the supply is plentiful; in the latter case, the price will be bid down by those sellers who find that their stock of goods simply is not moving at the higher price.

If everything has a price attached to it, a businessman can add up the costs of the inputs he would have to purchase in order to produce a certain product, compare this sum with the price of the product, and see whether the cost of production or the revenue from the sale of the product will be the larger amount. Of course, there is still a knowledge gap, even when everything has a price tag on it, because those prices might change, either favorably or unfavorably from the point of view of our businessman, after he has already committed himself to a line that looked profitable on paper. Nevertheless, knowledge of current prices and of price trends in the recent past are exceedingly valuable guides to economic decision-making.

Suppose, now, that for a particular product under consideration, it appears likely that costs will exceed revenue. The businessman will therefore decide not to produce this product. Is this a good decision from the point of view of the community as a whole?

Price of the product.—In order to answer this question, we must first understand a little more fully what it is that could cause input costs to exceed the price that buyers are willing to pay for the product. The inputs that business will need to purchase are seldom directly desired by consumers. Businesses are willing to pay a price for machinery, for man-hours of work, and for raw materials only because they expect consumer demand for the product that is ultimately turned out to be great enough to keep the price of the product above production costs. Now, quite a number of different kinds of businesses that turn out different products use some of the same kinds of inputs. Different product lines are thus competitors for each type of input.

But the businesses which produce those products for which consumer demand is strongest, as evidenced by the willingness of the consumers to keep the price up above the costs, will be the businesses which will be most aggressive about buying up the inputs they need. So long as a profit is to be made on each unit of output produced, it will pay someone to employ the needed inputs to turn out more of the product. If these inputs are scarce, it may be necessary to offer a slightly higher price for them in order to bid them away from other uses. (Of course, the price offered for inputs would never be high enough to wipe out the prospect of profits in all product lines. No businessman would offer to buy inputs at an unprofitable price.) The result will be that productive inputs will move out of those uses where consumer demand for the products is relatively weak and into those uses where consumer demand is strongest. This will not mean that all resources will move into production of some one product at the top of the popularity poll. Do not forget that, as the amount of any one product supplied to the market increases, the price of that product that will cause consumers to buy up the whole supply will generally fall. Conversely, as the production of the less desired items contracts, their market prices will, in general, rise. Thus there are market forces at work tending to depress profits in those industries for which demand was initially most strongly unsatisfied; the profitability falls *as output expands* and demand is more and more satisfied. At the same time, those industries in which consumer demand was initially over-satisfied (as compared to the more urgent consumer requests) will become profitable *as output contracts*—for those firms remaining in business. When the supply has become low, consumers whose needs for some amount of the product are sufficiently urgent will offer a cost-covering price. The result is that profitability tends to be equalized in all lines of endeavor. By the simple guide of profitability, productive resources are put to work in accordance with the priorities indicated by consumer demand. And more than this, the prices of those productive inputs that are most urgently needed (to satisfy the most urgent consumer demands) will be bid up relative to the prices of less needed resources.

Productive inputs do not arise from nowhere. They themselves must be produced. Labor skills must be cultivated, the various types of machinery must be manufactured, materials must be extracted from land and sea. If the choice of which productive input to produce (for example, which occupation shall a student prepare for) is also guided by the profitability rule, then the bidding up of the prices of the most needed inputs will cause them to be created in greater abundance. This, in turn, will allow the ultimate consumer demands to be met more fully and more rapidly.

Notice at this point that if monopolistic control of any line of production prevents output from expanding in response to high profits (because expansion causes costs to rise and price to fall, thus narrowing down those very profits), then the efficiency of the price system is vitiated, and the community suffers.

Source of consumer demand.—There is one more very important point to be made. It relates to the sources of consumer demand. While satisfaction of consumer demand may seem the ultimate aim of the economy, in some philosophical sense or other, it is actually the people's needs that ought to be satisfied. The technical (economics) meaning of *demand* is "desire" backed by purchasing power." From whence comes this purchasing power? The beauty of the price system is that it rewards productive inputs in accordance with their ability to contribute to the satisfaction of consumer demand. The owners of those productive resources that contribute most to the satisfaction of demand have first say of what that demand shall consist. The best part of this procedure is that, as people are induced to cultivate possession of superior skills and superior resources, the quantities of these skills and resources increase; the community as a whole becomes more productive, and everyone who is successful in following the guideposts to advancement is drawn into the orbit of enhanced prosperity. The unfortunate part is that, through no fault of their own, some people find it impossible to acquire the desirable skills or resources. Less common and less important nowadays is the fact that other people come into possession of desirable inputs through luck, inheritance, or fraud.

4. HOW DOES THE ECONOMY CHANGE AND GROW?

In the preceding section an economy was pictured as continually on the move, with the various members of the caravan forever scanning the guideposts to make out the most advantageous directions. What is the result of all this individual motion? Why has not a grand mutual adjustment been reached, in which profits are equalized in all lines of endeavor, and everyone has bettered himself as much as he is able?

Population changes.—One feature of our economy that continually prevents an equilibrium adjustment is the fact that some people die and others are born. In a traditional society, where everyone has certain tasks and rewards assigned at birth, these facts of life would not disturb the equilibrium. But in any economy in which each new arrival must use his wits and talents to make an economic niche for himself, young sprouts are forever pushing up in new places. Furthermore, an economy that accompanies increased population with increased division of labor, with all the productivity enhancement that such specialization entails, is very likely to be an economy that affords a material basis for population increase. The world population explosion brought on by the eighteenth century agricultural and industrial revolutions is a familiar fact of history. By coupling population growth with enhanced productivity, we have implicitly intertwined two types of change: quantitative change and qualitative change. It is the qualitative change that is primary, for it makes the quantitative change possible.

In a country that is still in a pre-industrial or early industrial stage, almost all the people are at work in agriculture. In Europe in the Middle Ages and the early Renaissance, and in the underdeveloped countries today, eight or nine people must till the soil in order to provide enough food to keep themselves plus one additional person—an aristocrat or a townsman—alive. In the United States today, the farm has become so mechanized that the situation is exactly reversed. It takes one farmer to provide nourishment for himself plus eight or nine urban dwellers. Furthermore, at the present time, the number of people a single farmer can keep supplied with food is rising faster than the rate of population increase. This means that, as time goes on, not only a smaller percentage of the total population but a smaller absolute number of people is required on the land. This means that some of the people already on the land are being forced to leave. Under a market price system, the signal for movement of resources out of a particular product line is decreased profitability. And indeed, since World War I, all but the most efficient farmers have experienced financial hardship, and this has resulted in a long-drawn-out migration to the cities. People have not usually been literally forced off the land. The forcing has been the result of a strong earnings differential.

The key new word in the paragraph above is *mechanized:* "the farm has become so mechanized." The farmer has learned to use new materials in new ways. Machinery has augmented and supplanted the efforts of men. Agriculture is being "automated." And that is progress. That is just the process described with much praise in sections relating to Questions 2 and 3 above. Resources, human resources included, are being released; when they are applied elsewhere in the economy, the total output produced by the economy increases with no increase in human drudgery. This is what we mean by productivity rise.

Changes in production technique.—When a person spends money on a commodity for personal need or enjoyment, that is called a "consumption expenditure." But when money is spent by a person or a corporation to enhance his own or his firm's commercial value, that is called an "investment expenditure." We call it "investment" when a person or a firm embarks on a new line of business or the expansion of an old line, when a worn-out machine is replaced by a new one, or when a student gives up leisure, tuition money, or the earnings he might have made in order to become a more proficient person.

Expenditures for investment are seldom made carelessly. The smaller the gratification obtained from the act-in-itself, the more care will be taken to try to ensure that the sacrifice will be well rewarded later. Investment involves sacrifice, in the sense that money spent on investment goods is money that might have been spent instead on consumption items. This was expressed in terms of fish and fishnets for Robinson Crusoe. The sacrifice, of course, may or may not be a very large one. The existence of a banking system which lends money for investments that look profitable greatly reduces the sacrifice which the investor himself experiences and greatly facilitates and encourages investment. If the banking system only lent money which was deposited with it, money which was evidently not wanted for immediate consumption or investment expenditures by the depositors, then the sacrifice would be small indeed. The investor still makes what is technically called a sacrifice, because he might have taken the money as a consumption loan instead. But as a matter of fact, most banking systems lend several times more money than is deposited with them. (The extra money is actually created by the banks. And conversely, when the debt is repaid the money passes out of existence again.) The newly borrowed money goes to increase demand for the investment goods the borrowers desire. Now if this means that resources are bid away from the production of consumption goods in order to increase the output of machinery, factory buildings, schools, and the like, then the total immediate output of consumption goods will fall. But then it is the consumers as a whole who are experiencing sacrifice of consumption goods that they might otherwise have enjoyed. And this sacrifice on their part is involuntary. Of course, these consumers are also likely to share in the increased consumption goods output that will occur when the investments bear fruit. (Notice that if the needed resources are lying idle, as in depressed times, then the investment expenditures involve no consumer sacrifice.)

To repeat, expenditures for investment are seldom made carelessly. Advice is usually solicited from marketing experts, from engineers and scientists, from private research laboratories, and from government research stations. The best way to install the new system is seldom to duplicate the old model. Even the educational system gets overhauled in content and method every few years. Investment is seldom engaged in without either introducing a way of producing the old product at lower cost, which means that smaller quantities of the old product are needed to produce the old quantity of output, or introducing a new product that was unheard of several years earlier, which might possibly attract demand away from some of the old products.

The fate of displaced workers.—To begin with, even when the number of workers needed to produce the old quantity of output falls, the lowering of cost per unit and the competitive lowering of price has often caused the new quantity of output to rise sufficiently to require the hiring of additional workers. Furthermore, even a small fall in the number of workers needed will be accomplished by normal attrition through quitting, retirement, and death. Nevertheless, workers today are being displaced in agriculture, in mining, and in certain transportation industries. These older workers, along with all the new young entrants to the labor force, must move to those industries where more workers are needed. Where are the jobs to be found?

Historically, employment in the goods-producing industries—agriculture, forestry, fishing, mining, construction, and manufacturing—appears to be levelling off. Between World War I and World War II, the expanding sectors were the service industries, but primarily those services that are hired by the goods-producing industries, such as white-collar work, wholesale and retail trade, banking and brokerage services, and other professional services to industry. Since World War II, the service industries remain the expanding sectors, but those which cater to the goods-producing industries are themselves feeling the bite of automation. The big trend is towards the service industries that cater to the consumer directly.

There are two ways in which consumers need servicing. First of all, automation has reached out beyond the farm and factory into the home. This means that a large amount of labor that does not count in labor force tallies—the labor of the housewife—has been progressively replaced by machinery plus a smaller amount of hired labor: the labor of the T.V. repairman, the automobile mechanic, and all the others who service the growing quantities of "consumer hardware." Second, the country has reached a stage of affluence and leisure in which people can receive more personal attention. The employment fields that are growing most rapidly of all are those which provide direct services to the body and mind, like medicine and teaching. But it is significant that a large part of medical care and education is supplied through nonprofit institutions and government.

It does not seem likely that person-to-person services will be rapidly automated out of existence, despite the programed teaching machines. People need people. What is not so certain is whether the "invisible hand" will lead them to seek each other in the marketplace.

5. WHAT CAN GO WRONG WITH THE ECONOMIC SYSTEM AND WHAT CAN BE DONE TO KEEP THE ECONOMY PROSPEROUS?

Throughout the discussion, some possible sources of trouble have been noted. And in fact, possible trouble has periodically turned into actual trouble. This country's extraordinary record of economic growth has been punctuated by geographical pockets of "sick" industries and temporal pockets of business cycle depression.

Before the Civil War, the agricultural frontier served as something of an escape valve for economic troubles. To revert once more to our farmer-hunter example: if the hunter had wanted to disengage himself from dependency upon the farmer, he could have picked up and moved westward to virgin country. There was no need for him to accept a disadvantageous economic arrangement with the farmer. And if he did move away, withdrawing his hunting contribution from the farmer's daily food supply, the farmer would not have been left in a hopeless position. He, too, could move back to independence without suffering disastrously. But the very abundance engendered by co-operation has moved us past the point of no return. The very population increase that was brought about by increased productive efficiency imposes upon us the need to go on co-operating. We can no longer disengage. There is no longer a farm to which each city dweller can retreat if the industrial mechanism develops a short circuit.

Observe the chain of reactions that might ensue when a number of mines close down in West Virginia. Hundreds of miners are thrown out of work. Even with unemployment insurance, their expenditures drop to less than half their accustomed amounts. Storekeepers in the district find sales sluggish, and they in turn cancel orders for shipments from afar. Real estate values drop. Local governments experience a smaller tax inflow and a larger welfare benefits outflow; they may find it necessary to economize on the salaries or hiring of teachers, policemen, garbage collectors, and so forth. This has further ill effects on retail business: some stores may fail and orders drop still further for cars from Detroit, fruit from California, washing machines from Pittsburgh and apparel from New York. The cutback in business spending in West Virginia reaches out all over the country.

Suppose now that the mine owners withdraw from the business scene, pay off their bank debts, and retire. If businessmen in some different, booming industry come to the banks and borrow the newly repaid money in order to augment business spending in their own line, then the total flow of spending and incomes all over the country will be unimpaired. The people doing the spending will have changed, and the products being purchased may have changed, but depressed revenues in businesses that have lost the mining district clientele will be counterbalanced by increased revenues in those businesses which receive increased orders from the newly expanding industry.

In the situation pictured, the mining community is an example of the backwash of progress. It would be very neat if the miners could pick themselves up and turn themselves into the kind of workers for whom demand .has increased. Whether new industry can be induced to set down roots in the mining district, or whether the miners have to uproot themselves and move to where the new industry is located, the problem remains that the miners have to be recast in a new die. Molding an old worker into a new shape is very, very difficult. But if the problem is not faced by the country as a whole, it will have to be faced piecemeal by each employer who is forced to bargain about labor security—about labor's right to a permanent job or a permanent income—with his own employees. The problem of labor security is endemic. If it is ignored in one context, it will pop up in another. "Feather-bedding" and stretching the job will not disappear until the country faces up to the security problem co-operatively. Each person must realize that, "There, but for the grace of God, go I." How many prosperous Yankees could have foretold that New England would lose its textile industry to the South, or Pennsylvania its coal industry to Texan and Oklahoman oil? And who knows when, in turn, Northern atomic energy plants will set back Texas and Oklahoma?

But there is a worse situation of the kind that was experienced in the Great Depression of the thirties. Suppose, in this second case, that the mine owners pay off their bank debts and retire, as before. But suppose that the closing of the mines is not quickly balanced by business expansion elsewhere. The drop in orders from the mining district will not then be masked by rising orders from other parts of the country. Cutbacks in orders, in production, in business spending, in employment, and then in consumer spending will spread out and reinforce each other throughout the country. In such a situation, it is clear that the country as a whole must act quickly and co-operatively to keep the flow of revenues from dropping off. The purchasing power of buyers must be maintained. Unemployment insurance, tax reduction, and even direct government spending may be needed in order to keep the demand for industry's products from falling to such an extent that *all* lines become unprofitable. To be sure, profits are equal to the difference between revenues and costs, but when the situation is one in which revenues are falling off in many lines at once, then forcing costs down, say by cutting wages, has very little effect on profits. Costs are nothing but incomes from the point of the people to whom these costs are paid. If incomes fall, then consumer expenditures and business revenues will also fall.

Conclusion

Economics is no longer known as "the dismal science." But neither is it unqualifiedly cheerful. Our economic system is designed to produce more for everybody, and on the whole it has done just that. But it is, after all, only a human creation, subject to human failings yet responsive to human corrections.

The Economic Background of the Ancient City of Rome

HELEN J. LOANE [*]

ON THE BASIS of the amount of imported grain, it seems almost certain that Rome—during the late Republic and early Empire—had a population of about a million. With this population, Rome was the largest residential centre of ancient times, with an intricate social and economic organization. Yet to say that, because of its size and structural modernity, the economy of Rome was like that of a modern industrial city, would be entirely misleading. Unlike New York, London, or even modern Rome, which pay for their imports by manufacture or the profits of trade, Rome balanced its imports by provincial tribute, imperial salaries, and the returns on Italian and foreign investments.

PRODUCTS IMPORTED

Consequently, when considering the economic background of Rome, we must start with imports. These include the bulk of all foodstuffs, clothing, household articles, and building materials—practically everything the Romans needed for sustenance. Most of these came by sea or by river, down the branches of the Tiber, for although the roads that led to Rome were graded and well paved, the immediate environment was generally unproductive, and ox-drawn wagons were too slow to bring in foodstuffs from any distance. Foodstuffs were floated on barges down the branches of the Tiber, for as Strabo says, the Anio, Nar, and the Clanis explain how Rome was

[*] Lecturer in Latin, Albright College, Reading, Pennsylvania.

The Economic Background of the Ancient City of Rome

able to support its population in spite of its location.[1] And Pliny the Younger sent cabbages and beets from his villa near Arretium down to Rome each spring.[2]

The sailing vessels that docked at Ostia, where a harbor of any depth appeared first in A.D. 64 (after Claudius), were, in general, small (about 80 ton), slow (the usual trip from Alexandria to Puteoli —about 1000 miles—took 20 days), and sailed only in summer, when storms did not obscure the stars.[3] In the time of Augustus, Strabo tells us,[4] ships either unloaded outside the sandbar beyond Ostia (16 miles down the river) or discharged cargo until they could be drawn up the shallow Tiber to Rome.

GRAIN

The transportation of tribute grain up the Tiber from Ostia illustrates the tremendous size of the barge traffic between Rome and its harbor city. Since the days of the Gracchi when the State assumed the responsibility of providing cheap grain for Roman citizens, the maintenance of an adequate supply of grain at a reasonable price was an accepted function of the Roman government and a political and commercial problem of grave importance.[5] Naturally, there were some men who considered it beneath their dignity to stand in line at the windows of the Porticus Minucius, but the right to free grain was the right of male plebian citizens resident at Rome. The earlier number of 320,000 recipients of a monthly allotment of 5 *modii* of wheat (about 1¼ bushels) was streamlined by Caesar to 150,000.[6] Augustus set the number at 200,000, and here it stayed during the early Empire.

The bureau of the *annona*, then, required nearly 4 million bushels annually to give away, and almost four times that amount for sale to the remainder of the population. In the early Empire, the Egyptian export to Rome was approximately 5 million bushels annually and

---

[1] Strabo *Geo.* v. 3. 7.
[2] Pliny the Younger *Ep.* v. 6.12.
[3] Pliny *Hist. Nat.* xix. 3-4.
[4] Strabo *Geo.* v. 3.5.
[5] See Rostovtzeff *"Frumentum"* P-W, VII. 174-177.
[6] Suet. *Jul.* 41.

that of Africa, twice as much. If we add the tribute from Sicily, it is clear that, after the *fiscus* had distributed the dole, it probably had enough grain to meet most of the needs of the home market. If the ordinary merchant vessel of 80 tons were used, then each summer some 6000 boats carrying Egyptian and African grain put in at Ostia. As many or more barges would be loaded to be drawn up the river to the capital. It is not surprising, then, that the barge-owners guild at Ostia had 258 members,[7] that Tacitus could report the destruction of 300 grain barges in one day,[8] and that inscriptions from Ostia show many thousands of stevedores, measurers, warehousemen, and barge men. Add to this the barges carrying wine, oil, building materials, and other products, and you can picture the oxen on the towpath forming a continuous line all day long.

Inscriptions seem to prove that the government disposed of the remainder of its tribute—some 13 million bushels—through independent traders, though it always kept a watchful eye on the sales price. Experience had taught that *inopia* and *discordia* go hand in hand. Suetonius tells us that, in a time of scarcity, Augustus regulated the price with no less regard for the interest of the farmers and merchants than for that of the populace.[9] How? Suetonius is silent. Tacitus does state that when, in the time of Tiberius, prices had reached a high level, the dealers were paid 2 *sesterces* (10 cents) for ¼ bushel to compensate them for selling at a lower rate.[10] Later, after the fire of 64, the Emperor set by edict a ceiling price of 3 *sesterces* a *modius*.[11] The price did rise, however, and Tacitus' price of 60 cents a bushel had risen, in the day of Pliny the Elder, to about a dollar.[12]

WINE

Wine, the second most important food item, though many Romans seem to have considered it the first, was imported in large quantities —on the basis of some modern comparisons, about 28 million gal-

[7] *CIL*, XIV 251 ff.
[8] Tacitus *Ann*. xv. 18.
[9] Suet. *Aug*. 42.
[10] Tacitus *Ann*. ii. 87.
[11] *Ibid*. xv. 39.
[12] Pliny *Hist. Nat*. xviii. 90.

lons annually. Much of it was brought to Rome in carts, as today, from vineyards in the Alban hills, but the greater part arrived by boat from southern Latium and Campanian, regions which developed the best vineyards in the world during the early Empire. It is possible to compare the three sources that name the most important wines drunk in Rome—the 14th book of Pliny,[13] the 13th book of Martial,[14] and the potsherds of wine *amphorae* found at Rome—and, *mirable dictu,* they check!

Interesting details of this wine trade with southern Italy are given by Petronius' account of Trimalchio's mercantile adventures.[15] We take them with two grains of salt. For the first enterprise, Trimalchio himself built five ships, loaded them with wine (*et tunc erat contra aurum*), hired captains, and sent them off to Rome. The boats and cargo, valued by Trimalchio at about a million and a half dollars, were lost in a storm. Undaunted, he prepared another shipment, this time of wine, bacon, beans, slaves, and the famous Capuan perfumes. From this enterprise, Trimalchio declared, 10 million dollars were realized. Knowing Trimalchio's propensities, we ignore the amount, but accept the source and type of imports, as well as the method of distribution.

By the middle of the second century, however, these famous wine-bearing districts of Italy were no longer so productive, and about half of Rome's supply was now shipped in from Spain. At Rome's emporium on the Tiber, the mound of potsherds called Monte Testacchio [16] consists of fragments of many million *amphorae,* most of which seem to have carried cheap Spanish wine (over half a billion gallons of it). The markings show that the normal price of an 80-pound jar was a little less than 60 cents, that the Spanish export tax was 2½ per cent, and that the shippers were Spaniards and Gauls.

BUILDING MATERIALS

Commerce in the various building materials may provide data on the size of the import problem. Take, for example, the materials

[13] Pliny *ibid.* xiv.
[14] Martial *Epigrammata* xiii.
[15] Petronius *Satyricon* 76.
[16] See *CIL*, XV, 4529-4685.

needed for the Colosseum. About 200,000 tons of travertine went into the exterior of the building, besides an equal amount of tufa, brick, and concrete.[17] The travertine, quarried below Tivoli, was barged down the Anio and Tiber to the docks, and then hauled by wagon to the building site. The deep ruts in the lava paving stones on the Sacred Way show the damage caused by the heavy wagons. If the travertine were laid in four years, as we know it was, then 180 wagons were required daily. Since the stone was hauled through the Forum, disrupting business along the way, Vespasian undoubtedly enlarged the Forum northward to take care of the city's needs.

Some idea of the quantities of marble imported for imperial projects can be shown by the amounts used for Trajan's Forum, with its enclosed buildings. Trajan's Column was probably imported in eighteen solid cubes of Parian marble, each weighing about 50 tons. Consider loading just one of these on a boat, transporting it to Ostia, transferring it to a barge, hoisting it up the river bank, and then moving it on rollers to the site. From Elba, also, came fifty granite columns to outline the nave of the Basilica Ulpia; each of these weighed about 40 tons. Then there were fifty columns of cipollino from Euboea, and so on and on. All in all, the shipment of marble for this one project was about 50,000 tons. Approximately 625 vessels, carrying this marble alone, must have docked at Rome's seaport within the space of a few years. Probably this is the reason Trajan enlarged the facilities of Rome's harbor at the mouth of the Tiber.

This is but a brief sketch of some of the chief imports of foods and building supplies, but it does illustrate, to some degree, the size and diversity of the traffic.

Roman Industry

ORGANIZATION

One of the problems to be considered in discussing industry at Rome is the degree of its similarity to the system at Pompeii, well-known because of the abundance of its remains and commonly regarded as

[17] See Helen J. Loane, *Industry and Commerce of the City of Rome* ("The Johns Hopkins Studies in Historical and Political Science," ser. LVI, no. 2 [Baltimore: The Johns Hopkins Press, 1938]).

The Economic Background of the Ancient City of Rome

typical of the Roman world. But in no single aspect was the contrast between the two cities greater than in domestic architecture. In picturing imperial Rome, one does not think of the familiar *atrium* houses of Pompeii but of the apartment houses of the contemporary harbor town of Ostia. This change in architecture carries with it implications of changes in industrial life, and some have been too ready to assume large-scale production in Rome and to believe that, just as the *atrium* house gave way to the large apartment houses, the economic system of the city was changed, and some type of "factory" superseded the old-fashioned individual shop.

Rome has been built-over too frequently to leave many traces of ancient houses, and the Marble Plan of the city of A.D. 200 is often difficult to interpret. After pouring over the plan, fragment by fragment, the only generalization I could reach was the frequency of the so-called Pompeian shop. In three fragments of a complex type of *insula,* the presence of an inner court, connected with the shops around the exterior, does suggest either a large workroom or a bazaar. But there is no proof. There is other evidence to prove, however, that although these *insulae* could provide unusual facilities for production or distribution, the small-shop system of Pompeii still prevailed at Rome.

In the first place, the great number of makers of individual articles whose names appear on Roman tombstones implies that custom work was much in vogue. Their mere presence is, of course, no proof that factories employing slaves did not exist (for slave names, unless put on an article of trade, rarely survive), but the very number of craftsmen argues against factory competition. Second, even more convincing are the groups of individual workmen organized into guilds, for slaves in factories—though they might form burial societies—would seldom belong to these *collegia;* and there are thousands of these *collegia* in the city—carpenters, glass blowers, shoemakers, jewelers, and makers of glass eyes. In the third place, streets and sections of the city often bore the name of an industry—just as in Medieval cities and Eastern cities today; so we find, in ancient Rome, Shoemakers' Street, Carpenters' Street, and Harness Makers' Street. If the location of a house could be designated as *inter falcariōs* (among the scythe-makers), there certainly were no scythe factories in operation at the time.

PRODUCTS

Bread.—Let us look now at individual items, such as the production of bread. In the wealthiest households, naturally, baking still continued as a part of home economy, but for most of the population bread was produced in small shops well distributed over the city. The usual type of baker is revealed by an edict of Trajan offering special privileges to those who milled and baked 25 bushels of wheat a day.[18] On the basis of Pliny's information that 70 loaves could be baked from a bushel of the finest flour, 25 bushels would mean a daily output of 1800 loaves.[19] Since the State had to offer special inducements to encourage work on this scale, the average establishment could not have been very large. Its size was determined by: the difficulty of storing fuel, the problem of grinding grain, the slow method of baking, and the problem of delivery—by hand or hand-drawn carts over narrow and congested streets. There was real difficulty with the traffic problem. Julius Caesar tackled it and prohibited wagons within the city after sunrise, and Martial tells us how they rattled along before that time, keeping everyone in Rome awake.[20] If there had been large bakeries, how could the producer deliver or how could the housewife get to them quickly?

Those who have seen the tomb of the baker Eurysaces at the Porta Maggiore—with its terra cotta reliefs showing the stages in the work of baking, even to a kneading machine turned by a donkey—will question how this baker made his money if not on large-scale production. The inscription tells how: He had contracts for supplying the *praetorian* cohorts and also the *vigiles,* the fire brigade. In the third century, moreover, large bakeries did become numerous, for then the dole was no longer wheat, but baked bread.

Clothing.—Next, let us take a look at the clothing industry. In the sheep country of the Po valley, among the Sequani in Gaul, and near Tarentum, much woolen cloth was produced in factories operated by slaves. This material was exported to Rome, where it was

[18] Gaius *Inst.* i. 34.
[19] Pliny *Hist. Nat.* xviii. 89-90.
[20] Martial *Ep.* xiv. 223.

made into clothing in small tailoring or dressmaking shops. Lack of inscriptions of weavers or weavers' guilds supports the conclusion that little production of cloth took place in the city, while more than thirty inscriptions of retail clothiers indicate many shops for sales of clothing. The needs of only a part of the city's million would be met by home industry, such as that in Lepidus' household, where the women were spinning at their looms when the mob broke in.[21] Augustus prided himself on wearing home-spun garments,[22] but this was, undoubtedly, part of his propaganda. Even a comparatively well-to-do lawyer like Cicero had to hire special weavers if he needed them on rare occasions.[23] Very few of Rome's apartment dwellers owned a slave or even a loom.

Jewelry.—Jewelry was also fashioned and sold by individual shopkeepers. The pearls and precious stones used by these artisans came largely from India, Egypt, and Arabia, and some of the stones were carved and made into ornaments at Alexandria. There were many jewelers along the Sacred Way, however, who showed great skill in cutting cameos and intaglios to order, and this craft prospered in small specialty shops, because Roman men took great pride in distinctive seals and individual signet rings. We know by name eighteen such jewelers along the Sacred Way.[24] In rich households, however, there would be young slaves, like Pagus,[25] who was put out as an apprentice at the age of twelve to learn the art of decorating gold bracelets with precious stones, or like Zosimus,[26] who, although his master gave him access to his gold and silver, never stole a penny's weight.

Implements.—Iron tools, knives, swords, and farm implements were apparently made to order in small shops at Rome, as elsewhere in the ancient world, and several fine reproductions of such workrooms have been preserved—the altar of Lucius Cornelius Atimetus in the Vatican Gallery and the tombstone from the Isola Sacra. Glassware was undoubtedly imported from factories near Cumae and

---

[21] Ascon. *Milo.* p. 38 st.
[22] Suet. *Aug.* 73.
[23] Nepos. *Atticus* 13.3
[24] *CIL*, VI, 9207 *et passim.*
[25] *Ibid.*, 9437.
[26] *Ibid.*, 9222.

Liternum, and fine furniture from Pompeii and Ostia. Most of the plates and bowls would undoubtedly be shipped down the Tiber branches from Arretium, and pots, pans, kettles, and buckets of copper or bronze would be shipped in wholesale lots from Capua. There are very few inscriptions of coppersmiths at Rome, and perhaps most of these would be employed in mending.

Silver.—Since silverplate was extensively used on rich Roman tables, it would not be surprising if production sometimes spread beyond the small individual shop. This development had already taken place at Capua, and silverware from there was probably sent in great quantities to the capital. That there *was* something like a modern assembly line at Rome, however, is suggested by the names of trained workers who worked at some special skill: the *caelator* (the engraver), the *inaurator* (the decorator), the *foreuticensis* (the embosser), the *flaturarius* (the caster), and so on. At a much later date, this implication of varied skills becomes a definite statement. St. Augustine writes: *"vel tamguam opifices in vico argentario ubi unum vasculum, ut perfectum exeat, her multos artifices transit cum ab uno perfecto perfici posset."* [27] Yet, on the other hand, the shops of thirty individual silversmiths at Rome are known. There are always some persons who desire individuality or want an old piece remade into a more fashionable design.

FACTORIES

Two pieces of literary evidence mention large manufacturers at Rome, but both these units were, however, concerned with processing state-owned materials. One handled the "Pompeian red" powdered *minium* used by potters, artists, and, most important of all, by people in the ritualistic state worship. All details of importation and processing were regulated by State decree.[28]

The other known Roman factory reprocessed the third grade of Egyptian papyrus, making it into the best paper called "Fanniana" from its owner's name.[29] It is probable that other industrialists

---

[27] *De Civitate Dei* vii. 4.
[28] Vetr. *De Arch.* vii. 9. 3-4.
[29] Pliny *Hist. Nat.* xiii. 75-76.

reprocessed other materials less well-made under State control. That is a problem on which I am still working.

It is impossible to go into detail about the production of brick, which at Rome did exemplify the clearest case of large-scale production. Most of you know the story, anyhow, from the books of my teacher, Professor Tenney Frank.[30] He explains that since brickmaking was originally a branch of farm work, it had always been free from the stigma attached to other industrial pursuits, and that the leading families at Rome had made their fortunes at it. Nero's fire demonstrated that the favorite Roman building stone, travertine, crumbled badly when subjected to heat, so that in the rebuilding of the city, Nero and succeeding emperors resorted to brick-faced concrete. Instead of limited quantities of roof tiles, vast quantities of brick were suddenly required. Thousands of slaves were bought for this service, and profits made by a few large brickyards, particularly those of the descendants of Domitius Afer, provided the fortune upon which the Antonine family rose to power. Marcus Aurelius, as a private citizen, inherited about fourteen yards and at his death, twenty. Since about 200 bricks a day was the average for a worker (we get this information from work details in the army)[31] and the period of production from April to September extended well over 100 days, an average yard, say of 50 workmen, would produce an annual output of over a million bricks.

If large-scale industries in bronze utensils, cloth, and pottery arose elsewhere in the empire, why were more not at Rome? In the first place, there was no more labor-saving machinery available here than at Pompeii, and even less respect for the success that came with business ventures. Moreover, neither metal nor fuel was procurable nearby, and transportation was slow and expensive. Rome, then, was not the natural location for large industries. Another very important decentralizing influence at the capital was the great number of rich households where slaves catered to the needs of the wealthy. To these contributing factors may be added lack of patents, Roman

---

[30] Tenney Frank, *Economic Survey of Ancient Rome*, Vol. V (Baltimore: Johns Hopkins University Press, 1940), p. 188 ff.
[31] *CIL,* III, 11381 ff.

law on partnership, and, above all else, the lack of respect that prevailed in ancient societies for success in trade.

Distribution

Although not all the problems associated with distribution can be solved with the data now available, it is clear that at Rome there existed both the Pompeii system, where the maker of a specialty displayed and sold his wares in a small shop, and also a method of marketing imported wares unconnected with any production.

SHOPS

Sales facilities offered small merchants at Rome were unusual. The streets of Rome, as we see them on the Marble Plan, were endless rows of galleries and arcades lined with shops. Then, as Martial tells us,[32] many dealers stood behind makeshift stands of boards on the sidewalk; others, by a tripod near a busy corner or near a column in the Forum. Barbers, innkeepers, cooks, and clothing dealers had carried their businesses so far onto the sidewalk, that the *praetor* had been forced to go into the gutter. The State, moreover, from the earliest period had established booths near the Forum where farmers could find wares in exchange for the produce they had brought to market. Later, the Basilica Aemilia and the Julia, although intended primarily for courts of law, offered shelter to purchasers on market days. After A.D. 64, a great arcade with a portico behind it, built by Nero across the Sacred Way below the Palatine, was converted by Vespasian into a Spice Market. A Basilica Argentaria, a silver warehouse near the Forum of Caesar, begun by Domitian, was completed on the Quirinal. By Hadrian's time, the State had as many as 500 shops to lease in the great *mercati* and basilicas of the city.

Nero's Portico.—Conjectures about the method of distributing imported wares have been fostered by excavations of Nero's great portico and the shops behind Trajan's Forum. Nero's extensive portico was intended primarily as an ornamental approach to the

[32] Martial *Ep.* vii. 61.

The Economic Background of the Ancient City of Rome

Palatine; low and spacious, the building covered a wide area that had been laid waste by the fire. The southern corridor, next to the Palatine, was let out for commercial stalls, and there is evidence that jewelers sold their wares in its 100 or more intercolumnar spaces. The inscriptions give the names of twenty-two jewelers from here, seventeen of which are styled *margaritarii,* pearl traders. Separating walls do not appear until the third century, and traces of grilles have disappeared; so it seems that each evening the dealer packed up his precious wares and reappeared with them each morning.

Vespasian and Domitian turned the whole structure to practical uses, and the larger part of the portico, north of the Sacra Via, came to be called the "Horrea Piperataria," the Spice Market. Vespasian, a businessman who directed much of his energy toward balancing the State budget (he said, on his accession, that he needed 2 million dollars [40 billion *sesterces*] to set the affairs of government in order),[33] apparently was interested in renting out space in the structure—for cash. It may even be that Vespasian not only rented out space here to dealers in Eastern wares, but also set apart shops for the sale of wares taken into the *fiscus* as tribute in kind. It is significant that the Elder Pliny, who was a member of "Vespasian's cabinet" as commander of his fleet, gives long lists of the prices of perfumes, spices, and other Oriental wares as would be sold in a state-owned spice market;[34] and Statius hints that taxes in kind, even at this period, came to the official *a rationibus*.[35] It is quite possible that the State went into merchandising long before Aurelian's time, and that the financier, Vespasian, was responsible for the practice. At any rate, Nero's pleasure portico became a series of shops at this time.

Campus Martius.—Another center of the luxury trade was the Campus Martius, around the voting booths (Saepta Julia) and the Porticus Argonautarum. Martial gives details of a shopping trip there by Mamurra.[36] In the first shop, he inspected carefully the

---

[33] Suet. *Vesp.* 16.
[34] See Pliny *Hist. Nat.* xii.
[35] Statius *Silvae* iii.3. 89ff.
[36] Martial *Ep.* ix. 59.

young slaves; in the next, he concentrated on table tops of rare wood and tortoise shell couches; then he went on to the shop where Corinthian bronzes were to be found; and then to the shop where he saw jasper and tinkling pearl earrings. Then finally, Mamurra made his purchase—a penny cup! Juvenal has a better story—of an ancient gold digger who went home from the Campus with a vase of crystal, a myrrhine vessel, and—a diamond! [37]

Mercato of Trajan.—A similar question of State interest in trade arises in regard to the 150 shops built into the Quirinal hillside, east of Trajan's Forum, the so-called Mercato of Trajan. Since there is little or no equipment for production, they were used, apparently, for sales booths. A few, however, do have small *piscinae* in the concrete floor, where fish could be kept and sold; another has a floor sloping to a central hole, where a vat could be stationed to catch oil or wine. Since, in Trajan's time, imports to the capital were constantly increasing and since the building of his Forum had destroyed many small shops, it seems clear that the State attempted to meet a definite need and erected this market. There is no evidence, whatever, that the *fiscus* used any of these shops for distribution of state-owned goods. That is to say, there is no evidence that the practice begun by Vespasian at the Spice Market was continued by Trajan's *fiscus* at the Mercato. State interference in merchandising on a large scale came only in the days of Diocletian and after.

AGENTS

With the exception of auctioneers—so important that Martial [38] equates one auctioneer to two *praetors,* four military tribunes, seven lawyers, and ten poets—and chance references to peddlers and shopkeepers, the sources have little to say about distributing agents, while wholesale dealers in foods, metalware, and clothing are scarcely mentioned. This may be due to the ambiguity of the term *negotiator* or absence of records of slaves or freed agents. Yet the persistence of the small-shop system, abetted by the traffic problems and domestic architecture, is revealed very clearly by conditions in the great

[37] Juvenal *Sat.* xi. 153-155.
[38] Martial *Ep.* vi. 8.

State porticos and markets. Even here the small independent retailer persisted.

Conclusion

I should like to conclude with an account, given by Suetonius [39] and Pliny [40] of Q. Remmius Palaemon, a schoolteacher who actually amassed a fortune. This famous teacher of rhetoric began life as a slave in a weaving mill near Vicetia. His annual income (he was subsidized by the government) from teaching finally reached 400,000 *sesterces* (at the moment, about $40,000), but he had made his original fortune from the sale of wine and of ready-to-wear clothing. To distribute this clothing, which he probably imported from the district where he had labored, Palaemon probably operated a chain of stores managed by his freedmen. In A.D. 45, from proceeds of this venture, he launched into a more respectable source of income. Buying a vineyard some 10 miles from Rome, he hoed, cultivated, and dressed vines and brought his estate to an almost incredible peak of perfection. Then, after eight years, he sold the vintage as it hung on the vines for 400,000 *sesterces*. The neighbors, by way of finding an excuse for their own indolence (thus says Pliny the moralizer) gave all the credit for this success to Palaemon's profound erudition. Finally, Seneca, who always admired erudition and success, bought the estate for four times its original price. There are no details of its further success; so it probably was not the erudition. It probably was the brawn, as good schoolteachers know it usually is.

[39] Suet. *De Gram.* 23.
[40] Pliny *Hist. Nat.* xiv. 49.

Home Economics Education Faces Another Challenge

CLIO S. REINWALD *

THE APPROVING of the Smith-Hughes Act, February 23, 1917, officially made home economics a part of vocational education. The funds made available and the standards established for programs did much to facilitate the growth and development of home economics as a part of the secondary and adult school programs. Recent legislation has created new opportunities for home economics education.[1]

Home economics, for over fifty years, has had as its major goal,

> to prepare youth and adults for responsibilities and activities involved in homemaking and in achieving family well being. This continues to be a major goal, but new emphasis and methods of instruction are necessary as one views changes in society, the changed and changing ways in which families live, and the new home problems with which both youth and adults are coping.[2]

ADAPTATION TO CHANGE

The year 1964 will go down in the history of home economics education as one of the most revolutionary of all. Changes formerly considered impossible will become the anticipated and expected. There is an anonymous saying, "Nothing is so sure as change itself." Eleanor Roosevelt, in her last book, put it this way, *Tomorrow is*

---

* Co-ordinator of Family, Migrant, and Nursing Education, Department of Public Instruction, Harrisburg, Pennsylvania.
[1] Public Law 88-210, 88th Congress, H. R. 4955, December 18, 1963.
[2] Edna P. Amidon, Paper presented to the State Directors of Vocational Education, Washington, D.C., May, 1962.

Home Economics Education Faces Another Challenge

Now, and at a recent meeting in Pittsburgh, Beth Peterson, home economist for the DuPont Company, said, "Monday's wonder becomes Tuesday's commonplace. By the weekend, it is 'ole hat.'" Change is a constant element in life. This is especially true with the human organism as one observes the rapidly changing behavioral patterns of a normal child. Recognition of how the human organism adjusts to its changing environment is necessary for those involved in bringing about educational change.

There is much in common with the way individuals and institutions adapt to change. Gradual change that occurs naturally is accepted with little or no discomfort and without being aware of its taking place. When change is accelerated, people and institutions are forced to adapt more rapidly by external forces over which they have little or no control. Some refuse even to recognize change; some resist actively; and others accept eagerly and are challenged by the tremendous possibilities opening before them. Taba explains the nature of change and its implications for individuals and society in this way:

> . . . Changes in the nature of society and in man's perception of the world have always involved difficulties in solving problems because under conditions of change, data lead in directions that diverge from our expectations and involve an alteration of accepted goals and values. Each new shift has involved a necessity for "disassembling a configuration of images" with which we have interpreted the world around us. These images are only partly explicit and are bound up with feelings rather than thought. This feeling-boundedness makes them difficult to alter, and unconscious valuations may outlast social realities.
>
> Changes today involve yet more than that. They are so massive and so radical that they create a sense of discontinuity with the past and uncertainty about the future. For the first time in man's history, it is difficult to foresee what the future will be and the ways in which to prepare for it. No longer can either the present or the future be seen as a mirror of the past, and no longer can we use either the present or the past as a measure of the future. We are faced perhaps with a greater discontinuity than we know how to span.[3]

[3] Hilda Taba, "Education for Independent Valuing," *New Insights and the Curriculum,* ASCD Yearbook 1963 (Washington, D.C.: Association for Supervision and Curriculum Development, a department of the National Education Association, 1963), pp. 222-223.

Like a person, the total home economics education program "is feeling the impact of accelerated change and the converging of social forces which present challenges to points of view and accustomed practices."[4]

Home Economics as a Field

PRESENT DEFINITION

The American Home Economics Association in *Home Economics, New Directions,* has defined home economics as

> the field of knowledge and service primarily concerned with strengthening family life through: educating the individual for family living, improving the services and goods used by families, conducting research to discover the changing needs of individuals and families and the means of satisfying these needs, [and] furthering community, national, and world conditions favorable to family living.[5]

The main responsibility of home economics educators has been with the education of the individual for homemaking and family living. Many in Pennsylvania have benefited as a result.

THE SITUATION FIFTY YEARS AGO

Fifty years ago, when home economics was in its infancy, what was the role of woman in the average income family? She was wife-mother-homemaker—with responsibility for making clothes, sheets, and curtains, for rearing children, preparing food, caring for the family during illness, and managing the family income. Services such as laundering, dry cleaning, frozen packaged foods, ready-to-wear clothing, minimum-care clothing, electrical appliances, plenty of hot water and many other labor-saving products were never in the minds of the most dreamy-eyed homemaker of fifty years ago. The policies developed to implement the Smith-Hughes Act in 1917 placed the

---

[4] Rua Van Horn, Speech presented at the American Vocational Association Convention, Atlantic City, N.J., 1963.
[5] Committee on Philosophy and Objectives of Home Economics, *Home Economics, New Directions: A Statement of Philosophy and Objectives* (Washington, D.C.: American Home Economics Association, 1959), p. 4.

emphasis in vocational home economics programs on homemaking, not on wage-earning. Homemakers needed assistance in maintaining their homes; so the emphasis was on this phase. Many have benefited, and the program has grown and expanded in the direction of homemaking as a vocation.

The federal laws, such as the Smith-Hughes or George Barden Acts, are administered through policies. The State Plan for Vocational Education is developed as a basis on which a state agrees to use federal funds within the policies established by a federal agency. Policies have a strange way of becoming a tradition, and traditions often become stronger than law. This may have been the reason why wage-earning was never considered a part of the program in home economics education.

THE SITUATION TODAY

Statistics in the March 30, 1964 edition of a Harrisburg newspaper, *The Evening News,* show that:

> . . . About 34 per cent of all workers are now women—compared to only 20 per cent of the over-all work force in 1920. The number of women in the labor force has climbed back to World War II peak levels. About 25 million women, both married and single, are now working. By 1970, the number of women in the labor force is expected to rise by 25 per cent—almost twice the rate of increase anticipated for men.[6]

Woman's role has changed very decisively in fifty years. It is becoming increasingly a dual role of homemaking and wage-earning. As more women are employed outside the home, the need for hiring services to maintain the home and family increases. Over the past year, the number of service workers, such as household employees, increased 5 per cent. These essential services are mainly home and community service oriented. This means that "essential services for family well-being may need to be provided by someone whom the homemaker can employ or secure the needed service in a community situation."[7]

---

[6] *The Evening News,* March 30, 1964, p. 6.
[7] Van Horn, *op. cit.,* p. 2.

HOME AND COMMUNITY SERVICE OCCUPATIONS

Passage of the Manpower Development Training Act provided funds and the necessary legislation to include programs in preparing workers for employment in home and community service occupations. Rua Van Horn was appointed to the staff of the Division of Vocational Education in the U. S. Office of Education, Washington, D. C., with a major responsibility to develop programs in the areas using the knowledge and skills of home economics. Nine such curriculum guides are in the process of being developed to show some of the important learnings to emphasize in training programs. These nine are for service occupations known to exist, but this in no way implies there are no others. These programs are only a beginning of what it is possible to develop if groups throughout a state concentrate and organize their efforts and creativity. The titles of the nine home and community service occupations accepted by the Department of Labor for inclusion in the *Dictionary of Occupational Titles* are as follows:

Community—Focused Occupations Which Use Home Economics Knowledge and Skills
    Child Day-Care Center Worker
    Management Aide in Federally Aided Low Rent Public Housing Projects
    Visiting Homemaker
    Hotel and Motel Housekeeping Aide
    Supervised Food Service Worker

Home—Focused Occupations Which Use Home Economics Knowledge and Skills
    Personal Wardrobe Maintenance Specialist
    Companion to an Elderly Person
    Family Dinner Service Specialist
    Homemaker's Assistant

TWO HOME ECONOMICS PROGRAMS

As one recognizes the accelerated changes taking place in home economics education, there are many decisions to be made and questions to be answered. Earlier, it was stated that many have benefited by the program which prepared women for homemaking. How will programs preparing women for wage-earning differ?

COMPARISON OF THE PROGRAMS

Both programs use home economics knowledge and skills as the basis for curriculum. Listed below are a few points that show the major differences in the two programs:

Homemaking	Wage-earning
Curriculum is broad in scope and content.	Limited and specialized instruction is based on the job analysis of a specific occupation.
Personal attitudes and behavioral development necessary to strengthening family well-being is stressed.	In preparing for wage-earning, emphasis is placed on the development of attitudes and behavior necessary to secure and hold a job.
All students are accepted because of the belief they can benefit from the program.	Personal qualities and aptitudes are the basis for selecting enrolees in a specific job-oriented program.
Marriage and maintaining a home are common to practically everyone; so programs are justifiable in all communities.	Programs are established only when evidence shows sufficient job opportunities are available for placement of trainees.
Counseling is an aid but not necessary.	Vocational counseling service is necessary to help the teacher in determining needs in the placement of students in the most satisfactory program, as well as employment opportunities.

Advisory committees have not been a "recommended" requirement.	The establishment of a local advisory committee helps determine work available and advise and evaluate the specific emphases of the training program.

Briefly, to summarize the need for both programs, "all communities need programs for instruction in homemaking, but programs for wage-earning will be provided only when there is established evidence of job opportunity." [8]

Home economics knowledge and skills may provide programs for training in wage-earning at four different levels or situations in our educational system: (1) upper secondary-school grades—skilled or semi-skilled; (2) post-high school in the area vocational-technical schools or institutes—skilled or semi-skilled; (3) junior or community colleges—technical in focus; and (4) adult programs, including (a) regular vocational education, (b) Manpower Development and Training, and (c) Area Redevelopment Act—skilled or semi-skilled.

TEACHERS FOR THE PROGRAMS

The question immediately arises as to how teachers will be secured and what qualifications will they need. There will be some common qualifications and a few differences for teachers of programs leading to gainful employment and of those for homemaking. The following are a few of the common elements: (1) both need current knowledge in home economics areas to be taught; (2) both need skill as a teacher; and (3) both need understanding of what is happening to individuals and families in our society.

The teacher of wage-earning course needs experienced insight into the competitive world of employment, which includes such things as: (1) getting a job and holding it; (2) pride in doing a skilled performance of work; and (3) effective relationships between employer and employee. This last qualification is so important that if a teacher with a baccalaureate degree has not had the wage-earning experience,

[8] *Ibid.*

the latter takes precedence and an experienced person without the degree will be chosen. An intensive program of in-service teacher education will be needed to provide assistance in preparing teachers for the wage-earning program.

Summary

As home economics educators reorient themselves to the changing educational picture and adjust their instructional programs to meet the needs of youth and adults, there are a few points which need to be considered in planning and implementing the home economics curriculum in Pennsylvania schools. Influential factors in developing this curriculum are as follows:

More women and more married women than previously are being employed outside the home.

An increasing number of women are assuming a dual role of homemaker and wage-earner.

Home economics is the basis for programs in wage-earning as well as homemaking.

Programs in wage-earning have different goals from those for homemaking.

Wage-earning programs are specifically directed to preparing for *one* occupation where homemaking, to be effective, must be broad in scope.

A broad homemaking program is a desirable prerequisite for wage-earning programs in the secondary school.

As more women assume the dual role of wage earner and homemaker, there is an increasing need for instruction in child development, management of home and finances, consumer, and other family problems.

Job-oriented programs in home economics may be offered at four different levels, starting with the upper secondary schools.

Homemaking programs are needed in all communities, but they should be geared to the needs of the group enroled.

Home and community service occupations programs are offered only where there is a specific need determined with the help of an advisory group which includes the State Employment representative.

Curriculum for job-oriented programs is developed on the basis of a specific job analysis.

The current needs of families in a community determine the program offerings for a broad homemaking program.

Home economics subject matter and skills are the underlying foundation of both instructional programs. With different information, methods, goals, and experiences, the curriculum provides effective instruction for those preparing for homemaking and for those training for gainful employment.

Consumer Textile Problems Stimulate Research

DOROTHY SIEGERT LYLE *

THE NATIONAL INSTITUTE of Drycleaning introduced its expanded "National Fair Claims Guide for Consumer Textile Products" on August 6, 1964. Albert E. Johnson, director of Textile Trade Relations for NID, is the author of the Guide. It is a document that will exert a force on practically every aspect of the textile-apparel industries.

INFLUENCE OF THE GUIDE

By bringing together nationwide consumer experience on the performance of 72 classes of textile apparel, and by providing definitions of terms relating to performance, service processes, and labeling, a whole new area of communication is opened.

Principles of product serviceability, both implied and specified, as related to the life expectancy of apparel will go far beyond attaining fair adjustments for consumers, dry cleaners, retailers, and manufacturers.

LABELING

Labeling in particular is likely to be stimulated, since the Guide specifies that without a label, minimum normal serviceability is to be expected. This is a new concept. It assumes that most articles of clothing and textiles for household use live up to their implied

* Director of Consumer Relations, National Institute of Drycleaning, Silver Spring, Maryland.

serviceability expectations as defined in the Guide, and that only those items which can fail to perform in this manner require precautionary information in the form of permanent labels.

Consumers have greatly appreciated the Federal Trade Commission's laws and rulings which have brought about accurate labeling of fiber content of textile products. However, there is a great need for improved textile product labeling. The continual introduction of new fibers, yarn constructions, fabric constructions, dyes, finishes, and decorative designs makes it imperative that purchasers, users, and cleansers of textile products also have accurate information regarding the quality of products, their use, and care.

Many approaches are being taken to label textiles today. With the development of the Common Market, labeling will become even more important. There are countries who have developed the "symbol" approach to labeling, and areas where symbols are preferred to written directions. However, the weaknesses of this system are that the proposed symbols can be confusing, for they are not always simple and clear, and the use of the symbol by consumers involves memorizing numerous details.

The National Institute of Drycleaning takes the position that the English language in the English-speaking countries is an adequate medium for describing the use and care of textiles; the use seems too complicated to be explained by a system that depends largely upon pictorial symbols.

Any labeling program to be sound must be based on standards. The "National Fair Claims Guide for Textile Products" is closely related to the testing requirements under the "American Standard Performance Requirements for Textile Products," L22, published by the American Standards Association. The Guide is intended for consideration as an American standard following its initial period of use.

ANALYSIS OF TEXTILE PERFORMANCE

The Textile Analysis Laboratories of the National Institute of Drycleaning and its branch office in Glendale, California, have accumulated textile performance statistics over a period of years. For example, in 1963, the laboratory handled a total of 24,312 problems involving textiles. Of this total, the dry cleaner was responsible for 21.8 per cent of the problems, the consumer was responsible for 37.8 per cent of the total, and the manufacturing source was responsible for 29.0 per cent. Garment construction problems accounted for 2.3 per cent, and new problems (unclassified), 5.6 per cent. Even with all the technical know-how of trained personnel and the latest in scientific equipment, in 3.5 per cent of the total items received for analysis, it was not possible to pinpoint responsibility for the damage.

CONSUMER SERVICE PROBLEMS

Let us look at the major items in each group. What complaints were classified under consumer service? A total of 9,185 items fell within this classification. Of this group, 9.9 per cent of the complaints were due to mineral acid (hydrochloric or sulfuric acid from batteries, laboratory contact, cleaning of bricks, and so on). Damage from cold wave solution ranks second, with 9.6 per cent. Damage from heat (this could be scorch or fusing due to the presence of heat-sensitive fibers) accounted for 8.4 per cent. Carmelized sugar stains resulting from contact with any juice or beverage that contains a reducing sugar accounts for 8.2 per cent, and oxidized oil for 7.2 per cent. Shrinkage of fabrics from improper handling makes up 6.3 per cent, and mechanical damage (rips, tears, holes, abrasion), 6.0 per cent. Contact dye, bleaching, and insect damage accounted for 5.1, 5.0, and 4.9 per cent, respectively. The misuse of antiperspirants and deodorants results in 3.1 per cent chloride damage to silk, while other complaints in this category include: streaks in draperies, 2.4 per cent; loss or change of finish, 2.3 per cent; albumin stains, 2.1 per cent; blood and perspiration stains, 2.0 per cent; adhesive stains, 2.0 per cent; and oxycellulose damage, 1.7 per cent.

FABRIC SERVICEABILITY

In the category of fabric serviceability, the total number of complaints was 7,053. Shrinkage ranked first, with 11.4 per cent. Knit garments appear to be the worst offender, and there is a great need to improve dimensional stability of fabrics.

Sun fading of dyes ranked second, with 10.1 per cent, and sun tendering of draperies accounted for 8.9 per cent. Dye problems are classified in several different categories. Solvent-soluble dyes accounted for 9.5 per cent; discoloration of fluorescent dyes, 8.6 per cent; and pigment prints, 8.0 per cent. Fume fading is still with us, and 4.8 per cent of problems in this group were due to this. The use of silk in unbalanced fabric constructions resulted in 7.1 per cent of the problems. Some dyes rub off with abrasion in wear and cleaning, and 3.0 per cent were caused by this. The worst offender is adlecian blue on cotton. Light-sensitive dyes, water-soluble dyes, and acid color change of dyes results in 2.5, 2.5, and 2.1 per cent, respectively. Some dark colored dyes on acetate and nylon under certain conditions of use and storage give off a gas that may deposit on and stain a lighter colored fabric used or hanging next to it. Last year NID received 64 or 0.9 per cent of complaints on sublimation of dye.

Sometimes fabric construction causes complaints. Last year, this amounted to 1.9 per cent, while low fabric strength accounted only for 1.1 per cent. Surface applied designs, on a serviceable fabric, may perform poorly. Metallic prints are unpredictable. For this reason, metallic prints were found responsible for 1.6 per cent of the complaints in this fabric service category. Surprisingly, the urethane foam laminates have resulted in a very few complaints, less than 1.0 per cent (0.9 per cent).

COMPLAINTS AGAINST THE DRY CLEANERS

In any service industry where one is dependent on people, there are bound to be consumer complaints. The dry cleaning industry is no exception. Dry cleaning processes or techniques accounted for 5,298 complaints of the total number analyzed. Mechanical damage accounted for 15.3 per cent of complaints against the dry cleaner, followed by soil redeposition, 11.6 per cent.

Many fabrics are dyed with colors that are sensitive to the reagents used to remove spots and stains. Color loss due to spotting and prespotting was 11.0 and 8.5 per cent, respectively. It is easy to chafe or abrade some fabrics. This accounted for 5.6 per cent. Certain controls must be exercised to avoid shrinkage or stretch in the cleaning and finishing of fabrics. Last year the laboratory received 5.4 per cent items in this category as shrinkage complaints and 4.8 per cent for stretching. Occasionally, a spotter will prespot a silk garment to remove stains. If the moisture is not controlled, the darker color in a print may stain the surrounding lighter area. This accounts for 3.4 per cent of the items in this group. Too, a spotter may put a prespotted garment into the dry cleaning cylinder while it is still moist. This can result in dye stains in dry cleaning, and 5.1 per cent were of this type.

The dry cleaning process must be controlled. If it is not, a cleaner may have problems with carbon stains, accounting for 2.6 per cent, or stains caused from non-volatile materials that may build up in the solvent, which accounted for 2.4 per cent. If heat is not controlled in the pressing of an item, the dry cleaner may also have complaints on scorching or fusing of the fibers, as was true in 2.8 per cent of our cases. New fabric developments, such as the new textured acetates, may bring new problems to the dry cleaner. They are very easily dulled, delusterized, or can develop shine during pressing. Acetate satin may be delustered very easily, and delustered acetate accounts for 1.5 per cent of the items in this group.

Some nylon and Dacron rainwear fabrics are made water-repellent with the use of a plasticizer. If these items are dry cleaned, the plasticizer is removed and the article becomes stiff. Last year, dry cleaners were responsible for 89 items, or 1.7 per cent of such complaints.

Velvets are very important in the fashion picture. Some velvets are made with an acetate pile. Acetate pile velvets cannot be tamped while wet to remove spots and stains, or the pile will be distorted permanently. In 1963, 76 items, or 1.4 per cent of the group, fell under the classification of distorted nap or pile.

Manufacturers state that Fiberglas curtains and draperies should be wet cleaned. Many of the colors are affected adversely with dry cleaning. We have issued a bulletin to NID members advising them to wet clean Fiberglas. If they fail to do this and color is lost, we feel the cleaner is responsible. We had 73 complaints, or 1.4 per cent of the total, in this category attributed to color loss in Fiberglas curtains and draperies.

GARMENT CONSTRUCTION

Garment construction problems numbered 548. Button damage, such as damage from nitrate buttons, adhesive stains, or fugitive dye stains accounted for 37.8 per cent of the complaints in this category. Rubber-lined jackets caused 72, or 13.1 per cent, of the complaints; loss of elasticity of waistbands or wrist bands, 11.1 per cent. Stretch pants that stretched resulted in 8.6 per cent of of the items; sequins that bled color or curled from heat in steaming were found in 4.7 per cent. Dress shields permanently attached to garments caused 3.1 per cent of the dissatisfaction with items in this classification. Complaints ranging below 3 per cent were shrinkage in built-in linings, 2.7 per cent; stains from foam rubber, 2.4 per cent; non-dry cleanable belts because of the solvent-soluble adhesives used, 1.8 per cent; neoprene coatings, 1.8 per cent; shoddy interfacings, 1.5 per cent; and fires from shoulder pads, 0.5 per cent.

UNKOWN

In the category labeled, "unknown," because we cannot pinpoint responsibility, we received 857 items. Shrinkage accounted for 33.0 per cent; miscellaneous stains, 27.8 per cent; color loss or change, 19.2 per cent; and mechanical damage, 6.5 per cent.

NEW PROBLEMS

Every year the Textile Analysis Laboratory receives problems they have not seen in previous years. This is understandable when we think of all the textile developments that result in new consumer merchandise each year. For example, there are many new developments in the simulated suedes and leathers that make these look like the genuine skins. The expanded vinyls that resemble suede must be wet cleaned; they cannot be dry cleaned. Many times, the garment maker combines a wet cleanable simulated suede with a dry cleanable fabric. It is little wonder, then, that we find 36.2 per cent of the items in this new problem classification under the heading of "stiff suedes."

Over the years, we have experienced difficulty with resin-bonded pigments on cotton. This past year, there was the identical problem on 100 per cent Dacron fabrics, or 65 per cent Dacron and 35 per cent cotton blends, with 22.2 per cent of our new problems of this type.

The technique of screen printing has been used to apply surface designs to knit sweaters. With dry cleaning, the print design is removed, and 9.6 per cent of our new problems were of this nature.

Because leather is so popular, we see it being used to a great degree as trim. Unfortunately, many of the dyes used to give leather color will bleed to dry cleaning solvent. So bleeding of leather trim accounts for 8.7 per cent of the items in this group. On the other hand, plastic trim that looks like leather is sometimes used. This may stiffen, shrink, or peel with dry cleaning, and 66 items, or 4.8 per cent of new problems, were like this.

We mentioned that some simulated expanded vinyls stiffen. In others, we may find that the flock separates from the base fabric with dry cleaning and this constituted 7.6 per cent of the items in this category.

Some fabrics that bind foam to fabric are affected by dry cleaning. The fabric partially separates from the foam, creating a blistered effect. We found this to be true in 53 items or 3.9 per cent.

Some metallic fabrics have a limitation as to what can and cannot be done to remove stains. For example, if the stain can be removed only with a rust remover, the acid will affect the metallic coating of the yarns in a metallic fabric. This accounted for 25 items or 1.8 per cent.

Plastic stains account for 1.7 per cent of the items in this group. These include glue, airplane glue, and the "Silly Putty" that children find so delightful. This past year we have also seen red dyes used on cotton and rayon fabrics that change color when in contact with moisture. For example, rain drops may change the red to dark blue or black. We had 21 items or 1.5 per cent where this had happened.

Rayon velvets that mat and crush and cannot be raised upright by any method appear to be on the increase. This is usually attributed to the improper application and curing of the resin. There were 21 items or 1.5 per cent, in this group.

The Consumer's Dilemma

Questions to Ask

Frequently, the consumer finds herself in a dilemma when she must select a fabric for a given use or when she decides how it should be cared for. She may inquire: "Will I need to launder it? Will it be better dry cleaned? What special care must I give it? In this era of wash and wear why should some garments still be dry cleaned?" Here are some of the answers:

(1) Many types of soil are not removed from fabrics by water. Dry cleaning solvents remove oily and greasy soil more readily than water.

(2) Removal of spots and stains requires a knowledge of fabrics, dyes, and finishes in relation to the spotting reagent used and the methods and techniques required to effect removal.

(3) Specialized finishing equipment used by dry cleaners is designed to accommodate the intricate garment details that cannot be pressed by a hand iron on the home ironing board.

(4) Some fabrics require the replacement of special finishes. These can be replaced more readily under commercial procedures that are not adaptable to home application.

(5) Cleaning a garment in a dry cleaning solvent rather than water has the advantage of minimizing shrinkage, preserving tailoring details, preserving many of the colors and finishes applied to modern day fabrics.

Fabric Qualities to Note

The selection and care of modern day fabrics has become quite complicated for the consumer. Fabric properties can be determined by laboratory tests, and many times test results are used by manufacturers to prepare the labels, the hang tags, and the advertising and promotional material on fabrics and garments.

There are many individual properties that combine to make a fabric or garment or household item perform satisfactorily in wear and in cleaning, whether it be laundering, wet cleaning, or dry cleaning. These qualities are:

Fiber content.—A fabric made of 100 per cent composition of any one given fiber may be expected to have different qualities from a fabric having one or more fibers blended together. For example, a 100 per cent silk fabric would not have the same qualities as a 20 per cent silk and 80 per cent wool fabric.

Yarn construction.—A fabric may be made from a filament yarn or a spun yarn, a woolen yarn or a worsted yarn, a relatively simple yarn to a complex novelty yarn. Each type of yarn construction contributes certain qualities to the fabric.

Fabric construction.—Fabric construction may be simple or complex. There are a variety of standard fabric weaves and knits that have become well known over the years. But every year, the ingenious fabric designer may produce new and attractive fabric constructions.

Dyeing or printing.—Dyeing or printing of a fabric offers a wide selection of colors and designs from which to choose. Dye chemistry and the proper application of dyes to fabrics play an important part in the satisfaction received from dyed and printed materials.

Finish.—There are many different physical and chemical finishes applied to fabrics to give them many added and desirable properties. But in some instances, a particular finish may also cause limitations in use and care.

Decorative designs.—Decorative designs may be applied to fabric surface or woven into the basic weave construction to add interest and variety. Many of these designs give very satisfactory performance in wear and in cleaning. In some cases, however, a design may limit the wear life of the fabric.

Garment construction.—The manner in which fabrics are combined in garment design is a very important consideration. An improperly cut garment or a poorly sewn garment can result in disappointment.

Garment findings and trim.—Findings and trim are just as important as the fabric itself in garment design. If the stitching thread shrinks or bleeds, if the bias or stay tape, ribbon, or embroidery trim do not perform satisfactorily in cleaning, the value of the entire garment is lost.

V

Teacher Education

The Education of a Professor of Education

JOHN WALTON*

WHEN THE MATTER of an appropriate education for college and university professors is discussed, the argument usually centers around the relative importance of preparation for research versus preparation for teaching. However, the topic assigned to me—the education of a professor of education—contains at least two implications that take priority over the research versus teaching argument. They are: (1) Should a professor of education have his graduate training in some other field? and (2) How can we arrange to have practical men in schools and departments of education who can meet the standards of scholarship required for academic recognition? Not only the priority but the very reality of these two implications reveal that there is something extraordinary about our position in the academic world. But this is not news; there always has been something unusual about our field and about us. I shall not hazard a guess as to what it is. Rather I prefer to make a proposal for the education of the professor of education which, although it appears at first glance to be most extraordinary, is, in reality, most conventional from the view of an academician.

First of all, I should like to say that I am not talking about "clinical" professors or "intermediary" professors,[1] so glibly recommended by Mr. Conant, who has attempted to put a gloss over the present situation. The first is a rather pretentious title borrowed from another profession which we respect and envy, perhaps, and the second

---

* Professor of Education and Chairman, Department of Education, Johns Hopkins University, Baltimore, Maryland.
[1] James Bryant Conant, *The Education of American Teachers* (New York: McGraw-Hill Book Company, Inc., 1963), pp. 122, 142.

connotes a position for us somewhere between the Heaven of pure scholarship and the Purgatory of pedagogy. I shall argue for the preparation of scholars in education, who mourn no lost opportunities to be psychologists, historians, sociologists, or philosophers, and who hold a voluntary allegiance to an autonomous discipline of "education."

The Discipline of Education

The suggestion for the training of scholars in education is likely to be countered at once with the pronouncement that it is not possible to train scholars in education because there is no scholarly discipline of education, although scholars trained in other disciplines should study the phenomena of education. The answer to this pronouncement will require some elaboration, but in brief it is this: the present state of education obviously affords a superb opportunity for original scholarship in its highest form. And this opportunity is twofold. First, there is the possibility of making sense of what we already know about education. Although most of the modern literature on the subject is incredibly bad, there is, in this vast accumulation, a great deal of information that is worthwhile and undoubtedly it represents the beginnings of a reputable field of academic study. Furthermore, an enormous amount of information and serious opinion about education lies scattered throughout the literature of other disciplines, where it remains isolate and unrelated.

Organization of Knowledge

Herein lies the opportunity for scholars, creative scholars, not merely to become encyclopedists, but to organize areas of systematic knowledge that will provide the means for understanding the phenomena and for pursuing investigation and research within a theoretical framework. For example, if one examines the numerous research studies on the improvement of instruction and finds the rather consistent conclusion that variations in the methods and conditions of teaching make precious little difference in measurable learning, one is immediately tempted to account for this phenomenon. If this research does indicate that there is, in formal education, a kind of "static state" which is difficult, if not impossible, to change, it might be possible to account for this by answering that, up to a point, teaching enhances learning and after that has no positive effect. A conclusion of this kind would change the emphasis in the study of education and give it a new direction.

ORIGINAL RESEARCH

Original research with a view to the discovering of socially new knowledge, i.e. knowledge no one now has, offers a second area of scholarship. The phenomena for investigation are present, and all the methods of research available to scholars in the other disciplines are available to educationists. Although logic, statistics, and experimental methodologists may in some instances enjoy departmental and disciplinary status and have scholar-devotees assiduously working for their improvement, they are in the academic domain, and the educationist as well as the psychologist and the sociologist may use them freely.

REASONS FOR THE PRESENT STATE

Two questions may arise at this point: Why, in view of all the effort that has gone into the study of education, do we not now have a reputable academic subject. And why not assign the study of education to scholars in the other social sciences who are eager to extend the boundaries of their disciplines? The answer to the first question is becoming increasingly clear;[2] students of education have been primarily concerned with the solution of practical problems, the development of a profession, and social reform. Even the true intellectuals in the field, Harold Rugg, for instance, have been more interested in using education as a means of social reform than in pursuing disinterested scholarship. Now this is laudable enough in its own right, but it has interfered with the development of a scholarly discipline.

[2] See Charles J. Brauner's, *American Educational Theory* (New York: Prentice-Hall, Inc., 1964).

Perhaps, we should admit here that the line between practical and pure scholarship is not so hard and fast as we have made it appear. It is questionable, for example, whether scientific research, even in its "purest" form, is disinterested research, since one of its primary objectives is ultimate improvement in our ability to predict and control the operations of nature. History, on the other hand, is a relatively "pure" discipline because it is less concerned with power and prediction. The social sciences are tending in the direction of science, but the events and activities they seek to control are deeply insolvent to ethical considerations with which they have little demonstrable competence to deal. It is true, also, that the natural sciences seem to be facing more insistent ethical questions, for example, in the questions about the use of nuclear power and the genetic control of the future of our species. But in education, the distinction between disinterested scholarship and the immediate, *ad hoc,* solution of practical problems has scarcely been made. As a matter of fact, the study of education has been justified only as practical and professional, and so urgent and controversial have been the problems with which it deals that the energies of the educationists have been exhausted in training teachers and defining emotional involvements.

The answer to the question, Why not assign the study of education to other disciplines? seems obvious and cogent. The information other disciplines acquire is appropriated by them and made an obscure part of their subject matter. There it remains, scattered throughout a number of subjects and disguised under the names of psychology, philosophy, and sociology. Furthermore, there are important aspects of the educational enterprise, curriculum and teaching, for example, that rarely come within the purview of other academic disciplines. I make no claim that all we know about education can be organized into a comprehensive body of systematic knowledge, but there may be several smaller organized bodies of knowledge about education that should stand in close proximity to one another; that is within the discipline and the departments of education.

Therefore, the kind of professor of education I am concerned with is one who organizes, discovers, and teaches knowledge about education, not primarily with a view to training teachers and administrators any more than the professor of economics is primarily concerned

The Education of a Professor of Education

with teaching future bankers and business men, but because he believes that education is a subject worth teaching all students and worthy of scholars who will make their life work the extension of knowledge. The professor of education should resemble graduate professors in the academic disciplines more than he resembles professors of medicine, law, engineering, or business administration.

THE ACADEMIC PREPARATION OF THE PROFESSOR OF EDUCATION

Having assumed that the professor of education is to be a scholar in education, whose principal responsibilities are the advancement of knowledge and the preparation of other scholars, I shall now attempt a description of the kind of academic preparation he should have. Let us begin with the undergraduate years.

UNDERGRADUATE EDUCATION

Certainly we are not prepared to give undergraduate majors in education (it might be well if some other disciplines would admit this also, however important they are at the graduate level), and, therefore, our program will have to be different from those in many other fields in which students complete an undergraduate major before going on to graduate work. The undergraduate major for the prospective scholar in education need not be specified, but it probably should not be in the social sciences. A more humanistic and rigorous preparation is needed. Perhaps, it should be in literature, history, or science, with some work in the history and philosophy of these subjects. Certainly, his general education should include substantial work in these studies. And there should be considerable technical preparation in mathematics, logic, and writing. In the junior and senior years, two or three seminars in education should be offered, in which there is a systematic coverage of the literature and the intellectual problems in education. Thus, the undergraduate would have some encouragement to pursue a graduate work in the field.

GRADUATE EDUCATION

The graduate program should have one central idea—the organization and extension of our systematic knowledge about education. An attempt to develop a discipline of education will surely be attended by an intellectual excitement that should attract capable and imaginative students. It should also maintain the focus on education, for all too often students in graduate departments of education who do some of their work in the other social sciences—which they should do—are drawn by a kind of centrifugal force into an identification with them. A familiar feature on the academic landscape is the professor or graduate student in education who claims to be a psychologist, a sociologist, a historian, or a philosopher, but who has no recognition in these disciplines. Furthermore, it should obviate another problem: Education has generally looked to the other social sciences for its models of scholarship, which so far have not been very promising; therefore, the paleness of educational scholarship. A concern for an autonomous discipline may well result in new and appropriate models by which knowledge about education can be organized, transmitted, and extended.

Research methods.—Furthermore, research methods in education should be taught in departments of education, for as long as they are taught in other departments, education will be regarded as not having any; although, in reality, statistics, survey techniques, logic, experimentation, analysis, and theory belong to education in precisely the same degree that they belong to psychology, sociology, or political science. Admittedly, history may offer an exception, but even this is doubtful; the history of science, for example, is now being taught in separate departments.

Seminars.—As for the graduate work in the substantive work, it will depend, first, upon the success of scholars in organizing the information that is now available and in conducting continued research. Graduate students should participate in the initial phases of the organization. Series of seminars should be organized around significant aspects of the enterprise of formal education that may become general divisions of the discipline. As an example, there may be seminars on the curriculum in which there is investigation into the ways in which subjects get into the curriculum, how they are organized and transmitted, and under what conditions they combine or disappear. These are problems unique to education; they have not been investigated by scholars in education, probably because they are uniquely educational.

Other seminars in such subjects as the nature of instruction, school learning, the uses of formal education, the relations between organization and education, comparative education, the history of education, and general educational theory may be organized. Let us leave to psychology the study of general learning, including that of rats and pigeons, and to sociology general social relations. Certainly our subject will overlap with others—nearly all subjects do—and we should use what we can from other disciplines to enhance the study of education.

Research.—In the graduate study of education great emphasis should be placed on research. The doctoral dissertation in each instance should be a contribution to knowledge, to the development of a discipline of education. This research should not be narrowly conceived; it should not be limited to those problems that lend themselves to the traditional statistical or experimental methods, for this indicates a premature assumption that our subject will ultimately yield its secrets to the quantitative method. Rather, we should recognize the fact that in education we shall be forced to deal with both factual and normative problems, and that a meaningful reorganization of knowledge can often be a significant contribution to knowledge. And certainly, scholars in education should begin at once in the transformation of the language in which research in the social sciences is written.

The Education of the Teacher of Teachers

The students who complete the program that we have outlined will be expected to teach and continue their research in graduate departments or schools of education. This proposal leaves unanswered the question: What kind of education should the teacher of teachers have? This is a different but not unrelated problem. Certainly, the theoretical courses in education can be taught by the scholars we propose to turn out; and an occasional one may well be able to offer a practical course, also. For the methods courses, I think we should have scholars from other disciplines who have taught or are teaching in the schools and who have the interest to keep up with developments in both their subject and teaching methods. In the training of school teachers, the scholar in education will have about the same contribution to make as economists have in the training of business administrators, which is considerable but somewhat oblique. This analogy is far from perfect, since teachers should be scholars in the subject matter they teach, but there are some similarities. The educationist should take his place in the academic community beside the other social scientists, and, although he may lose some of his immediate importance for the vast and urgent educational enterprise, he will in the long run contribute a great deal more to our understanding of this increasingly important social activity.

The Professional and Practical Preparation of the Professor of Education

JAMES L. GRACE, JR.*

To DESCRIBE the professional and practical preparation of the professor of education is a most difficult task. It is difficult for three reasons.

First, he is not so easily identified as are his collegiate colleagues. A professor of physics is a physicist, a professor of chemistry, a chemist. Most subject-matter professors can be easily recognized in this manner, and the preparation of such professors can be fairly well delineated. But the professor of education presents a less exact picture. To be sure, he is an educator, but so are his academic friends.

The image of the professor of education is a composite of a variety of specialists with a diversity of backgrounds. He may be a historian, a mathematician, a statistician, or a scholar in any field who is engaged in teacher education. He may have taught in the elementary or secondary schools, or his experience in teaching may have been entirely at the college level. He may teach all the education courses in a small college, or he may teach in a large institution with responsibility for only one segment of the professional sequence. The significant feature that distinguishes him from his academic associates is his particular involvement in the preparation of teachers and other educational specialists for the elementary and secondary schools.

* Acting Chairman, Department of Education, St. Joseph's College, Philadelphia, Pennsylvania.

Secondly, the image of the professional educator at the elementary and secondary levels presents an equally varied picture. As a classroom teacher, he may teach all the subjects in the elementary school or instruct in a single area at the secondary level. As a school administrator, he may be an elementary or secondary school principal, a school superintendent, or a business manager. He could be a guidance counselor, a director of public relations, or a curriculum specialist in anything from art to vocational education. The professional educator may hold any one of these positions or still others that have not been mentioned, so vast is the field. And the preparation of these professionals is the particular responsibility of professors of education.

A third point which adds difficulty to this task is the question of the disciplinary nature of education itself. While this ancient debate will not be elaborated here, it is certainly germane to the topic of professional preparation. As a professional discipline, education has its own internal dynamics and approach based upon its proper object of concern—the professional act itself. In addition, it is specifically concerned, where other disciplines are not, with the schools—their curricula and their varied services to society.

Because schools and departments of education prepare professionals for a variety of positions in the schools and because professors of education with differing preparations are needed to train them, there can be no single ideal preparation of *the* professor of education.

Three Professors of Education

Therefore, this paper will consider the professional preparation of three professors of education, corresponding to the three major areas of competence in the field. They shall be termed "the professor of pedagogy," "the professor of school administration," and "the professor of professional studies." The dominion of professors of pedagogy covers methodology, curriculum, teaching and learning theory, educational psychology, and human growth and development. Of concern to professors of school administration are the administration and financing of schools and school systems, school laws and regu-

Preparation of the Professor of Education 243

lations, and personnel. Educational sociology, history and philosophy of education, and research are the interests of professors of professional studies.

The professor of pedagogy would deal primarily, but not necessarily exclusively, with undergraduates preparing to teach. The professor of professional studies would function primarily at the graduate level, extending and deepening the students' knowledge of professional education, while the professor of educational administration would function exclusively at the graduate level. Their particular responsibility in teacher education and the practical and professional preparation of these three professors of education will now be considered.

THE PROFESSOR OF PEDAGOGY

Responsibilities.—Pedagogy is defined by Webster as "the art, practice, or profession of teaching; especially, systematized learning or instruction concerning principles and methods of teaching." As an undergraduate professor, the professor of pedagogy should be prepared to instruct the teacher education student in the methods and techniques of guiding the learning process. He should also be competent to teach the introductory courses in education, educational psychology, and human growth and development. He should also be a skillful supervisor of student teaching if given this responsibility. And above all, he should be, in the words of the National Commission on Teacher Education and Professional Standards, "particularly aware of the influence on the student of his own performance as a teacher." [1] The professor of pedagogy has the major responsibility for developing master teachers and should be a master teacher himself.

The importance of good teaching on the part of the professor of education on the undergraduate level cannot be overstressed. We cannot tolerate mediocrity in the elementary or secondary schools. Education is too vital to our society. If we cannot tolerate it there,

---

[1] National Commission on Teacher Education and Professional Standards, *A Position Paper on Teacher Education and Professional Standards* (Washington, D.C.: National Education Association, 1963), p. 13.

we cannot tolerate it in schools or departments of education. If the children of America are to be taught by expert professionals, their teachers must exemplify the best in college teaching. Again, in the words of the TEPS commission, "Teaching skills and artistry should rank first among the attributes of the college teacher, particularly the teacher in professional education."[2]

This is not to say that the professor of pedagogy must typify every teaching technique appropriate to the elementary school or to treat his college students as young adolescents. He is a college teacher and should use methods and techniques appropriate to that level of schooling, but he should, at the same time, exemplify the basic and fundamental qualities of good teaching: motivation, concern for the individual student and his needs, planning in terms of goals, stimulation of students to relate and interpret knowledge in terms of these goals, and a belief in the potentiality of the learner.

As a graduate professor, the professor of pedagogy would be engaged in the development of curriculum specialists for the schools and of other professors of pedagogy, and would conduct pedagogical research and experimentation. He should be especially competent to render such service because of previous experience as an undergraduate professor preparing teachers and because of his advanced study in the field.

Undergraduate preparation.—It is proposed that professional and practical preparation of the professor of pedagogy consist of the following sequence: (1) undergraduate preparation for elementary or secondary teaching, (2) a minimum of five years of professional experience in the schools, and (3) a graduate program emphasizing curriculum study and experimentation, teaching and learning theory, and interdisciplinary study in psychology and sociology.

As an undergraduate, it is essential that the future professor of pedagogy prepare himself as a teacher for the lower schools. The college teacher of teachers cannot give proper professional treatment to his instruction unless he has been prepared as a teacher. This professional preparation must be scholarly and liberal as well as practical. Early indication of interest in college teaching while desirable, is not vital. What *is* vital is an early interest and enthu-

[2] *Ibid.*

Preparation of the Professor of Education

siasm for teaching. Hopefully, some professors of education are responsible for this enthusiasm, or possibly a high school or elementary teacher may have been the source of encouragement and inspiration. Regardless of who is responsible, the potential professor of pedagogy has it.

After college, the future professor would teach. No graduate school for him. The first-year teacher should not take graduate courses. While many states require a piling up of additional credits for permanent certification, this places too great a burden upon the beginning teacher. Yet no sooner is he graduated than he is signing up for more courses, when he has his hands full preparing his classes without taking upon himself the additional responsibility of a graduate program.

Consider how often undergraduate professors of education stress the importance of planning in teaching. The key to success as a teacher is the well-planned lesson and the well-prepared teacher. This takes time. The conscientious teacher who takes his responsibility to his students seriously burns the candle at both ends when beginning graduate school and doing classroom teaching at the same time. The future professor of pedagogy does not consider his education complete, but at this point his classroom teaching must receive priority. Hopefully, all teachers entering classrooms for the first time would have this attitude.

Experience.—The practical experience of the future professor should be as broad as possible. As a classroom teacher, he would actively participate in all aspects of the educational program, for a teacher's responsibility is not limited to the classroom. He would welcome opportunities to serve on curriculum committees, administrative cabinets, and the like. Through participation in parent-teacher organizations, he obtains first-hand knowledge of what parents expect of the school and in turn acquires experience in interpreting the school's program to one of its most interested publics. As a professional, he would associate himself with his professional organizations, keep up to date by reading professional journals, and collaborate with his professional colleagues in improving the educational program of the school, while continuing always to improve his skill as a teacher. Later, as a teacher of teachers, he will be responsible for portraying to his students a complete picture of the school and its place in American society.

Experience as a co-operating teacher in a college program of student teaching would be of great practical worth to the prospective teacher of teachers. Working with student teachers provides valuable opportunities for direct instruction of college students in pedagogy, for association with different undergraduate programs of student teaching and with professors of pedagogy, and for greater understanding and recognition of the importance of student teaching in the development of professionals for the schools. This experience in working with prospective members of the profession is invaluable to the future teacher of teachers.

Graduate study.—After one or two years of teaching experience, the future professor would begin his graduate studies—during summers in the beginning and later possibly in an afternoon or Saturday class. He begins with courses that will help him become a better teacher. Through in-service teaching and graduate study, the individual sees theory and practice develop together. While his early graduate work would stress pedagogy, other professional studies should not be ignored. Since the undergraduate professor of education must introduce the undergraduate student to the study of teaching and schooling, it is important that the former be a scholar in professional education, a student of his profession. Therefore, part of his graduate studies must deal with such areas as comparative education, history of education, educational sociology, or the like. Attention to these areas of professional study broadens his background and produces the knowledgeable professional.

Throughout his graduate work for the Master's degree, maximum opportunity for experimentation and research should be permitted. It is urgent that graduate schools develop in classroom teachers, as well as future professors, a respect for research. Too many in-service teachers taking graduate courses ignore research findings because of limited practical experience in the classroom. It is amazing how adept some in-service teachers are in refuting educational principles supported by extensive research on the basis of thirty students in the classroom. Since it is doubtful that the requirement of a Master's thesis will return, the responsibility now lies with each graduate school professor to require truly graduate papers and not elongated and warmed-over undergraduate work. Too often haphazard and poorly co-ordinated work is accepted under the aegis of action-research. Everything that does not meet the strict standards of bona fide research is baptized "action research." Opportunities for good solid research exist in the schools, and in-service graduate students should be doing it.

It is not intended that this research activity of the future professor of pedagogy should make him a research specialist. Technical research is not the central purpose of pedagogy. This research on the Master's level is intended to make the future professor a demanding and knowledgeable consumer of research. Stratemeyer describes him rather effectively:

> . . . The teacher is first a consumer and interpreter of research. He seeks knowledge of the findings of research, discovers relationships among those findings, subjects them to critical analysis, and through skillful interpretation helps others and himself to understand their implications for use in life situations.[3]

The professor of pedagogy as an interpreter of research to his students must relate research to the classroom situation. The future professor must not rely solely upon his practical experience to teach prospective teachers, but also upon the collective experimentation and research of the profession. Practical experience adds meaning to theory and research. Together with scholarship, they provide a firm foundation for the professional discipline of pedagogy.

The prospective professor would intensify his study, teaching, theory, and practice in the doctoral program. Teacher education would have a prominent place in the program, and related professional studies would continue to make a significant contribution to his professional preparation.

A year of full-time study at this level is recommended for the candidate, and it is important for a number of reasons: It would give impetus to the attainment of the degree, and the prospective

---

[3] Florence B. Stratemeyer, "College Teaching and Teacher Education," *Teacher Education For a Free People,* ed. Donald P. Cottrell (Oneonta, N.Y.: American Association of Colleges for Teacher Education, 1956), p. 275.

professor would be in more intimate association with practicing professors of education. In addition, the future professor could get a taste of college teaching, possibly a methods course or supervision of student teachers. This year of graduate study is also the most advantageous time for the prospective professor to enter college teaching, because he is not so far advanced on the salary scale for classroom teachers that the move is financially difficult.

In-service growth.—After becoming a college teacher, he must continue to grow professionally and make his contribution to the discipline. Publication and research, as well as attention to good teaching, must be part of the in-service training of the professor of pedagogy, as for all college teachers.

The Professor of School Administration

Responsibilities.—As a graduate professor, the professor of school administration does not deal with prospective teachers but with prospective administrators of educational facilities. His students are practicing or future principals and superintendents. As a professional educator, he must be no less a teacher than his pedagogical counterpart at the undergraduate level, and his contribution to the educational enterprise is no less important. But his experiential background need not be so extensive. To be sure, experience in school administration is important, but knowledge and appreciation of the administrative process need not be obtained through actual tenure in school administration. Administrative intern programs and graduate fellowships in collaboration with school systems could serve the same purpose as a long period of service in a principalship or superintendency and be a more intensive and efficient learning experience.

Elementary or secondary classroom experience is also helpful but not imperative. A knowledge of curriculum and pedagogy is necessary, since this is the milieu of educational administration. But while the elementary principal should be a former elementary teacher, the professor of educational administration who is teaching prospective elementary school principals need not be.

Professional preparation.—Therefore, the following sequence is proposed as professional preparation for the professor of educational administration: (1) an undergraduate program with a minor in education; (2) practical experience gained through an administrative internship of one year in conjunction with graduate study; and (3) a graduate program emphasizing school administration and finance, the school and its legal status, and the dynamics of the administrative process.

It is not necessary that this prospective professor pursue an undergraduate program in education. A major in government or business with a minor in education would provide a better foundation for his future career. Since the educational enterprise is a major function of government and since it is certainly big business, these areas of undergraduate study seem appropriate. A minor in education would serve as an introduction and orientation to professional education.

After college, the prospective professor of educational administration would enter graduate school. Since his area of competence would be administration, not pedagogy, a graduate program in administration with an intern program in the schools leading to the Master's degree would be appropriate. The intern program must be varied, yet intensive. The intern must be given opportunities for working with elementary and secondary school principals, business managers, and superintendents.

Like the professor of pedagogy, the prospective professor of educational administration would be a student of his profession and part of his graduate study would deal with its philosophical, historical, and sociological background. In addition, as a knowledgeable professional, learning theory and the principles of teaching would also be studied. This related study would be continued in the doctoral program.

The doctoral program of the prospective professor would provide opportunities for research and specialization in his area of interest. Advanced field research and opportunity to work with mature professors of administration in a consulting capacity to school systems would also be very valuable.

The Professor of Professional Studies

Responsibilities.—The professor of professional studies may be a philosopher of education, an educational historian, an educational sociologist, or an educational researcher. His is an interdisciplinary approach to the study of education. At the undergraduate level, he would probably teach in another academic area in addition to education. As a graduate professor, his teaching of advanced students in education, coupled with extensive research and study of the profession, provides the academic adhesive to education as a professional discipline.

Just as physics draws on mathematics, biology on chemistry, and the social sciences on each other, education as a subject draws upon all disciplines. This fact should not lessen education's claims to disciplinary status. Therefore, the position of the professor of professional studies is a sound one. His professional preparation, by necessity, must be interdisciplinary.

Professional preparation.—Therefore, the following professional sequence is proposed for the prospective professor of professional studies: (1) undergraduate preparation in a related or basic field, such as history or psychology, with elective courses in education; (2) an interdisciplinary graduate program, with major attention given to the study of professional education. The professional preparation of the professor of professional studies would be taken on a full-time basis through the doctorate. Some, because of financial reasons, may teach in secondary schools while pursuing advanced study, but this practical experience is not necessary to their preparation as professors of professional studies.

The research worker in education is also included among the professors of professional studies. This placement is based upon the position taken by Nathaniel Gage in his speech to the American Association of Colleges for Teacher Education in February. He says this about the research worker in education:

> We need what other scholarly disciplines have—a tradition of graduate work into which young people move directly from the bachelor's degree. Without first spending years as teachers (any more than young people do in psychology, chemistry, anthropology, or history) these young people will get a thorough grounding in research methodology, including statistics, measurement, and experimental design. At the same time, these students will participate actively in the research projects of their professors. Thus, early in their graduate careers, they will begin to gain research experience,

rather than first passing the qualifying examinations and then writing a thesis proposal.[4]

Whereas, the professor of pedagogy is primarily a teacher, the professor of professional studies is primarily a researcher and student of professional education. His preparation would include pedagogy, but his function is not to teach teachers. Major emphasis in his preparation would be upon the research tools of the related fields as applied to education.

Conclusion

In spite of the vastness of education with its vague and ill-defined limits, an attempt has been made to define the functions of the professor of education and then to provide some guidelines for his preparation. Three professional areas of competence have been sketched, and proposals have been made for the preparation of professors of education in these areas.

Many questions on this topic still remain unanswered: Should professors of education be responsible for the training of all school personnel? How can specific programs be developed at the undergraduate level for preparing scholars and students of the discipline of education? What specific programs of selection can be established for recruiting professors of education? Should the practicing professional educator in the elementary or secondary schools continue to be a major source of professors of education? These and other questions must be answered if the field of education is to be given disciplinary status in the eyes of the academic world.

[4] Nathaniel Gage, "Psychological Theory and Empirical Research for Teacher Education," *Freedom With Responsibility in Teacher Education* (Chicago, Ill.: American Association of Colleges for Teacher Education, 1964), p. 104.

VI

International Education

Art Education; International Aspects

ARTHUR R. YOUNG*

DEVELOPMENTS in international art education parallel our global thinking and define a pattern of expanding growth. The desire to share, not just goods and material things but knowledge and the enjoyment of the arts, characterizes the international scene today. At no time in history have countries participated in this give-and-take with greater frequency and with more show of enthusiasm. Had this cultural interchange focused on business or the sciences alone, much would have been lost. Some of the most compelling and effective examples of successful interchange have occurred in the area of the arts. What our image is abroad has been modified and even transformed through our mediation of music, theatre, films, painting, sculpture, graphics, and dance into countries which previously were disposed to view us as being industrial-minded to the exclusion of all else. And, in a somewhat similar fashion, the image we held of others was often modified by their arts when they reached our shores.

CULTURAL EXCHANGE PROGRAMS

In such interchange, the arts are singularly fortunate in that their communication is, in large part, not dependent on language, which often sets up a formidable barrier. Ease of communication and assimilation characterize the visual and auditory arts. These arts are responded to by large audiences in numbers far exceeding the potential of agronomy, physics, husbandry, and medicine—all needful in international exchange, but all restricted to smaller audiences. The

* Professor of Art Education, Pratt Institute, Brooklyn, New York.

arts have the added advantage of capturing audiences through their emotional and aesthetic responses. Cultural exchanges are today a growing front, and the demands for such exchanges between nations increase with the years. More recently, through the co-operation of art organizations and individuals on five continents, cultural exchange programs have been including material bearing on art education.

EXHIBITS OF CHILDREN'S ART

In any given year, it is now possible to see exhibits of children's art from all corners of the earth. As the organizations sponsoring exchanges of students' work, from preschool to college, are better supplied with funds, these exhibits will multiply. Programs for such interchange work best through established agencies, governmental, private, educational, and so on. In due time, professional art schools, schools of architecture, industrial design, commercial art, and regional and urban planning will be invited to subscribe to traveling international exhibits.

How little most of us know of the practices of such schools beyond our borders! The arts and art education need no longer remain insular and confined. We have long since realized how salutary such exchanges are. We learn from each other, and no single center of learning is so richly endowed and so self-sufficient that it cannot better its status through sharing with others. The publicizing of top creative achievements in the arts of one nation to others beyond its borders is no new phenomenon. The history of art is but a recounting of just such mediation. But at no time save the present has it seemed necessary to disseminate the values and rewards of art education. It is certainly no accident that in this century, in answer to this need for global interchange, UNESCO came into being. It is now a fond hope that the cultural insularity once so prevalent will no longer continue, and that, wherever the desire to share exists or a need arises, there will be a readiness on the part of others to contribute their resources and co-operate to the extent of their ability.

With gains in technology speeding cultural inter-communication on every level, it is conceivable that a degree of cultural intimacy will be achieved unequaled in any previous age. All peoples speak from their point of origin, and the folklore, rituals, pageantry, costumes, handicrafts, and symbols produced are expressions of their character and uniqueness. It has been observed that the art work of young children is identified and shaped by this enfolding indigenous culture.

RECOGNITION OF INDIGENOUS ART

It is generally a matter of regret that so much of the spirit and vitality of indigenous art has succumbed to wars, disasters, and colonization. The introduction of art idioms and ideologies alien to a given culture usually results in the dessication of the extant, indigenous art. In any cultural exchange, there is always present the latent danger of destroying that which marks the uniqueness of a given people. Though such influence may not be intended, it is desirable to make sure that cultures are not pressured or down-graded; rather efforts should be made to instill respect and confidence and to confirm in all people a recognition of their essential artistry. In the past half century, many museums throughout the world have included art works of all major cultures, rather than display their own to the exclusion of all else. So today, the East is knowledgeable about Western art, as we in the West are of theirs. But what is also taking place is the recognition of the contributions of primitive cultures, and examples of such art can now be found in museums everywhere. Such primitive art, once viewed as captivating curiosities, is now esteemed for its aesthetic accomplishment.

EXCHANGE OF STUDENT ART WORK

Mutual respect and admiration for a given people is often achieved through the study and enjoyment of their arts. Similarly, appreciation could be further enhanced through a vigorous and effective exchange of student art work. Extremely valuable to art education would be the exchange of precepts, procedures, and practices. How little we know of the art education literature in other tongues—certainly, no one part of the world has a "corner" on educational methodology. How important it would be to know what articles, books, films, and slides significant to art education are available.

A project aimed to achieve just this was introduced in 1949, but it failed to fulfill its early promise due to budgetary limitations. This initial step came out of UNESCO, but only two issues of a publication were introduced before the project was abandoned. An outgrowth of UNESCO was the International Society for Education through Art—INSEA—an organization holding as an objective a world image for art education. Distinguished art educators have brought much effort, determination, and spirit to its program. Edwin Ziegfeld of Teachers College, Columbia University, Charles D. Gaitskell of Ontario, Canada, and J. A. Soika of Berlin, West Germany, have done much to move this vast project ahead.

The International Society for Education Through Art

POSITION

The position taken by INSEA is evident from its Preamble, as follows:

> That: *Creative activity* in art is a basic need common to all people; and *Art* is one of man's highest forms of expression and communication;
>
> That: *Education through art* is a natural means of learning at all periods of the development of the individual, fostering values and disciplines essential for full intellectual, emotional and social development of human beings in a community;
>
> That: *Association* on a world-wide basis of those concerned with education through art is necessary in order that they may share experiences, improve practices and strengthen the position of art in relation to all education;
>
> That: *Co-operation* with those concerned in other disciplines of study outside the teaching profession and domains of education would be of mutual advantage in securing closer co-ordination of activities directed to solving problems in common;
>
> That: *International co-operation* and the better

understanding between peoples would be furthered by a more completely integrated design and permanent structure for the diffusion of beliefs and practices . . . , so that the right of man "freely to participate in the cultural life of the community, to enjoy the arts" and to create beauty for himself in reciprocal relationship with his environment, would become a living reality.[1]

MEETINGS

Members of INSEA have met in widely dispersed geographical centers since the first meeting in 1955. Meetings have taken place in Paris, The Hague, Manila, and Montreal, and the meeting in 1965 will be in Tokyo. Those fortunate enough to be part of these conferences have come away feeling rewarded and, more than ever, dedicated to further service. It is hoped that increased budgets will enable INSEA further to enrich its program of offerings, that more exhibits of school arts will be available, and that the growing demands for such exhibits can be met in full.

ACTIVITIES

But whether INSEA, the National Art Education Association, and other art education organizations, government, or private resources sponsor international exchange of educational material, the fact remains there is a job to be done. Such resourceful groups could work conjointly or, when desirable, perform separately, but never losing sight of the need of making all pertinent resources available to art educators wherever they may be. The beginnings of such a far-flung objective have been made, and already it is apparent on what basic "grass-root" levels such programs tend to operate. No country can boast such advanced and accomplished achievements in art education as not to benefit from an interchange of ideas and procedures; certainly no country can lay sole claim to inspirational

[1] International Society for Education Through Art, *Constitution, Rules, Procedures* ('s-Gravenhage: N. V. Drukkerij Trio, n.d.), p. 3.

teachers who possess qualities and capacities that set the creative energies of their students in motion.

We all tend to approve wholeheartedly programs and activities focused on international exchange. We all agree that such objectives are worthy and in line with our global attitudes. At the same time, we express some hesitance when asked to become personally identified and involved. Where does one begin? Any single art educator could arrange an exchange of art exhibits with an art educator abroad, but usually this is best accomplished when inaugurated by an art association, a government agency, or an organization like INSEA, which is structured to utilize exchange material whenever possible.

To many people, the ambitious objectives of an organization like INSEA seem idealistic and out of reach. But is this really so? In the broader sense are such objectives dealing with interchange of art and art education so unlike the aims of the modern Olympic Games, wherein skilled athletes from all parts of the world are invited to compete together? Tomorrow in Tokyo, the eighteenth Olympiad will start bringing the first contestants together, and when the final events have been completed—win, lose or draw—the thousands of competitors will have made significant gains. They will have learned, through fraternizing, through camaraderie, and through competition, what could not possibly be learned in any other way. And though we do not view the exchange of the arts and art education as competitive enterprises, benefits similar to the Olympics could be realized through the interchange of aesthetic values.

An Art Specialist in the Caribbean

Perhaps, at this time, it would be well to introduce a related experience of mine and remove this discussion from a purely theoretical level. In 1962, it was my good fortune to act as Art Specialist under the auspices of the United States Information Service.

THE ASSIGNMENT

My assignment was to teach art on all levels and to lecture. The areas of instruction were painting, sculpture, and the graphic arts, and other activities relating to the age groups taught. The location of this assignment was the Caribbean, with one unit of teaching devoted to Georgetown, British Guiana, on the mainland. My itinerary included Trinidad, Tobago, Barbados, Martinique, Grenada, and Jamaica, with stop-overs in Haiti, St. Lucia, Antigua, Puerto Rico, and Curaçao.

THE PROGRAM

The program varied somewhat from one location to another, but in most instances consisted of the following activities: Classes in art were conducted mornings and afternoons, Monday through Saturday. These classes cut across all levels, from elementary to teacher education. There were also artist groups, members of local art societies, and lay groups sandwiched into this program. Included in this schedule were classes in silk screen printing, the initial introduction of this graphic art in the Caribbean. The response to all of these activities was most gratifying.

The artist groups who enroled for silk screen printing far exceeded our expectations, and after one month the materials were exhausted. Forty students enroled in a class planned for twenty. The enthusiasm, the eagerness to learn, the creative fervor were in evidence throughout the trip. The silk screen group completed enough work to cover the many partitions set up in the empty public market which was our studio in Port of Spain, Trinidad.

It was in this market that classes in figure drawing and painting were also conducted. The working hours were 8:00 a.m. to 5:00 p.m., and there was never a need to check on attendance. Students were present at all times. The local radio company brought in their equipment and broadcast studio criticisms on a number of occasions. If Port of Spain is spot-lighted here, it is because this city is the largest in the Caribbean and has an excellent cultural program underway. Cultural Director M. P. Aladdin and Miss Sibyl C. Atteck did much to make my stay in Trinidad a memorable one.

In many schools visited in the Caribbean area, there were no art programs—no materials to draw on other than a slate. In some elementary classes, I had children bring in flowers and leaves, both in rich abundance, and, with the petals of flowers dampened with water, they made designs on their board desks. In most cases it was necessary to improvise with what was at hand in the natural environment.

In Georgetown, British Guiana, my schedule included teaching in denominational schools—Catholic, Baptist, Anglican—and in government schools, on all levels. A worker's club held art classes in the late afternoons, and criticisms were given each day. Also the artist group in Georgetown was very prolific and put on a large exhibit of their work during my stay there. One could go on at great length describing the many exciting facets of this State Department assignment. Every moment was a challenge, and every day brought new experiences.

Conclusion

In retrospect, beyond all else is the memory of excited and avid students. The desire to learn, to master new materials, to know what was best for them in meeting their expressional needs—these were always in evidence. At the end of the tour and somewhat frayed by the demanding schedule, I was supported by the memory of the many exciting happenings, the warmth of response of the hundreds of students encountered. There can be no greater reward. Our gains were reciprocal, and the experiences were learnings shared. I was convinced, as never before, that the arts and art education assume a new dimension when enacted in an international setting.

Explosion in Higher Education in Britain

HARRY K. HUTTON [*]

IT IS ONLY to utter the merest truism to say that no system of education can be studied intelligently in isolation. It cannot be separated from a particular people, in a particular place, at a particular time. Whether in America or Borneo or England, education is a social institution, inevitably reflecting and transmitting a culture, possibly helping change it. To see a good school as both creation and creator of culture is to see it whole. Thus, for instance, we should see Rugby under (Dr. Thomas) Arnold.

The bewildering diversity of English schools and their educational vocabulary abounding in such terms as "catchment area" and "ordinary level" are enough to discourage a Pennsylvanian whose interest in the whole subject is new. But to begin, let me first say a few things about the country and the people. We shall arrive at higher education and its "explosive" aspects in due course.

THE COUNTRY AND THE PEOPLE

To an American, England and Wales are comparatively small and incredibly old. By taking only slight liberty with the actual statistics, one finds that Pennsylvania is five-sixths of the size of England, and California is nearly three times as large. When it comes to population, if England, Wales, and Scotland are taken together—in short Great Britain—there are fifty million people, compared with the United States total, which is almost four times as large. But in the matter of age, there is no comparison!

[*] Professor of Education, Pennsylvania State University, University Park, Pennsylvania.

AN OLD COUNTRY

It is some fifteen centuries since the last of the Roman legions left Britain. A wall here and a road there still stand as serviceable souvenirs. As for churches, one built in the fourteenth century enjoys no special fame on that account. St. Martin's, Canterbury, is a little out of the ordinary in dating from the eighth.

Schools and colleges founded in the 1300's and 1400's would make up a considerable list. I have visited one of the three which can prove conclusively that it is the oldest in the country. The original date is somewhat vague but declared to be near A.D. 600. It is necessary to understand certain regrettable gaps and make allowance for missing records. English schools, of course, are not unique for claiming the earliest possible founding dates. The incontestable grounds on which the University of Pennsylvania rests its case for 1740 has been explained to me, and I have gladly revised my earlier impression that it developed from Franklin's Academy. But even 1740 or Harvard's 1636 is modern in comparison with Oxford's reputed 1167. Cambridge became a university town some thirty-five years later. Six centuries were to pass before London and Durham entered the field of higher education. There is nothing "explosive" in that much of the bald record!

The point of England's age need be labored no further. It is not emphasized as any obvious claim to educational wisdom. (I see little disposition among English educationists to justify any educational institution or practice by an appeal to antiquity. More typical today may be the grammar school headmaster who said, "We are old, almost at the stage of senility.")

But age *does* mean traditions, customs, often values and ways of thinking that the stranger must not underestimate. These may even be significantly different in different parts of a small but ancient country. Yorkshire is not Dorset. Devon is not to be confused with Lancashire or even with Kent. The North and the Midlands and the South all have special cultural characteristics. London is the heart, but no non-Londoner equates it with the whole body.

NATIONAL CHARACTERISTICS

Anyone is on slippery ground when he tries to characterize an entire people. Mr. Gladstone did well to warn his countrymen against ever "indicting a whole nation." He might have added, "or idealizing it." I shall content myself with a few careful generalizations about Englishmen and shall be the more cautious because I am often amazed, and occasionally stupefied, by things that I hear or read about Canadians, my own people.

Whatever his Tudor and Stuart ancestors may have been, the modern Englishman is surely tolerant, given to compromise, fond of his own idea of comfort, somewhat distrustful of theory, impatient with detailed plans and instructions, something of a sportsman and a bit of a gambler, an avowed believer in fair play. He is secular rather than religious, but may be seen between Sunday services peering reverently at the monstrosities with which cathedrals and abbeys are cluttered. He is satisfied that education is a good thing, if only for its cash value. He seems not to have anything remotely approaching the sociologists' interest in "class stratification," and it was Lord James who said that American educationists on quick tour of England are apt to be fatally obsessed with ideas about the class structure of English society.

This is not to ridicule or discount the value of sociological studies. They are going forward in Britain, as in the United States. There, as here, they reveal some deplorable conditions and underline the manifold problems of industrial societies, but at least they show that the "class structure" is changing, that what is called "upward social mobility" is no longer a phenomenon, and that, in fact, its connection with education is clear. One of the greatest of modern English educationists, Sir Fred Clarke, was justly critical of government reports on education, because they tended to ignore completely the psychological and sociological origins and implications of educational problems. He would have felt better on that score had he lived to read the Newsom Report of 1963, aptly titled *Half our Future*. It deals critically and sympathetically with the education of "children

—the average and the less than average ability between the ages of 13 and 16."[1] To the list of common English characteristics should be added the deep conviction that far too little has been done for the education of those who are average and below average. At the same time, it is an American, not an English theory, that equality of opportunity will ensure equality of attainment. An Englishman is more likely to say that people should have equal opportunity to find out that they are unequal and then just face it, with no medals or stigmas attached.

The generalizations about the English are largely my own. They have been refined or strengthened by reading the observations and opinions of both American and English writers, such as Norwood,[2] Sadler,[3] Collier[4] and Baldwin.[5]

"Baldwin" refers to the Rt. Hon. Stanley, Prime Minister during that sorry episode which ended with the abdication of Edward VIII. What Baldwin wrote and said about his fellow-countrymen reflects his political astuteness but has a certain ring of authority.

> We always have grumbled, but we never worry . . . (and) by the absence of worry he (the Englishman) keeps his nervous system sound and sane, with the result that in times of emergency the nervous system stands when the nervous system of other peoples breaks. . . . He (the Englishman) may not look ahead, he may not heed warnings, he may not prepare, but when he once starts he is persistent to the death, and he is ruthless in action.[6]

Were he alive today, Baldwin would be quick to see that England is finally aroused to the need for more and better education, however practical or mixed the motives may be.

[1] *Times (London) Education Supplement,* October 18, 1963, sup. ii-iv; Ministry of Education, *Half our Future*: A Report of the Central Advisory Council for Education (England) (London: Her Majesty's Stationery Office, 1963).
[2] Cyril Norwood, *The English Tradition of Education* (London: John Murray, 1929).
[3] Michael Sadler, *The Two-Mindedness of England* (Reading [Berkshire], England: Reading College, 1901).
[4] Price Collier, *England and the English*: *from an American Point of View* (London: Duckworth, 1909; New York: Charles Scribner's Sons, 1916).
[5] Stanley Baldwin, *On England* (London: Philip Allan & Co., Ltd., 1926), pp. 1-9; 141-167.
[6] *Ibid.,* p. 3.

Forty years ago he was rather complacent on the whole subject. He thought that there had been "remarkable progress," in education if one remembered the fact that "we have only occupied ourselves seriously, with the problem for two generations."[7] Consider the full significance of that! In 1924, the Prime Minister of Great Britain could make a proud reference to "progress," which was really impressive only in the light of century upon century of general political indifference to popular education.

The Development of Education

slow development of state action

Not until 1870 did the State assume some responsibility for providing elementary education. Thirty-seven years earlier, a "half-empty House of Commons" had made a token grant to two voluntary organizations that were providing a modicum of schooling for the masses. (A curious researcher has discovered that it compared badly with the cost of maintaining the Royal stables.) In 1839, a bare majority of two saved what had become an annual grant from being abolished.[8]

There is little or no inspiration in the general story of popular education in England until comparatively recent times. Church control of education had been broken in the sixteenth century. Until the nineteenth, a reformed Church, determined Dissenters, occasional philanthropists, and a scattering of charitable organizations did good work but hardly began to fill the gaps. State secondary education came only in 1902, in spite of all the warnings and supplications that had come from Matthew Arnold and a few others over the years. Balfour, who as Prime Minister piloted the 1902 Act through Parliament when probably no lesser light could have done it, had much stronger views than those of Baldwin, though there was no startling change in English education in the years intervening between their leadership of Tory governments. "The existing educational system of this country," said Balfour, who was never one to

---
[7] *Ibid.*, p. 161.
[8] S. J. Curtis, *Education in Britain Since 1900* (London: Andrew Dakers, Ltd., 1952), p. 7.

exaggerate or be carried away by emotion, "is chaotic, is ineffectual, is utterly behind the age, makes us the laughing-stock of every advanced nation in Europe and America, puts us behind, not only our American cousins, but the German, and the Frenchman, and the Italian." [9]

THE 1944 BREAKTHROUGH

There were bright and brightening spots in the English educational scene when World War II overwhelmed the nation. But on the whole, secondary and higher education were for small and smaller minorities. The mass of children and young people received elementary education only, first in the regular six-year state or church schools, then in "higher tops" of those schools, or in "central schools." At a liberal estimate, 10 per cent of the academically brightest, including suspiciously few from the "lower classes," went to grammar school at about age twelve. Carefully selected though they were, well under half of them ever qualified for university. A third and smaller group went to technical schools. The vast majority called it a day at fourteen. The dependable and traditional sources of supply for universities and colleges were: (a) the Public Schools (which are actually "private")—Winchester, Eton, Harrow and a host of others which do not mesh with the general run of other schools, since they take their boys at thirteen, drawing them from special and private "prep schools," and (b) grammar schools like Manchester and Bradford.

Educational questions were not shelved during the war. Planning went ahead through the Battle of Britain, the V1's and the V2's. In 1944, what is commonly called "the Butler Act" was passed by Parliament. It heralded a new day.

Most of the act's provisions need not concern us here. But its theme was "secondary education for all." The very term "elementary education" with its non-academic and class connotations was removed from the official vocabulary. The school-leaving age was raised to fifteen, with notice of a further move to sixteen when the

---

[9] Quoted in Collier, *op. cit.*, p. 98.

time was propitious. All fees in state-maintained secondary schools were to be abolished after April of 1945.

The 1944 act was characteristically permissive in not prescribing any particular forms of secondary education for local authorities to set up. Whatever was provided was to be in accordance with the age, ability, and aptitude of the pupil. The main types of secondary schools, as you know, are now secondary modern, grammar, technical, and comprehensive.

A British educational historian says of the Butler Act that

> taken as a whole, it constitutes the most important single advance ever made in English education. . . . For the first time the nation will possess a fully co-ordinated system of schools based on the idea that education is a progressive development through the successive stages of primary, secondary, and further education.[10]

Once secondary education is provided, indeed mandated, for everyone, the final step is taken when higher education is made readily available for all who can profit from it and have the will to undertake it. The expression "readily available" and the inclusive "all" were revolutionary concepts in the England of yesterday. Today they are universally accepted. No reasonably sane person in Britain would deny that restricted secondary and higher education have resulted in a criminal waste of ability. Whichever party wins the national election this fall will not only devote special attention to the extension of higher education but will give it high priority.

RECENT GROWTH OF HIGHER EDUCATION

Among the new universities are those at Keele and Brighton. Scientists know that those ten institutions called "college of advance technology" are to be given the status of universities, which they should have had long ago. Whereas there were 216,000 students in full-time higher education in Great Britain in 1962-63, places are to be available for 392,000 in 1973-74 and, on present estimates, for 558,000 in 1980-81.[11] Those figures will not leave an American breathless,

[10] Curtis, op. cit., p. 139.
[11] Ministry of Education, *Higher Education*, Report of the Committee appointed by the Prime Minister under the Chairmanship of Lord Robbins, 1961-63. Cmnd. 2154 (London: Her Majesty's Stationery Office, 1963), p. 69.

but to an Englishman they signify an explosion of atomic proportions. Against the historical background, they stand out in blinding brilliance.

Oxford and Cambridge were synonymous with university education in England for more than six hundred years. And neither of them has ever had an enrolment in all of its colleges approaching the 12,000 that a 1964 almanac lists in the four leading institutions of the sovereign state of Mississippi.[12]

The Oxford-Cambridge (now "Oxbridge") monopoly ended when Durham and London received their charters in the second quarter of the nineteenth century. London, which is a baffling federation of some forty different schools and colleges, has long been considered to have a colossal enrolment—13,000 before the war and about 25,000 now. Six of the older civic universities, Manchester, Birmingham, Liverpool, Leeds, Sheffield, and Bristol, all founded in the nineteenth century or before the first world war, have a combined enrolment of not quite 40,000. The University of Wales accounts for some 8,000. The younger civic universities, Reading, Nottingham, Southampton, Hull, Exeter, and Leicester, founded in the years just before and after World War I, have upwards of 13,000 students altogether. Now add Keele, chartered in 1962, and seven more either in operation or in process of formation, Sussex, Norwich, York, Canterbury, Colchester, Coventry, and Lancaster, and there are a round two dozen universities in England and Wales. But seven new ones since World War II is a revolutionary development.

THE ROBBINS COMMITTEE

But even such unheard-of expansion satisfied no one. Much more must be done. The post-war population bulge would hit the universities in 1965. And if universities were to be of manageable size (with the wild exception of London), seven new ones would never meet the growing demand for higher education. The First Lord of the Treasury, My Lords concurring, accordingly issued an historic Minute on February 8, 1961, proposing that a committee under Lord Robbins' chairmanship review the pattern of full-time higher

[12] *Information Please Almanac,* Atlas and Yearbook, 1964 (New York: Simon and Schuster, 1963), p. 356.

education in Great Britain. Note that this action was not taken by the Minister of Education. University grants are made in Britain by the Treasury on the recommendation of the University Grants Committee, a system in effect since 1919 and apparently one that in many ways has worked almost ideally, with high regard for the universities' autonomy.

The complete charge to the Robbins Committee takes up eight lines of type. Here is a prime example of economy of words! It was

> "to review the pattern of full-time higher education in Great Britain and in the light of national needs and resources to advise Her Majesty's Government on what principles its long-term development should be based. In particular, to advise, in the light of these principles, whether there should be any changes in that pattern, whether any new types of institution are desirable and whether any modifications should be made in the present arrangements for planning and co-ordinating the developments of the various types of institution." [13]

And so the Robbins Committee of a dozen members went to work. It held 111 meetings, commissioned 6 surveys, made 7 overseas visits (including one of three weeks in the United States), collected a mass of data, received and read more than 400 documents of written evidence, had discussions with representatives of 90 organizations, with 31 individual witnesses, and so on. There can be no question about the industry and the thoroughness with which the charge was carried out. The main report was released in October, 1963. It will run to five volumes, two of which are not yet published.

Robbins had a good press in England, as news and in editorial comments. It seems providential that the report appeared after a first-class national scandal had practically blown itself out. If the report had acclaiming headlines in British papers and periodicals, it also had considerable publicity in America, for *School and Society* gave it some prominence. That magazine published both the Government Statement [14] and an admirable summary of Robbins [15] by Stuart Maclure, able editor of *Education,* a London weekly.

[13] Ministry of Education, *op. cit.,* p. 1.
[14] "The British Government Endorses the Robbins Report," *School and Society,* XCII (Summer, 1964), 107-108.
[15] J. Stuart Maclure, "Britain's Plan for Higher Education," *School and Society,* XCII (Summer, 1964), 228-231.

Highlights of the report.—When the main text of a report runs to 323 pages, and the recommendations reach a total of 178—and when it can be said in good conscience that every one of 19 chapters and 837 sections is important—a reviewer has a formidable task indeed. Controversial parts of the report are largely irrelevant to my topic and will therefore be omitted.

1. The report gets off to a good start by emphasizing some hard facts, e.g. "Unless higher education is speedily reformed . . . there is little hope of this densely populated island maintaining an adequate position in the fiercely competitive world of the future." Again, "However well the country may have been served by the largely unco-ordinated activities and initiatives of the past, we are clear that from now on these are not good enough." And while there is no need for controlling higher education from the centre, highly subsidized though it is from the public purse, "there should be co-ordinating principles; and . . . individual initiative must not result in mutual frustration." [16]

2. The committee assumes "as an axiom that courses of higher education should be available for all those who are qualified by ability and attainment to pursue them and who wish to do so." [17] And the report comes out for grants rather than loans to students who need financial help. It is moved by the argument that "it is a bad thing . . . for young people to emerge from the process of education with a load of debt. It is an anxiety and an incentive to caution at a time when willingness to take risks is desirable." [18] Has the thing ever been better expressed? One cannot resist throwing in a further quotation along the same line.

> In particular, where women are concerned, the effect might well be either that British parents would be strengthened in their age-long disinclination to consider their daughters to be as deserving of higher education as their sons, or that the eligibility for marriage of the more educated would be diminished by the addition to their charms of what would be in effect a negative dowry.[19]

[16] Ministry of Education, *op. cit.*, p. 5.
[17] *Ibid.*, p. 8.
[18] *Ibid.*, p. 211.
[19] *Ibid.*

Explosion in Higher Education in Britain 273

To add the postscript now, approximately 80 per cent of British students in higher education receive grants, and in half of the cases, the grants cover total expenses. This is at once a sound national investment and deserved encouragement of able students from families with low incomes. But though grants are no new thing in English education, the scale on which they are awarded today would have seemed utopian or mad to the liberal or conservative of the Victorian era.

To round out my list of highlights, part of the summary that appeared in *Education* of October 25, 1963, under "The Robbins Report" is reproduced here. Numerals are changed to follow my sequence.

> 3. The number of students in full-time higher education should be increased from the present 216,000 to 560,000 in 1980, of which the university share would increase from 130,000 to 350,000. This means an increase in the proportion of the relevant age group in full-time higher education from the present eight per cent to 17 per cent.
>
> 4. Twenty-six more universities are proposed (making 57 in all for England, Wales, and Scotland)—10 upgraded CATS, 10 upgraded Regional Colleges and Teacher Training Colleges and six entirely new universities. Five "special Institutions for Technological Education and Research" are proposed, four of them to be developed from existing institutions and the other to be one of the new universities. The "Liberal Arts College" concept is rejected.
>
> 5. Teacher Training Colleges should be called Colleges of Education, taken away from the Local Education Authorities and put under the aegis of University "Schools of Education," but the LEA's should have one third of the places on the Colleges' Governing Bodies.
>
> 6. Expenditure on full-time higher education will increase, through these proposals, from £206 million in 1962–63 to £742 million in 1980–81; in terms of percentage of Gross National Product, a rise from 0.8 to 1.6 per cent.[20]

Immediate action and reaction.—Her Majesty's Government accepted without delay or demur the main report recommendations about increasing the number of places in higher education and gave

[20] "The Robbins Report—A Summary," *Education* (London), CXXII (October 25, 1963), 729-730.

assurance that the proposed foundations of six brand new universities would be considered.[21] There was no questioning of the clear case made for according university status to the colleges of advanced technology or of that for "building up technological universities" (like M.I.T. in this country). The training colleges for teachers will share in the largesse, and no objection was taken to a somewhat vague suggestion in the report that arrangements should be worked out for the ablest students in those colleges to receive degrees.

The most significant feature of the statement was the apparent readiness to accept the fact that governmental expenditure on education must increase on a scale unprecedented for Britain. There was just a reminder that "it will be essential to get the fullest possible value for money from this massive allocation of scarce resources." [22] Although one editor could not get over "the manic haste" with which the government accepted the chief recommendations of the committee, in general there was strong approval of its action.

If there was less excitement over Robbins in Scotland than in England, a dispatch to the *Times Educational Supplement* of November 8, 1963, explained why. It said in general that what are revolutionary concepts in English education are not necessarily novel in a more enlightened country. Thus, as far as Scotland was concerned, "the case for technological education at the highest level was won before the (Robbins) report was published and its arguments found their inclusion in the transformation of the Royal College of Science and Technology into the University of Strathclyde." [23]

The governmental commitment to a vast expenditure on higher education aroused no gasps or protests of any account. For one thing, it afforded no ground for political attack. If the Tories can talk calmly about twenty to thirty new universities, some Labor leaders say that sixty would be more like it, though this is probably pre-election exaggeration. For another thing, there is much more money about in England now than there was a few years ago. My

[21] *Higher Education,* Government Statement on the Report of the Committee under the Chairmanship of Lord Robbins, 1961-63. Presented to Parliament by the Prime Minister by Command of Her Majesty, November, 1963, Cmnd. 2165 (London: Her Majesty's Stationery Office, 1963)), p. 4.
[22] *Ibid.*
[23] *Times* (London) *Educational Supplement,* November 8, 1963. Reprinted by permission.

own apology last summer to a cashier for tendering a pound note for a six-penny cup of tea was brushed aside lightly with the comment, "Think nothing of it, dear. Everybody's got pound notes these days."

A FILLIP FOR SCIENCE

A Scottish item in the *Times Educational Supplement* of November 8, 1963, has already been quoted. Another story in that issue really "shook" me. I could imagine something like it appearing in our American magazine, *Mad,* but it would be far-fetched even for that unusual publication. Here is the actual item:

> Engineering was worthy of the best boys in the secondary schools and should not be regarded as a second-class profession, said Mr. R. F. Marshall, university liaison officer for Associated Electrical Industries Ltd., at a one-day study conference on education for engineering at The Polytechnic, Regent Street, on Wednesday.
>
> The case for regarding engineering as a profession rested on the qualification of its members. The professional engineer had an adequate and sound education, special training, experience of taking responsibility and integrity of purpose and character. The definition of a professional engineer was of a man whose work was predominantly intellectual and varied and not of a routine mental or physical character. Engineering required original thought, judgment and supervising ability and the professional engineer was able to make contributions to the development of engineering science and its application.
>
> Mr. Marshall also pointed out that the distinctions between science and engineering were sometimes confused. "An engineer, whatever he does, can never ignore the human factor," (*sic·*) he said. "One can be an excellent scientist and have no regard for the human factor. Whatever an engineer may do, I suggest it is a profession worthy of the best of our young people."
>
> Many types of employment were available for those who became professional engineers. These included design and development, research, manufacturing, selling, installation and commissioning, teaching and training. Professional engineers also had their place in management, if they acquired extra knowledge through postgraduate and other courses, reading, travel and other experience.
>
> It was difficult for schoolmasters to give boys an adequate idea of the opportunities in the profession but school-leavers should be better informed.

Mr. C. E. Quekett, group recruitment officer, Guest, Keen and Nettlefolds, said that schoolmasters should be careful to recommend engineering to boys with aptitude and interest in it but they should not regard it as the answer for boys who did physics and mathematics but were not considered good enough for other professions.[24]

At the grave risk of being anticlimactic, I ask you if you can picture a meeting in the United States with two speakers trying hard to establish a convincing case for engineering as a profession. The astounding fact is that, in England, applied science has not enjoyed any great prestige. This is an amazing study in itself and has many ramifications. Sir Charles Snow touches on the subject in his *Two Cultures,* not in the main text but in the Notes at the end, one part of even a good book that is likely to be unread.

He emphasizes that the Soviet Union exports engineers. Thousands upon thousands of them are needed in Asian and African countries. But England can do very little to help in meeting the demand. She is low in engineers to start with and in particularly short supply of the types suitable for foreign service who "need all the human development that university education can give them." [25] This statement is clarified in Note 22, which says:

> The English temptation is to educate such men in sub-university institutions, which carry an inferior class-label. Nothing could be more ill-judged. One often meets American engineers who, in a narrow professional sense, are less rigorously trained than English products from technical colleges; but the Americans have the confidence, both social and individual, that is helped through having mixed with their equals at universities.[26]

There should be a great change for the better, now that the colleges of advanced technology are to be given university status. Other types of technical colleges should increase in prestige and enrolments. An educationist quoted in the London *Sunday Times* of September 22, 1963, may not have over-stated it when he attributed an alarming number of vacancies at technical colleges to "bumble-

[24] *Ibid.,* p. 667.
[25] C. P. Snow, *The Two Cultures and the Scientific Revolution* (Cambridge University Press, 1960), p. 36.
[26] *Ibid.,* p. 51.

dom, ignorance and snobbery."[27] But at long last the problem is being taken in hand. The Robbins Committee has done its bit to ensure something like explosive developments in applied science. Pure science seems always to have a good supply of promising recruits in England.

TEACHER TRAINING

Like Mr. Conant and Mr. Koerner, we have a special interest in teacher education. And surely none of us feels complacent about it. One hundred and twenty-five years after state normal schools were first founded in the United States we are far from having reduced the preparation of teachers to a science. So are the English. They have taken the whole matter seriously for a far shorter time than we have. Two old and thoroughly discredited ideas persisted through the centuries in England. One is that elementary teachers do not need much education beyond the elementary level, perhaps just a smattering of secondary. The other is that reasonable mastery of advanced subject matter, and certainly a university degree, will automatically qualify a person to be a secondary school teacher. The first idea has disappeared, and the second is on the way out.

The great majority of English teachers are prepared in some 150 three-year training colleges whose entrance requirements are much less demanding than those of the universities. Forty-odd of these institutions are under a religious denomination; the others, under local education authorities. The denominational ones are treated generously by the State, subsidized for all of their recurrent and up to 75 per cent of approved capital expenditures. About 50,000 students are enroled in these colleges, nearly half of which have fewer than 500 students, and 46 of them have fewer than 250.[28] Only 1 per cent of students in training colleges are graduates; they take a one-year course.[29] Most graduates who take any teacher training (and it must be remembered that this is not compulsory as yet) take a year's course in a university department of education.

[27] *Sunday Times* (London), September 22, 1963.
[28] Ministry of Education, *op. cit.*, pp. 109-110.
[29] *Ibid.*, p. 27.

It is hard to think of anything in the whole scheme of English teacher education that could be adopted or adapted in the United States. The customary minimum of fifteen weeks of practice teaching (27 at one institution that I visited) is good. So is the practice of requiring an applicant to write an essay paper on some broad topic within his specialty.

As a result of recommendations in the Robbins Report, the training colleges will probably be called "Colleges of Education" and will be federated in university Schools of Education. An individual enrolment of 750 is seen as a satisfactory minimum.[30] All colleges of education are to be financed by the body responsible for university grants if Robbins is heeded.

And the number story, the "explosive" part of the picture? By 1970 it is expected that there will be 82,000 students in the colleges, compared with between 49 and 50,000 in 1962. Ten institutions should have enrolments of at least 1,000 by then, compared with one now.[31]

It seems safe to predict that within the near future *all* teachers in primary and secondary schools will be required to have training. The Newsom Report does not mince words on that subject, so far as teachers of average and below average young people are concerned. The National Union of Teachers is solidly in favor of compulsory training. The Ministry is now pledged to it—at an unspecified future date. At least the force and the direction of the wind are clear. Scotland is not concerned. It has long required all teachers in the state schools to have training.

THE BALANCE SHEET

To an American, familiar only with education in his own country or state, the English developments may hardly add up to a deafening explosion. After all, more than 25 per cent of our population is pursuing formal education. We envisage seven million in higher education by 1970. About 40 per cent of high school graduates are now going on to our 2,000 universities, about 1,300 of which offer

[30] *Ibid.*, p. 111.
[31] *Ibid.*, p. 110.

teacher education. The Robbins Report itself says plainly that higher education in Britain compares unfavorably with that in two other countries—the United States and the Soviet Union.[32] Only in one or two respects, e.g. a student-teacher ratio of eight to one and the massive subsidization of students, is there anything remarkable by American standards.[33]

Yet the English speak of developments in their country's educational system as revolutionary. And they should know. They call the present one "the fourth revolution"—one in elementary in 1870, one in secondary in 1902, the Butler Act of 1944 mandating secondary education for all, and now one in higher education.

There can be no doubt that some of the new universities are living up to the official expectation that they will be "centers of innovation." Sussex, for instance, is typical in getting away from the narrow specialization which may be considered both a strength and a weakness of Oxbridge. All arts students have a common course for their first two terms; all science students for their first three. Moreover, Sussex has no "departments" as we know them; the School of Atlantic Studies deals with American and British literature and history, the School of European Studies offers the principal languages of Europe and its literature and history, and so on.[34] The University of North Staffordshire, at Keele, completely residential for students and staff, has a Foundation Year for all students to introduce them to the cultural heritage of Western Europe. This idea came from the first Vice-Chancellor, Lord Lindsay, a former Master of Balliol, one of the most ancient of Oxford colleges.[35] I recall a famous remark of Asquith's to the effect that Balliol graduates were distinguished for "a tranquil consciousness of effortless superiority." There has been no suggestion that Keele is reserved for some limited group of the intellectually élite.

A word must be said about York. Here, where Lord James is Vice-Chancellor—and there has been no more vigorous critic of what he considers to be the fluffy side of teacher education—profes-

[32] *Ibid.*, pp. 44, 268.
[33] *Ibid.*, p. 41.
[34] H. A. Rée, "The New Universities in Britain," *Comparative Education Review*, VIII (June, 1964), 95.
[35] *Ibid.*

sional education has a status that is lamentably rare in English universities. But a student at York can take a degree in mathematics *and* education, or English *and* education, and so on in some other combinations. This, if you please, is a sort of breakthrough. It is a result of the new universities being empowered from the first to award degrees and plan their own courses, instead of following the old tradition of starting off as "university colleges" in the maternal care of the University of London.

Conclusion

In sum, great things are expected of the infant universities. And they look like a lusty group. The avowed intent is to keep them comparatively small, with maximum enrolments of about 3,000; that may be a good size for "a community of scholars."

The Robbins Report and the increasingly impressive statistics speak for themselves. But it would be a bad mistake to conclude that English educationists join in one grand chorus of praise and thanksgiving. Talk with leaders like Sir Ronald Gould of the National Union of Teachers, or Sir William Alexander of the Association of Education Committees, or Her Majesty's Senior Chief Inspector Percy Wilson, or read the books by Peterson of Oxford, or Pedley of Exeter, or Vaizey of London, and whatever else you detect you will not discover any complacency. Read a sociological study like Hopkins' *New Look: A Social History of the Forties and Fifties in Britain*,[36] and you will find nothing of the smugness that outsiders often associate with the Englishman. Rigorous criticism from within may be the healthiest sign of all. Nor are professional educationists, sociologists, and psychologists alone in their concern and suggestions. The political parties, to a remarkable extent, give high importance to their educational platforms. The press and the parents are interested as never before. To a friendly observer who enjoyed their hospitality and visited a good cross-section of their schools, it does appear that as far as education is concerned, the British have struck their tents and are really on the march.

[36] Harry Hopkins, *The New Look: A Social History of the Forties and Fifties in Britain* (London: Secker and Warburg, 1963).

In the beginning I mentioned Arnold of Rugby who "moulded a generation of English school-boys by making character as important as classics." Whether there are comparable figures in English education today is not for me to say. I *can* say, however, that I was highly impressed by leaders like Lord James at York, Sir Desmond Lee at Winchester, A. B. Clegg in the West Riding, and Mrs. H. R. Chetwynd of Woodberry Down. Such a list could be extended indefinitely. Depend upon it, there is no dearth of leadership in English education.

Wales can stand on its own. Aberystwyth and Cardiff, Bangor, Swansea, and Lampeter are proud names in Welsh history and in higher education. None of them should wane. Wales, and Anglesey in particular, is a trail-blazer in organizing comprehensive, co-educational secondary schools,[37] and this with no sacrifice of academic standards. However explosive educational developments may become in Wales, that nation will still manage to export scholars, the Jones's and the Lloyd's, the Williams's and the Evans's, and those with equally familiar Welsh names in colleges and universities throughout the English-speaking world.

Since all too little has been said about Scotland, let my closing words be taken from the rectorial address given by Sir James Barrie years ago to the students at St. Andrew's. That classic speech on "Courage" has a moving passage that bespeaks the spirit of Scottish education, whether in pre- or post-Robbins days. Barrie said to the young men at St. Andrew's:

> Mighty are the Universities of Scotland, and they will prevail. But even in your highest exultations never forget that they are not four, but five. The greatest of them is the poor, proud homes you come out of, which said so long ago: "There shall be education in this land." She, not St. Andrew's, is the oldest university in Scotland, and all the others are her whelps.[38]

[37] Robin Pedley, *The Comprehensive School* (Baltimore: Penguin Books, 1963), p. 59.
[38] James Barrie, *Courage,* The Rectorial Address Delivered at St. Andrew's University, May 3, 1922 (New York: Scribner's, 1928), p. 48.

Bibliography

CHARLTON, KENNETH. " 'What is the University for?'—The Keele Experiment," *Notes and Abstracts* in the Social Foundations of American and International Education. Ann Arbor: University of Michigan, School of Education, Summer, 1964, pp. 6–9.

DENT, H. C. *Universities in Transition*. London: Cohen & West, 1961.

FLEXNER, ABRAHAM. *Universities, American, English, German*. New York: Oxford University Press, 1930.

GREEN, MARTIN. *A Mirror for Anglo-Saxons*. London: Longmans, 1961.

HUTCHINSON, MICHAEL and YOUNG, CHRISTOPHER. *Educating the Intelligent*. Baltimore: Penguin Books, 1962.

KNELLER, GEORGE F. *Higher Learning in Britain*. Berkeley: University of California Press, 1955.

LLOYD, JOHN W. "British and American Education in Cultural Perspectives," *Comparative Education Review,* VI (June, 1962), 16–24.

MOBERLY, WALTER H. *The Crisis in the University*. London: S. C. M. Press, 1949.

PETERSON, A. D. C. *A Hundred Years of Education*. New York: Collier Books, 1962.

Times (London) *Educational Supplement,* issues for October, November and December of 1963, especially those of November 1, 8, 15, 22, and 29, which have editorial comment, news items, and letters to the editor about the Robbins Report.

UNIVERSITY OF LONDON INSTITUTE OF EDUCATION. *The Year Book of Education, 1950*. London: Evans Brothers, Ltd., 1950. See especially Section 11, "The British Isles," pp. 154–258.

VAIZEY, JOHN. *Britain in the Sixties: Education for Tomorrow*. Baltimore: Penguin Books, 1962.

Appendix

Schoolmen's Week Committees and Program, 1964

ADMINISTRATIVE OFFICERS OF THE UNIVERSITY

GAYLORD P. HARNWELL, *President*

DAVID R. GODDARD, *Provost;* CARL C. CHAMBERS, *Vice-President for Engineering Affairs;* I. S. RAVDIN, *Vice-President for Medical Affairs;* GENE D. GISBURNE, *Vice-President for Student Affairs;* STUART H. CARROLL, *Secretary.*

SCHOOLMEN'S WEEK STAFF

General Chairman—HELEN HUUS, Associate Professor of Education
Executive Secretary—RICHARD S. HEISLER, Assistant to the Dean, Graduate School of Education
Administrative Assistant—ALICE M. LAVELLE
Co-ordinators:
    Higher Education—WILLIAM W. BRICKMAN, Professor of Education
    Elementary Education—RICHARD D. BUCKLEY, Instructor of Education
    Secondary Education—HELEN R. BURCHELL, Lecturer on Education

GENERAL COMMITTEE FOR SCHOOLMEN'S WEEK

Members Representing the University:
HELEN C. BAILEY, Former Visiting Professor of Education
FRANCIS BETTS, Director, Houston Hall
R. JEAN BROWNLEE, Dean, College for Women
JACK D. BURKE, Director, Office of Foreign Students
MARVIN FARBER, Professor of Philosophy
JOHN F. FOGG, JR., Director, Morris Arboretum
JEREMIAH FORD, II, Director, Intercollegiate Athletics
MRS. ALBERT M. GREENFIELD, Associate Trustee
ROBERT C. HAMMOCK, Professor of Education
MORRIS HAMBURG, Associate Professor, Economic and Social Statistics
J. FREDERICK HAZEL, Professor of Chemistry
JOHN H. KEYES, Business Manager
CHARLES LEE, Vice-Dean, Annenberg School of Communications
MRS. JOHN F. LEWIS, JR., Associate Trustee
THERESA S. LYNCH, Dean, School of Nursing
ROY F. NICHOLS, Vice-Provost
ARTHUR R. OWENS, Registrar
FROELICH G. RAINEY, Director, University Museum
OTTO SPRINGER, Dean of the College
E. CRAIG SWEETEN, Director of Development
MRS. THOMAS RAEBURN WHITE, Associate Trustee

Members Outside the University:
E. CARLTON ABBOTT, Superintendent, Lansdowne-Aldan Joint Schools, Lansdowne, Pa.
ANTHONY R. CATRAMBONE, Superintendent, Camden Public Schools, Camden, New Jersey
G. C. GALPHIN, Dean of Admissions, Drexel Institute of Technology, Philadelphia, Pa.
ALLEN C. HARMAN, Superintendent, Montgomery County Schools, Norristown, Pa.
HARRY K. HEIGES, Superintendent, Collingdale School District, Collingdale, Pa.
WEBSTER C. HERZOG, Superintendent, Chester County Schools, West Chester, Pa.
THOMAS HOWIE, Superintendent, Alexis I. duPont Special School District, Wilmington, Delaware
EMILIE M. MILLER, Principal, Tinicum Township Schools, Chester, Pa.
GEORGE E. RAAB, Superintendent, Bucks County Schools, Doylestown, Pa.
EARL F. SYKES, President, West Chester State College, West Chester, Pa.
G. BAKER THOMPSON, Superintendent, Delaware County Schools, Media, Pa.

UNIVERSITY of PENNSYLVANIA

Schoolmen's Week Program

FIFTY-SECOND CONFERENCE
OCTOBER 7-10, 1964

Schoolmen's Week is supported financially by, and planned co-operatively with, the University of Pennsylvania, Association for Childhood Education, Delaware Valley Reading Association, Drexel Institute of Technology, Pennsylvania Association of Private Academic Schools, Philadelphia Suburban Elementary Principals Association, Philadelphia Teachers Association, Private School Teachers Association of Philadelphia and Vicinity, and the following school districts: Avon-Grove Area Jointure, Camden City, Central Bucks Jointure, Cheltenham Township, Chester City, Chichester Jointure, Clifton Heights, Coatesville Area, Collingdale, Conshohocken, Council Rock, Darby-Colwyn Jointure, Deep Run Valley Jointure, Delaware County, Downingtown Jointure, Doylestown Borough, Folcroft Borough, Garnet Valley Jointure, Haverford Township, Interboro, Kennett Consolidated, Lansdowne-Aldan Jointure, Lower Merion Township, Marple-Newtown, Media, Montgomery County, Narberth, Nether Providence, New Hope-Solebury Jointure, Norristown, North Penn Jointure, Octorara, Oxford Area Consolidated, Penn-Delco Union, Pennridge Jointure, Phoenixville, Phoenixville Area Jointure, Pottstown, Radnor Township, Ridley Park, Ridley Township, Rose Tree Union, Sharon Hill, Springfield Township (Delaware County), Springfield Township (Montgomery County), Swarthmore-Rutledge Union, Tredyffrin-Easttown-Paoli Area, Unionville-Chadds Ford, Upland Borough, Upper Darby Township, Upper Merion Township, West Chester Borough, West Chester Jointure, and Yeadon.

Headquarters and Registration
The Palestra
33rd and Chancellor Streets
Philadelphia 4, Pennsylvania

Acknowledgements

Schoolmen's Week wishes to acknowledge its indebtedness to the following individuals and organizations for their co-operation in developing the 1964 program:

CONTRIBUTING SPECIALISTS

Administration—WILLIAM E. ARNOLD, Professor of Education, University of Pennsylvania; *Art*—LOUISE B. BALLINGER, Lecturer on Education, University of Pennsylvania; *Guidance*—JOHN E. FREE, Director of Counseling Service, University of Pennsylvania; *Library*—RONALD K. SCHAFER, Librarian, Pottsgrove High School, Pottstown; *Modern Foreign Language*—ARNOLD G. REICHENBERGER, Professor of Romance Languages, University of Pennsylvania; HARRY WEINMANN, Teacher, Schuylkill Township Elementary School; Phoenixville, Pa.; RUTH CORNFIELD, Visiting Lecturer, University of Pennsylvania; *Music Education*—HELEN E. MARTIN, Assistant Professor of Education, University of Pennsylvania; *Nursery-Kindergarten*—ALICE K. WATSON, Lecturer on Education, University of Pennsylvania; *Mathematics*—ALBERT I. OLIVER, Associate Professor of Education, University of Pennsylvania; *Reading*—MARY E. COLEMAN, Associate Professor of Education, University of Pennsylvania; E. GILLET KETCHUM, President, Delaware Valley Reading Association; *Science*—R. J. CHINNIS, Assistant Professor, American University, Washington, D. C.; RICHARD SNYDER, Teacher of Biology, Radnor Senior High School, Radnor, Pa.; HAROLD FERGUSON, Teacher of Science, Harriton High School, Rosemont, Pa.; *Vocational Education and Practical Arts*—H. HALLECK SINGER, Director, Vocational Teacher Education, University of Pennsylvania.

PLANNING COMMITTEE

KATHRYN ABBOTT, School Nurse, Pennbrook Junior High School, North Wales, Pa.; WILLIAM E. ARNOLD, Professor of Education, University of Pennsylvania; HAZEL ASHHURST, Chairman of Professional Committee, Educational Secretaries Association, Philadelphia; BROTHER F. AZARIAS, Chairman, Department of Education, LaSalle College, Philadelphia; MARIAN BAILLIE, Supervisor of Special Education, Delaware County Schools, Media, Pa.; LOUISE BALLINGER, Lecturer on Education, University of Pennsylvania; ROSS BORTNER, Assistant Superintendent, Chester County Schools, West Chester, Pa.; MARVIN BRESSLER, Professor of Sociology, Princeton University, Princeton, N. J.; NORMAN CALHOUN, Assistant Superintendent, Delaware County Schools, Media, Pa.; ERNESTO A. CANALES, Teacher of Spanish, Upper Darby High School, Upper Darby, Pa.; EDNA CARROLL, Adult Education Council of Philadelphia; MARY CARTER, Principal, Radnor Senior High School, Radnor, Pa.; ROBERT J. CHINNIS, Assistant Professor, American University, Washington, D. C.; MARY E. COLEMAN, Associate Professor of Education, University of Pennsylvania; ADELE COLUMBIA, Head, Home Economics Education Department, Drexel Institute of Technology, Philadelphia; MURIEL CROSBY, Associate Superintendent, Wilmington Public Schools, Wilmington, Delaware; RICHARD L. CURRIER, Assistant

Acknowledgements

Regional Superintendent in Charge of Secondary Education, The Pennsbury Schools, Fallsington, Pa.; HALL CUSHMAN, Head, Lower School, Germantown Friends School, Philadelphia; JEAN DALY, Assistant Professor, College of Nursing, Villanova University, Villanova, Pa.; FREDERICK G. DENT, Suburban Elementary Principals Association, Kennett Square, Pa.; ETHEL G. ENCKE, Southeastern Association for Health, Physical Education and Recreation, Radnor, Pa.; JOHN FREE, Director, Counseling Service, University of Pennsylvania; WILLIAM MARSHALL FRENCH, Chairman, Education Department, Muhlenberg College, Allentown, Pa.; MARTHA A. GABLE, Director of Radio and Television Education, School District of Philadelphia; HARRY GASSER, Assistant to County Superintendent, Montgomery County Schools, Norristown, Pa.; CATHERINE E. GEARY, Director, Elementary Education, Cheltenham Township School District, Elkins Park, Pa.; WILLIAM LEE GERMAN, Chairman, Art Department, Radnor Senior High School, Radnor, Pa.; O. GRANT GOODEN, President, Suburban Philadelphia Business Education, Springfield, Delaware County, Pa.; JAMES GRACE, Chairman, Education Department, St. Joseph's College, Philadelphia; FREDERICK C. GRUBER, Professor of Education, University of Pennsylvania; THEODORE F. GUTH, President, Phi Delta Kappa, Philadelphia; JOSEPH C. HALL, Assistant Professor of Psychology, Cheyney State College, Cheyney, Pa.; ROBERT C. HAMMOCK, Professor of Education, University of Pennsylvania; ALLEN C. HARMAN, Superintendent, Montgomery County Schools, Norristown, Pa.; GEORGE HARRIS, Chairman, Education Department, Villanova University, Villanova, Pa.; HENRY HOFMANN, Assistant to the Superintendent, Rose Tree Union School District, Rutledge, Pa.; DAVID A. HOROWITZ, Associate Superintendent, School District of Philadelphia; MARTIN HUBBLEY, President, Association of Teachers of Mathematics of Philadelphia and Vicinity, Abington High School, Abington, Pa.; ROLAND HUGHES, Pennsylvania School Counselors Association, Abington Senior High School, Abington, Pa.; ELEANOR ISARD, Personnel and Guidance Association, Department of Psychology, Temple University, Philadelphia; WILLIAM E. JOHNSON, Chairman, Department of Foundations of Education, University of Pittsburgh, Pittsburgh, Pa.; E. GILLET KETCHUM, President, Delaware Valley Reading Association, Philadelphia; CHARLOTTE E. KING, Associate Professor of Education, West Chester State College, West Chester, Pa.; MARJORIE E. KING, Teacher of Foreign Languages, Springfield Township Public Schools, Montgomery County, Chestnut Hill, Pa.; FRANCES LINK, Co-ordinator of Secondary Education, Cheltenham School District, Elkins Park, Pa.; CHARLES LONG, Superintendent, Chester City School District, Chester, Pa.; FLORENCE LOOSE, Counselor, Wilmington High School, Wilmington, Delaware; REV. THOMAS F. LOUGHREY, President, Greater Philadelphia Council for Teachers of English, Philadelphia; MARION MACSKIMMING, Pennsylvania Home Economics Association, Southeastern District, Coatesville, Pa.; JUDITH MARCUS, Librarian, Masterman Laboratory and Demonstration School, Philadelphia; BEATRICE MARKS, President, Philadelphia Home and School Council, Philadelphia; HELEN E. MARTIN, Assistant Professor of Education, University of Pennsylvania; SAMUEL E. MCDONALD, Business Manager, Coatesville Area School District, Coatesville, Pa.; RUTH MELSON, Mathematics Coordinator in Elementary Schools, Haverford Township School District, Havertown, Pa.; KEITH MERRIMAN, President, Southeastern District Council of Social Studies, Hatboro-Horsham Junior High School, Hatboro, Pa.; RUTH WEIR MILLER, Executive Director, World Affairs Council of Philadelphia; JOSEPH D. MOORE, Director

Acknowledgements

of Secondary Education, Tredyffrin-Easttown-Paoli Joint Schools, Berwyn, Pa.; MARK C. NAGY, Principal, Ithan Elementary School, Bryn Mawr, Pa.; ALBERT I. OLIVER, Associate Professor of Education, University of Pennsylvania; BARBARA OLIVER, Assistant to Dean of Women, University of Pennsylvania; WESTON C. OPDYKE, Director of Elementary Education, Tredyffrin-Easttown-Paoli Joint Schools, Berwyn, Pa.; ANNE M. OSBORNE, Director of Curriculum, Upper Darby Township Schools, Upper Darby, Pa.; ELIZABETH OSTERLUND, Associate Professor of Education, Temple University, Philadelphia, Pa.; WILLIAM G. OWEN, Dean of Admissions, University of Pennsylvania; ELWOOD PRESTWOOD, Assistant Superintendent, Lower Merion Township Schools, Ardmore, Pa.; ARNOLD REICHENBERGER, Professor of Romance Languages, University of Pennsylvania; EDNA M. RENOUF, Elementary Supervisor, Springfield Township Schools, Delaware County, Springfield, Pa.; LAWRENCE V. ROTH, William Dick School, Philadelphia; RONALD SCHAFER, Librarian, Pottsgrove High School, Pottstown, Pa.; BENJAMIN SCHLEIFER, Chairman, Department of General Studies, Philadelphia College of Art; JOSEPH S. SCHMUCKLER, Teacher of Chemistry, Haverford Senior High School, Havertown, Pa.; HUGH SHAFER, Associate Professor of Education, University of Pennsylvania; HELEN SHIELDS, Assistant Professor of Education, Beaver College, Glenside, Pa.; H. HALLECK SINGER, Director, Vocational Teacher Education, University of Pennsylvania; I. EZRA STAPLES, Assistant to Associate Superintendent, School District of Philadelphia; MARION STEET, President, Philadelphia Teachers Association, Philadelphia; KERMIT M. STOVER, Superintendent, Marple-Newtown Joint Schools, Newtown Square, Pa.; MALVENA TAIZ, Assistant Professor, Physical Education for Women, University of Pennsylvania; CLEORA TEFFEAU, Principal, Francis X. McGraw School, Camden, New Jersey; FRANCES THOMSON, Association for Childhood Education, Philadelphia; ABRAM VANDERMEER, Dean, College of Education, Pennsylvania State University, University Park, Pa.; TED VARBALO, President, Philadelphia Science Teachers Association; JOHN WALTON, Chairman, Department of Education, Johns Hopkins University, Baltimore, Maryland; HARRY WEINMANN, President, Modern Language Association, Paoli, Pa.; HAROLD H. WINGERD, Assistant Superintendent, West Chester Public Schools, West Chester, Pa.; MARECHAL-NEIL YOUNG, Superintendent, District #3, School District of Philadelphia.

Organizations

Adult Education Council of Philadelphia; American Chemical Society of Philadelphia; Association for Childhood Education; Association of Teachers of Mathematics of Philadelphia and Vicinity; Commission on Secondary Schools, Middle States Association; Delaware Valley Programing Association of the National Society for Programed Instruction; Department of Elementary School Principals, Southeastern District; Educational Secretaries Association; English Club of Philadelphia; Folk Dance Leaders Council of Philadelphia; Greater Philadelphia Council for Teachers of English; Home Economics Association of Philadelphia; International Reading Association, Delaware Valley Branch; Kappa Delta Epsilon; Kappa Phi Kappa; Modern Language Association of Philadelphia and Vicnity; Montgomery County School Nurses

Acknowledgements

Association; Pennsylvania Association of Women Deans and Counselors; Pennsylvania Home Economics Association, Southeastern District; Pennsylvania Learning Resources Association; Pennsylvania Music Educators Association, Southeastern District; Pennsylvania School Administrators Association, Eastern Division; Pennsylvania School Counselors Association; Personnel and Guidance Association of Greater Philadelphia; Phi Delta Kappa; Philadelphia Board of Trade and Conventions; Philadelphia Home and School Council; Philadelphia Science Teachers Association; Philadelphia Teachers Association; Pi Lambda Theta; School of Education Alumni Association, University of Pennsylvania; School Librarians Association of Delaware, Montgomery, and Chester Counties; School Librarians Association of Philadelphia and Vicinity; Seventy-Five Club; Southeastern Association for Health, Physical Education and Recreation; Southeastern District Council of Social Studies; Special Education Association; Suburban Philadelphia Business Education Association; World Affairs Council of Philadelphia.

Wednesday, October 7

9:30 A.M.

1—Helping Teachers Make Better Classroom Tests .... **Auditorium, Houston Hall, 3417 Spruce Street**

Chairman: RICHARD R. BOCCHINI, Counselor, University of Pennsylvania

Speaker: BENJAMIN SHIMBERG, Director of Educational Relations, Cooperative Test Division, Educational Testing Service, Princeton, New Jersey

2—The Education of the Professor of Education .... **Franklin Room, Houston Hall, 3417 Spruce Street**

(An All-Day Conference)

9:30 A.M.-11:30 A.M.

First Session:

Chairman: SAUL SACK, Professor of Education, University of Pennsylvania

The Scholarly Preparation of the Professor of Education

Speaker: JOHN WALTON, Professor of Education and Chairman, Department of Education, Johns Hopkins University, Baltimore, Maryland

The Professional and Practical Preparation of the Professor of Education

Speaker: JAMES L. GRACE, JR., Acting Chairman, Department of Education, St. Joseph's College, Philadelphia

The Professor of Education in Relation to his Academic Colleagues

Speaker: ROY F. NICHOLS, Dean, Graduate School of Arts and Sciences, University of Pennsylvania

1:00 P.M.-3:00 P.M.

Second Session:

Chairman: WILLIAM W. BRICKMAN, Professor of Education, University of Pennsylvania

In-Service Growth of the Professor of Education

Speaker: WILLIAM M. FRENCH, Professor of Educaton and Chairman, Department of Education, Muhlenberg College, Allentown.

3:00 P.M.-3:15 P.M.

Coffee Break.

3:15 P.M.-4:00 P.M.

Additional discussion and summary.

Wednesday, October 7, 9:30 A.M.

3—Workshop for Evaluation Chairmen (In co-operation with the Commission on Secondary Schools, Middle States Association) ....
*Room 100, Illman Building,
3944 Walnut Street*

(An All-Day Conference)

(This is a workshop to acquaint beginning chairmen with their responsibilities in the 1964-65 secondary school evaluations. Participation is by invitation.)

Chairman: SYDNEY V. ROWLAND, Associate Executive Secretary, Commission on Secondary Schools, Philadelphia

Greetings: ABLETT H. FLURY, Executive Secretary, Commission on Secondary Schools, Philadelphia

Consultants:
B. ANTON HESS, Regional Superintendent, Central Bucks Joint Schools, Doylestown; JAMES H. McK. QUINN, Headmaster, Episcopal Academy, Philadelphia

4:00 P.M.

4—Art Appreciation (In co-operation with the Educational Secretaries Association of Philadelphia) .... *Auditorium, Illman Building, 3944 Walnut Street*

Chairman: HAZEL M. ASHHURST, Senior Secretary, Penn Treaty Junior High School, Philadelphia

Speaker: MARGUERITE J. WALTER, Assistant Director of Art Education, School District of Philadelphia

Thursday, October 8

9:30 A.M.

5—The Uses of Programed Instruction in Schools in the United States (In co-operation with the Delaware Valley Programing Association of the National Society for Programed Instruction—Part 1 of a Two-Part Sequence) .... *Auditorium, Asbury Church, 33rd and Chestnut Streets*

Chairman: ROBERT H. JENSEN, Staff Assistant, Personnel Research Division, Industrial Relations Department, Sun Oil Company, Philadelphia

Speakers:
HAROLD L. MOON, Principal Associate and Director of the Training Division, Stevenson, Jordon, and Harrison Management Consultants, Inc., New York City; LINCOLN HANSON, Editor, *Journal of Programed Instruction,* Center for Programed Instruction, New York City

6—Testing: Common and Unique Roles of Teachers, Counselors, Administrators, and Psychologists .... *Auditorium, Christian Association, 3601 Locust Street*

Chairman: MARIE A. SMITH, Counselor, Cheltenham High School, Wyncote

Speaker: HAROLD G. SEASHORE, Director, Test Division, The Psychological Corporation, New York City

7—The Parents' Relations to the Dropout Problem (In co-operation with the Philadelphia Home and School Council) .... *Auditorium, Houston Hall, 3417 Spruce Street*

Moderator: BEATRICE MARKS, President, Philadelphia Home and School Council

Panel:
HELEN F. FAUST, Assistant Director of Vocational Guidance, Pupil Personnel and Counseling, School District of Philadelphia; MARJORIE DUCKREY, Assistant Director, Philadelphia Council for Community Advancement; MARY LONG, Parent, Philadelphia, BETTY ANNE FUNK, Parent, Philadelphia

8—The Explosion in Higher Education in Great Britain .... *Franklin Room, Houston Hall, 3417 Spruce Street*

Chairman: ROBERT C. HAMMOCK, Professor of Education, University of Pennsylvania

Speaker: HARRY K. HUTTON, Professor of Education, College of Education, Pennsylvania State University, University Park

9—The Methods Controversy in Reading (In co-operation with the Delaware Valley Reading Association) .... *Irvine Auditorium, 3401 Spruce Street*

Thursday, October 8, 9:30 A.M.

Chairman: E. Gillet Ketchum, Supervisor of Re-education Clinic, Psychological Services, Institute of the Pennsylvania Hospital, Philadelphia

Speaker: Leo C. Fay, Professor of Education, University of Indiana, Bloomington, Indiana

10—Summerhill: A Radical Approach to Education ....
McClelland Hall Lounge, 37th and Spruce Streets

(The Lounge may be reached through the dormitory tower at 37th and Spruce Streets. Turn left within the dormitory area, pass through arch, and descend the stone steps. The Lounge is located under the arcade, extending to the right.)

Chairman: Frances M. Taylor, Teacher, Hillcrest Elementary School, Drexel Hill

Speaker: George Von Hilsheimer, Headmaster, Summerlane School, Mileses, New York

11—Teaching of Genetics in the Secondary School Science Program ......
Medical Alumni Hall, Maloney Building, University of Pennsylvania Hospital, Spruce Street at 36th Street

Chairman: Richard Snyder, Teacher of Biology, Radnor Senior High School, Radnor

Speaker: Erwin I. Oster, Assistant Member, Division of Chemotherapy, The Institute for Cancer Research, Philadelphia

12—The Non-College-Bound Student .... **Auditorium, University Museum, 33rd and Spruce Streets**

Chairman: Matthew J. Pillard, Associate Professor of Education, University of Pennsylvania

Speaker: Philip U. Koopman, Superintendent, Lower Merion School District

13—Improving Human Relations through Homeroom Guidance (A Demonstration) .... **Auditorium, Illman Building, 3944 Walnut Street**

Chairman: Marechal-Neil E. Young, Superintendent, District #3, School District of Philadelphia

Demonstration Lesson: Mary Speece, Teacher of English, Jay Cooke Junior High School, Philadelphia

Demonstration Group: Pupils from 8th grade class Jay Cooke Junior High School, Philadelphia

Discussants:
Bernard Glantz, Principal, Jay Cooke Junior High School, Philadelphia;
Richard B. Anliot, Director, Pennsylvania Human Relations Commission, Department of Public Instruction, Harrisburg

Thursday, October 8, 9:30 A.M.

14—Arithmetic Evaluation Techniques .... **Room 300,**
Convention Hall, 34th and Convention Avenue

Chairman: RUTH V. MELSON, Mathematics Co-ordinator, Haverford Township Elementary Schools

Speaker: BEN A. SUELTZ, Professor of Education, State University College, Cortland, New York

15—Art Workshop .... **Room 301,**
Illman Building, 3944 Walnut Street
(The same as Program 94)

Chairman: MARY C. RENNER, Director of Audio-Visual Instruction, Upper Darby Township Schools

Director: JANE BETSEY WELLING, Emeritus Professor of Education, Wayne State University, Detroit, Michigan

Assistant: LUCILLE W. CARLTON, Teacher of Art, Beverly Hills Junior High School, Upper Darby

Note:
Only 40 persons can be accommodated at each session. Cards of admission may be obtained by writing to Schoolmen's Week, Attention: Art Workshop, Graduate School of Education, University of Pennsylvania, Philadelphia, Pa. 19104. Enclose a self-addressed, stamped envelope.

16—The New Image of Music .... **Room 100,**
Hare Building, 36th and Spruce Streets

Chairman: FOLKERT H. KADYK, Great Valley High School, Malvern

Speaker: GEORGE ROCHBERG, Chairman of the Music Department, University of Pennsylvania

---

11:00 A.M.
17—First General Session .... **Irvine Auditorium,**
3401 Spruce Street

Organ Prelude at 10:45 a.m. .... Muriel Draper
At the Curtis Memorial Organ

VALUES FOR A CHANGING AMERICA

Chairman: HELEN HUUS, Associate Professor of Education, University of Pennsylvania

Introduction of the Speaker: GAYLORD P. HARNWELL, President, University of Pennsylvania

Speaker: ARTHUR LARSON, Director, World Rule of Law Center, Duke University, Durham, North Carolina

Thursday, October 8, 2:00 P.M.

2:00 P.M.

18—Creation, Evaluation, and Uses of Programed Instruction in the Delaware Valley (In co-operation with the Delaware Valley Programing Association of the National Society for Programed Instruction—Part II of a Two-Part Sequence) .... *Auditorium, Asbury Church, 33rd and Chestnut Streets*

Chairman: Charles S. Wakefield, Sales-Marketing, RCA Educational Programs, RCA, Cherry Hill, N. J.

Speakers: To be announced. Various sub-group discussions under leadership of the Delaware Valley Programing Association.

19—Counseling for Vocational-Technical Education
Sunday School Room, Asbury Church, 33rd and Chestnut Streets

Chairman: John H. Althouse, Director of Curriculum and Guidance, Abington High School (South Campus), Abington

Speakers:
Larney Gump, Head, Guidance Department, William Tennent High School, Johnsville, Pa.; Harold Albright, Co-ordinator of Trade and Industrial Education, Department of Public Instruction, Harrisburg

20—The Poet and the Dancers .... *Auditorium, Christian Association, 3601 Locust Street*

Chairman: Benjamin Schleifer, Chairman, Department of General Studies, Philadelphia College of Art

Participating Dance Groups:
Bryn Mawr College—*Leader,* Ann Mason; Swarthmore College—*Leader,* Alyn Terata; Temple University—*Leader,* Cathie Pira; University of Pennsylvania—*Leader,* Malvena Taiz

21—Music and Art of France .... *Main Auditorium, Drexel, 32nd and Chestnut Streets*

(The story of France through piano music of master composers and colored slides of master paintings.)

Chairman: Louise Rohrback, Supervisor of Elementary School Music, Springfield Township, Montgomery County

Concert: Ruth Luty Campbell, Concert Pianist, Abington

Analyst: Emeline C. Weakley, Division of Art Education, School District of Philadelphia

Showing of Slides: E. Virgil Cooper, Division of Audio-Visual Education, School District of Philadelphia

THURSDAY, OCTOBER 8, 2:00 P.M.

**22—A Descriptive Analysis of Approaches to School Desegregation ....
Room 101 N, Student Activities Center,
Drexel, Southwest Corner, 32nd and Chestnut Streets**

Chairman: WILLIAM CASTETTER, Professor of Education, University of Pennsylvania

Speaker: PETER BINZEN, Reporter for *The Evening Bulletin*, Philadelphia

**23—Developing Critical Thinking Skills through Varied Instructional Techniques .... Auditorium, Houston Hall,
3417 Spruce Street**

Chairman: HELEN C. BAILEY, Former Visiting Professor of Education, University of Pennsylvania

Speaker: EDWARD J. SCHAEFFER, Head, Social Studies Department, The Masterman Laboratory and Demonstration School, Philadelphia

Demonstration: Students from The Masterman School, Philadelphia

**24—Help for the Left-Handed Writer .... Franklin Room,
Houston Hall, 3417 Spruce Street**

Chairman: JUDITH F. BRONSTEIN, Teacher, Gladwyne Elementary School, Gladwyne

Speaker: E. A. ENSTROM, Director of Research, The Peterson System, Inc., Greensburg

**25—New Developments in Elementary School Science Curricula ....
McClelland Hall Lounge,
37th and Spruce Streets**

(The Lounge may be reached through the dormitory tower at 37th and Spruce Streets. Turn left within the dormitory area, pass through arch, and descend the stone steps. The Lounge is located under the arcade, extending to the right.)

Chairman: JANE HARRIS, Teacher, Harris Elementary School, Collingdale

Speaker: JOHN G. NAVARRA, Professor of Science and Chairman, Science Department, Jersey City State College, New Jersey

**26—Major Concepts in Political Science: Implications for the Secondary School Social Studies Program .... Medical Alumni Hall,
Maloney Building, University of Pennsylvania
Hospital, Spruce Street at 36th Street**

Chairman: WILLARD R. HANCOCK, Superintendent, Yeadon School District

Speaker: THOMAS M. WATTS, Associate Professor of Political Science, University of Pennsylvania

**27—Children's Language, Literature, and Composition ...... Auditorium,
University Museum, 33rd and Spruce Streets
(The same as Program 54)**

Thursday, October 8, 2:00 P.M.

Chairman: Ross Bortner, Assistant Superintendent, Chester County School District

Speaker: Ruth G. Strickland, Research Professor of Education, Indiana University, Bloomington, Indiana

28—Continuing Crises in Continuing Education (In co-operation with the Adult Education Council of Philadelphia and the Division of School Extension, School District of Philadelphia) ...... *Room 2, University Museum, 33rd and Spruce Streets*

Chairman: Robert H. Coates, Director of School Extension, School District of Philadelphia

Panel:
Robert A. Luke, Director of Adult Services, National Education Association, Washington, D. C.; Oliver Gordon, Department of Christian Education, Greater Philadelphia Council of Churches

29—The Role of the Kindergarten in Reading Instruction .... *Auditorium, Illman Building, 3944 Walnut Street*

(The same as Program 65)

Chairman: Dorothy G. Hardy, Supervisor of Child Development and Kindergarten Education, School District of Philadelphia

Speaker: Helen A. Murphy, Professor of Education and Director of Educational Clinic, Boston University

30—Trade and Industry of the City of Rome .... *C. I. V. Lounge, Commercial Museum, 34th and Convention Avenue*

Chairman: Laura Junkins, Chairman, Foreign Language Department, Nether Providence Junior-Senior High School, Wallingford

Speaker: Helen S. Loane, Lecturer in Latin, Albright College, Reading

31—Social Studies Curriculum Development Trends .... *Room 101, Convention Hall, 34th and Convention Avenue*

Chairman: Richard D. Buckley, Instructor of Education, University of Pennsylvania

Speaker: John D. McAulay, Professor of Education, Pennsylvania State University, University Park

32—The Humanities: A Color Film Based on *Macbeth* (In co-operation with the English Club of Philadelphia) .... *Room 300, Convention Hall, 34th and Convention Avenue*

Thursday, October 8, 2:00 P.M.

Chairman: RICHARD R. ROBINSON, Teacher of English, Abraham Lincoln High School, Philadelphia

Demonstrator: ARTHUR CURTIS, District Manager for Pennsylvania, Encyclopedia Britannica Films, Inc., Paoli

33—Some Problems in Higher Education in Communist China ....
**Room 304, Convention Hall,
34th and Convention Avenue**

Chairman: AASE BREDAHL-PETERSEN, Lecturer on Education, University of Pennsylvania

Speaker: C. T. HU, Professor of Education, Teachers College, Columbia University, New York City

**34—Teacher Behavior in the Classroom: How Might It Be Evaluated?
Room 200, Convention Hall,
34th and Convention Avenue**

Chairman: ROBERT L. GRIMM, Director of Elementary Education, Upper Darby Township School District

Speaker: MICHAEL GIAMMATTEO, Instructor of Education, Temple University, Philadelphia

35—A Conference Approach to Unifying Auxiliary Services ....
**Room 213,
Keedy Hall, Law School,
100 South 34th Street**

Chairman: WILHELMINA BRITSCH, Nurse-Coordinator, District #4, School District of Philadelphia

Panel:
GERALD H. KRIEBEL, Principal, Pennfield Junior High School, Hatfield; JANET SEIP, Home and School Visitor, North Penn Joint School District, Lansdale; MARIE ANDREWS, Guidance Counselor, Pennfield Junior High School, Hatfield; JOHN FAZZINI, Guidance Counselor, Pennbrook Junior High School, North Wales; KATHRYN N. ABBOTT, School Nurse, Pennbrook Junior High School, North Wales

36—The Use of Models in Teaching Orbital Concepts of Chemistry ......
**Room A4, Rittenhouse Laboratory,
33rd and Walnut Streets**

Chairman: FRANCES LINK, Co-ordinator of Secondary Education, Cheltenham School District

Speaker: A. HARRIS STONE, Assistant Professor of Science Education, Southern Connecticut State College, New Haven, Connecticut

THURSDAY, OCTOBER 8, 3:45 P.M.

3:45 P.M.
37—Secondary School Evaluations: A Problems Clinic .... *Auditorium, Christian Association, 3601 Locust Street*

(This meeting is designed especially for schools that will be evaluated in 1964-65, but others interested in school evaluation procedures are invited.)

Chairman: ALBERT I. OLIVER, Associate Professor of Education, University of Pennsylvania

Panel:
WILLIAM T. BEAN, Principal, Lower Merion Senior High School, Ardmore; JEAN HOOPER, Headmistress, Prospect Hill Country Day School, Newark, New Jersey; LEONARD B. IRWIN, Superintendent, Haddon Heights High School, Haddon Heights, New Jersey; J. ALLEN MINNICH, Professor of Education, Ursinus College, Collegeville, Pa.; REVEREND FRANCIS D. DOUGHERTY, Rector, Salesianum School for Boys, Wilmington, Delaware

38—Home Economics Education Faces Another Challenge (In co-operation with the Home Economics Association of Philadelphia)
Room 101C, Student Activities Center, Drexel, Southwest Corner, 32nd and Chestnut Streets

Chairman: GRACE E. WOODWARD, Assistant Professor of Home Economics, Temple University, Philadelphia

Greetings: ROSEMERE BAUM, Teacher of Home Economics, George Washington High School, Philadelphia

Speaker: CLIO REINWALD, Co-ordinator of Family, Migrant and Nursing Education, Department of Public Instruction, Harrisburg

39—A Realistic Composition Program for Adolescents ....
Auditorium, Houston Hall, 3417 Spruce Street

Chairman: REV. THOMAS F. LOUGHREY, Head, English Department, Cardinal Dougherty High School, Philadelphia

Speaker: V. LOUISE HIGGINS, Director of English, Westport Public Schools, Westport, Connecticut

40—Better Private-Public School Co-operation .... *Franklin Room, Houston Hall, 3417 Spruce Street*

Chairman: HOMER N. STEWART, Principal, Media Elementary School, Media

Speaker: ERIC W. JOHNSON, Vice-Principal, Germantown Friends School, Philadelphia

41—Teacher Participation in Counseling Parents of the Handicapped Child (In co-operation with the Special Education Association)
McClelland Hall Lounge, 37th and Spruce Streets

THURSDAY, OCTOBER 8, 3:45 P.M.

(The Lounge may be reached through the dormitory tower at 37th and Spruce Streets. Turn left within the dormitory area, pass through arch, and descend the stone steps. The Lounge is located under the arcade, extending to the right)

Greetings: SANDRA CUNNINGHAM, Teacher of Retarded Educable Children, School District of Philadelphia

Chairman: CLAIR LECOMPTE, Teacher of Retarded Educable Children, Torresdale School, Philadelphia

Speaker: EUGENE MACDONALD, Speech and Hearing Clinic, Pennsylvania State University, University Park

42—Major Concepts in Economics: Implications for the Secondary School Social Studies Program .... *Room 101, Convention Hall, 34th and Convention Avenue*

Chairman: JOHN J. KUSHMA, Supervising Principal, Clifton Heights School District

Speaker: HELEN RAFFEL, Assistant Professor of Economics, University of Pennsylvania

43—Potential Mathematics for Elementary School Children (In cooperation with the Association for Childhood Education, Philadelphia) .... *Auditorium, University Museum, 33rd and Spruce Streets*

(The same as Program 73)

Chairman: FRANCES THOMSON, Teacher, Friends Select School, Philadelphia

Speaker: HOWARD F. FEHR, Head, Department of Mathematical Education, Teachers College, Columbia University, New York City

44—Medieval Arts in a Contemporary Setting .... *Auditorium, Illman Building, 3944 Walnut Street*

Chairman: JANE D. BONELLI, Supervisor of Student Teachers, Tyler School of Fine Arts, Temple University, Philadelphia

Speaker: MARY LOU SCULL, Head, Art Department, Germantown Friends School, Philadelphia

45—The Newspaper As A Potential Force in Education ....
C. I. V. Lounge, Commercial Museum, 34th and Convention Avenue

Chairman: LOUISE WENTZ, Teacher, Central Elementary School, Springfield, Delaware County

Speaker: LESLIE J. NASON, Educational Consultant, and Syndicated Columnist for Associated Press and *The Philadelphia Inquirer*

Thursday, October 8, 3:45 P.M.

46—Higher Literacy: Reading in the Content Fields .... *Room 300, Convention Hall, 34th and Convention Avenue*

Chairman: MARK C. NAGY, Principal, Ithan Elementary School, Bryn Mawr

Speaker: LEO C. FAY, Professor of Education, University of Indiana, Bloomington, Indiana

47—The Contribution of the Library Instructional Materials Center to Quality Education for Every Child (In co-operation with the School Librarians Association of Philadelphia and Vicinity) ...... *Rooms 246 A-B, Library Center, Drexel, 3243 Woodland Avenue*

Chairman: DOROTHY P. NASSAU, Director, Division of Libraries, School District of Philadelphia

Speaker: PAUL W. F. WITT, Professor of Education, Teachers College, Columbia University, New York City

Demonstration: Pupils from 4th grade class, Lea School, Philadelphia

Leaders:
YVONNE EDWARDS, Teacher, Lea School, Philadelphia; ELEANOR SERINSKY, Librarian, Lea School, Philadelphia

Commentator: RACHAEL W. DEANGELO, Professor, Graduate School of Library Science, Drexel Institute of Technology, Philadelphia

Friday, October 9

9:00 A.M.
48—Pennsylvania Music Educators Association, Southeastern District
Drexel Hill Junior High School,
State Road and Harper Avenue, Upper Darby, Pa.

(An All-Day Conference)

9:00 A.M.

PMEA Southeastern District Executive Committee Meeting

10:00 A.M.

PMEA General Session

Chairman: WILLIAM IFERT, Head of the Music Department, Downingtown Joint Senior High School, Downingtown

Greetings: CLYDE DENGLER, Director of Music, Upper Darby Township Schools, Upper Darby

Combined String Orchestra—Bala-Cynwyd Junior High School, Welsh Valley Junior High School, and Harriton High School—ANDREW FRECH, Director

A Look at the American Musical Scene

Speaker: WARNER LAWSON, Dean of the College of Fine Arts, Howard University, Washington, D. C.

Upper Darby Senior High School Choir—CLYDE DENGLER, JR., Director

12:00 NOON

Luncheon in School Cafeteria

The Madrigales, Haverford Township High School— PAUL FINK, Conductor

Group Singing— CLYDE DENGLER, Conductor

1:15 P.M.

Instrumental Music Clinic

Chairman: ANDREW FRECH, Conductor, Harriton High School Orchestra, Rosemont

Strings—Where and How to Get Them

Panel:

ANDREW FRECH, Harriton High School, Rosemont; MARIO TEREZZA, William Tennent High School, Johnsville, FREDERICK SWINGLE, Welsh Valley Junior High School, Penn Valley; HERMAN GIERSCH, Bala-Cynwyd Junior High School, Bala-Cynwyd

Brass Versus Plastic Instruments

Trombone with a G Attachment for Elementary School

Demonstrator: FRANCIS GLOSTER, Jenkintown High School

Choral Music Reading Clinic for Junior and Senior High School Music

FRIDAY, OCTOBER 9, 9:00 A.M.

Chairman: RONALD TEARE, Harriton High School, Rosemont

(Audience will form the chorus)

Conductors:
CLEM SMITH, Haverford Township Junior High School; JOSEPH SALANTINO, Springfield Junior High School, Delaware County; PAUL FINK, Haverford Township Senior High School; JESSE ZERR, Radnor Township Senior High School

Accompanist: VIVIAN WALTON, Drexel Hill Junior High School, Upper Darby

Music in the Elementary School

Chairman: ROBERT VAUGHAN, Director of Music, Chester City Schools

Music Reading: Three Dimensional

Speaker: ELIZABETH CROOK, Music Department, University of Delaware, Newark, Delaware

49—Resources Available to School Groups: An Extension of Classroom Study .... **Philadelphia Museum of Art, Parkway at 26th Street, Philadelphia**

Co-Chairmen:
WILLIAM LEE GERMAN, Chairman, Art Department, Radnor Senior High School, Radnor; FRANK P. GRAHAM, Chief, Division of Education, Philadelphia Museum of Art

Admission by showing Schoolmen's Week program or proper identification

1. General tours of the Museum—handled by volunteer guides

2. Museum lessons or gallery talks—conducted by docents on special sections of the Museum, such as English, French, East (Far or Near), European, Fashion Wing, and Decorative Arts

3. Films and slides—Museum Auditorium
(Lists available for rental or purchase)

4. Special studio demonstrations
   a. Sculpture
   b. Printmaking
   c. Drawing and painting

5. Special exhibition of students' work—6-18 years old—Education Galleries

The maximum number of tours that can be handled at any hour is ten groups of thirty each. If tours are filled for that hour, participants may attend the viewing of the films and slides, the special studio, demonstrations, or the special student exhibition. Tours will be repeated hourly to 3:00 p.m., except 12:00 Noon to 1:00 p.m.

50—School Nurse Workshop .... **Lankenau Hospital, Lankenau and City Line Avenues, Overbrook, Pa.**

(An All-Day Conference)

Friday, October 9, 9:00 A.M.

9:00 A.M.

Registration

9:30 A.M.

Which Child Needs Psychiatry? Emotional Conflicts, Normal and Abnormal
Chairman: GERDA LEWIS, School Nurse, Marple-Newtown School District
Speakers:
KENNETH H. GORDON, Medical Director, Child Guidance Clinic, Lankenau Hospital, Philadelphia; CAROL KRUSEN SCHOLZ, Chief Psychiatric Social Worker, Child Guidance Clinic, Lankenau Hospital, Philadelphia

11:30 A.M.

Exhibits—Health Museum
Film Reviews (A program of films and schedule for viewing will be distributed at meeting so that you may preview films which interest you.)

12:30 P.M.

A luncheon for school nurses wil be served in the cafeteria
Reservations must be made by September 25, 1964, and payment sent to DOROTHY FRABLE, Candlebrook School, King of Prussia, Pa. Price—$1.25

1:30 P.M.

Exhibits and Film Reviews

2:00 P.M.

The Fundamental Goal in the Profession of Nursing
Speaker: FAYE ABDELLAH, Chief, Research Grants Branch Division of Nursing, Department of Health, Education, and Welfare, Washington, D. C.

3:30 P.M.

Exhibits and Film Reviews

51—Partners: Administrators, Teachers, Librarians (In co-operation with the School Librarians of Chester, Montgomery, and Delaware Counties) .... **Upper Merion Senior High School, 435 Crossfield Road, King of Prussia, Pa.**

(An All-Day Conference)

(An invitation is extended to administrators, teachers, guidance counselors, curriculum personnel, department heads, and librarians.)

9:00 A.M.-9:45 A.M.

Registration and Coffee

10:00 A.M.-11:30 A.M.

General Session
Chairman: RONALD K. SCHAFER, Librarian, Pottsgrove High School, Pottstown

Friday, October 9, 9:00 A.M.

Greetings: CATHERINE F. HAND, Librarian, Upper Merion Senior High School, King of Prussia

Progress Report: School Libraries in Pennsylvania—JOHN A. ROWELL, Director of School Libraries, Department of Public Instruction, Harrisburg

Speaker: MARY GAVER, Professor of Library Service, Rutgers University, New Brunswick, New Jersey

11:30 A.M.-12:15 P.M.

Library Visitations (Guests are welcome in all three libraries.)

12:15 P.M.-1:15 P.M.

Lunch in School Cafeteria
Reservations, accompanied by check for $2.00 (choice of chicken a la king or shrimp creole) should be sent by October 2, 1964, to CATHERINE F. HAND, Librarian, Upper Merion Senior High School, King of Prussia, Pa. Tickets will not be mailed. Reservations will be checked at the door. Friends and guests of Schoolmen's Week are welcome to attend the luncheon.

1:30 P.M.-3:00 P.M.

Elementary School Session .... **Candlebrook Elementary School, Prince Frederick Street, King of Prussia, Pa.**

Chairman: MIRIAM SANTORO, Librarian, Abington Township Elementary Schools, Abington

Panel:
MARIAN GARRISON, Principal, Cedar Road Elementary School, Abington Township; MARY BAKER, Teacher, Lower Merion Elementary School, Merion; ROSEMARY WEBER, Librarian, Wayne Elementary School, Wayne

Junior High School Session .... **Upper Merion Junior High School, Route 23 and Henderson Road, King of Prussia, Pa.**

Chairman: STELLA PARRY, Librarian, North Brandywine Junior High School, Coatesville

Panel:
JOHN MCKENNA, Principal, Shady Grove Junior High School, Ambler; ENID VAN RYPER, Teacher, Plymouth-Whitemarsh Junior High School, Plymouth Meeting; ALBERTA A. GLADECK, Librarian, Thomas Williams Junior High School, Wyncote

Senior High School Sessions .... **Upper Merion Senior High School, 435 Crossfield Road, King of Prussia, Pa.**

Chairman: KATHERINE P. ROGERS, Librarian, Spring-Ford Senior High School, Royersford

FRIDAY, OCTOBER 9, 9:00 A.M.

Panel:
H. CURWEN SCHLOSSER, Superintendent, Upper Darby Township Schools, Upper Darby; PAUL N. REHNIG, Teacher, Eisenhower Senior High School, Norristown; MINDA SANDERS, Librarian, Downingtown Senior High School, Downingtown

9:30 A.M.

52—Vocational Agriculture .... *Downingtown Joint Senior High School, 445 Manor Avenue, Downingtown, Pa.*
(An All-Day Conference)

Opening Session
Chairman: H. M. KLINGER, Vocational-Agriculture Instructor, Downingtown

10:00 A.M.

Agriculture in the Area Technical School
Speaker: HAROLD B. ALBRIGHT, Area Co-ordinator, Trade and Technical Education, Department of Public Instruction, Harrisburg

12:00 NOON

Luncheon at Downingtown Joint Senior High School

1:30 P.M.

Agriculture and the Vocational Education Act of 1963
Discussion Leader: To be announced

53—How Well Are We Teaching Biological Sciences in the Elementary School Program? .... *Sunday School Room, Asbury Church, 33rd and Chestnut Streets*

Chairman: ROBERT C. THOMPSON, Teacher, Spring Mill Elementary School, Whitemarsh Township

Speaker: JOHN G. NAVARRA, Professor of Science and Chairman of Department of Science, Jersey City State College, New Jersey

54—Children's Language, Literature, and Composition .... *Auditorium, Christian Association, 3601 Locust Street*
(The same as Program 27)

Chairman: ALETHA PITTS SCARANGELLO, Teacher, Newark Special School District, Newark, Delaware

Speaker: RUTH G. STRICKLAND, Research Professor of Education, Indiana University, Bloomington, Indiana

FRIDAY, OCTOBER 9, 9:30 A.M.

55—Beginning Reading with the Initial Teaching Alphabet ....
Main Auditorium, Drexel, 32nd and Chestnut Streets

Chairman: NONA CHERN, Reading Consultant, Media Borough School District

Speaker: ALBERT J. MAZURKIEWICZ, Director, Reading and Study Clinic, Lehigh University, Bethlehem

56—Automation Business Machines in the High School (A Demonstration; in co-operation with the Suburban Philadelphia Business Education Association) .... **Rooms 246 A-B Library Center, Drexel, 3243 Woodland Avenue**

Chairman: O. GRANT GOODEN, Head, Business Education Department, Springfield Senior High School, Springfield, Delaware County

Panel:
A. ELIZABETH HUTCHINSON, Head, Business Education Department, Collingdale High School, Collingdale; CLAIRE HAMMER, Head, Business Education Department, Sharon Hill High School, Sharon Hill; DOROTHEA C. WARREN, Head, Business Education Department, Chichester Senior High School, Boothwyn; MARJORIE K. DOYLE, Teacher, Business Education Department, Springfield Senior High School, Springfield, Delaware County; DONNA WILSON, Educational Services Representative, International Business Machines Corporation, Washington, D. C.

57—The Public Relations Guide for School Lunch .... **Room 101 N, Student Activities Center, Drexel, Southwest Corner, 32nd and Chestnut Streets**

Chairman: ANNE EIFLER, Supervisor, School Lunch and Nutrition, Department of Public Instruction, Harrisburg

Speaker: PHILIP B. HEARN, Northeast Area Field Supervisor, Food Distribution Division, U. S. Department of Agriculture, New York City

58—The Education of Socially Disadvantaged Youth .... **Auditorium, Houston Hall, 3417 Spruce Street**

Chairman: WILLIAM E. ARNOLD, Professor of Education, University of Pennsylvania

Speaker: N. NEUBERT JAFFA, Supervisor of Special Projects, Baltimore Public School System, Baltimore, Maryland

59—The Amidon Elementary School ...... **Franklin Room, Houston Hall, 3417 Spruce Street**

Chairman: FREDERICK G. DENT, Principal, Greenwood Elementary School, Kennett Square

Speaker: CARL F. HANSEN, Superintendent of Schools, Washington, D. C.

FRIDAY, OCTOBER 9, 9:30 A.M.

60—Physical Education and Athletics (In co-operation with the Southeastern District for Health, Physical Education, and Recreation) *Irvine Auditorium, 3401 Spruce Street*

Chairman: ETHEL G. ENCKE, Director of Girls' Physical Education and Athletics, Radnor Senior High School, Radnor

Team Teaching and Staff Utilization in Physical Educaton

Speaker: KENT A. BUIKEMA, Athletic Director and Co-ordinator of Physical Education, Ridgewood High School, Norridge, Illinois

Question and answer session

61—Scope and Sequence in Foreign Language Instruction (In co-operation with the Modern Language Association of Philadelphia .... *McClelland Hall Lounge, 37th and Spruce Streets*

(The Lounge may be reached through the dormitory tower at 37th and Spruce Streets. Turn left within the dormitory area, pass through arch, and descend the stone steps. The Lounge is located under the arcade, extending to the right.)

Chairman: HARRY WEINMANN, Teacher, Schuylkill Township Elementary School, Phoenixville

Speaker: CONRAD J. SCHMIDT, Co-ordinator of Foreign Languages, Hackensack School District, Hackensack, New Jersey

62—Chemical Reactions: How? How Much? How Fast? How Far? (In co-operation with the American Chemical Society of Philadelphia —Part I of a Two-Part Sequence) .... *Medical Alumni Hall, Maloney Building, University of Pennsylvania Hospital, 36th and Spruce Streets*

Chairman: HAROLD W. FERGUSON, Teacher of Science, Harriton High School, Rosemont

Speaker: ARTHUR C. BREYER, Professor of Chemistry, Harvey Mudd College, Claremont, California

63—Educational Television Moves Ahead .... *Auditorium, University Museum, 33rd and Spruce Streets*

Chairman: WILLARD HANCOCK, Superintendent, Yeadon School District

Secondary School Social Studies

Television Program from WHYY-TV—*Footnote to Freedom*—MARTHA A. GABLE, Director, Division of Radio-Television, School District of Philadelphia

(This program is presented with the co-operation of the Philadelphia Bar Association.)

Producers: ABNER A. MILLER, CECILIA G. GLEESON, BYRON LUKENS

Curriculum Offerings on Channel 12—Present and Future

Speaker: T. EDWARD RUTTER, Superintendent, Radnor Township School District

Friday, October 9, 9:30 A.M.

Educational Television—A Service to the Community
Speaker: WARREN A. KRAETZER, Executive Vice President and General Manager, Station WHYY, Philadelphia
What a Parent Thinks of Instructional TV
Speaker: RHODA KATZ, President, Mann Elementary School Home and School Association, Philadelphia

64—Museum Educational Programs and Practices for the Elementary School .... *Room 2, University Museum, 33rd and Spruce Streets*

Chairman: KENNETH D. MATTHEWS, JR., Assistant Curator, Education Department, University Museum

Speakers:
ROBERT NEATHERY, Museum Director, Franklin Institute, Philadelphia; GILBERT MERRILL, Chairman, Education Department, The Academy of Natural Sciences, Philadelphia

65—The Role of the Kindergarten in Reading Instruction .. *Auditorium, Illman Building, 3944 Walnut Street*
(The same as Program 29)

Chairman: MYRNA LEVIN, Teacher, Penn Wynne Elementary School, Lower Merion Township

Speaker: HELEN A. MURPHY, Professor of Education and Director, Educational Clinic, Boston University

66—Linguistic Grammar in the Secondary School Classroom .... *Ballroom, Convention Hall, 34th and Convention Avenue*

Chairman: EDGAR H. SCHUSTER, Editorial Consultant, McGraw-Hill Book Company, New York City

Speaker: V. LOUISE HIGGINS, Director of English, Westport Public Schools, Westport, Connecticut

67—A New Era for Vocational Education .... *Classroom A, Commercial Museum, 34th and Convention Avenue*

Chairman: H. HALLECK SINGER, Director, Vocational Teacher Education, University of Pennsylvania
Speaker: To be announced

68—Teaching Moral and Spiritual Values in the Public Schools: The Philosophical Issues .... *Classroom B, Commercial Museum, 34th and Convention Avenue*

Chairman: FREDERICK C. GRUBER, Professor of Education, University of Pennsylvania

Speaker: ROBERT E. MASON, Professor of Education, University of Pittsburgh, Pittsburgh

FRIDAY, OCTOBER 9, 9:30 A.M.

69—Maps and Globes in Elementary School Social Studies ....
*C. I. V. Lounge, Commercial Museum,
34th and Convention Avenue*

Chairman: THERESE SENESKY, Universities Related Co-ordinator, Lea School, Philadelphia

Speaker: JOHN D. MCAULAY, Professor of Education, Pennsylvania State University, University Park

70—Art Education: International Aspects .... *Room 101,
Convention Hall, 34th and Convention Avenue*

Chairman: LOUISE B. BALLINGER, Lecturer on Education, University of Pennsylvania

Speaker: ARTHUR R. YOUNG, Professor of Art Education, Pratt Institute, Brooklyn, New York

71—Major Concepts in Sociology: Implications for the Secondary School Social Studies Program .... *Room 300, Convention Hall,
34th and Convention Avenue*

Chairman: MARION KUBIAK, Chairman, Social Studies Department, Upper Merion Senior High School, King of Prussia

Speaker: EVERETT S. LEE, Associate Professor of Sociology, University of Pennsylvania

72—Driver Education and Traffic Safety .... *Room 304,
Convention Hall, 34th and Convention Avenue*

Chairman: HARRY R. WIKE, Teacher of Driver Education, Upper Darby High School, Upper Darby

Speaker: IVAN J. STEHMAN, Supervisor, Highway Safety Education, Department of Public Instruction, Harrisburg

Demonstration Topic: Use of the Overhead Projector as a Trend in Driver Education—Technifax Corporation, Holyoke, Massachusetts

Moderator: RAY COLEMAN, Teacher of Driver Education, Abington Senior High School, Abington

73—Potential Mathematics for Elementary School Children ....
*Room 200, Convention Hall,
34th and Convention Avenue*

(The same as Program 43)

Chairman: ALFRED CASTALDI, Principal, Cynwyd Elementary School, Bala-Cynwyd

Speaker: HOWARD F. FEHR, Head, Department of Mathematical Education, Teachers College, Columbia University, New York City

Friday, October 9, 9:30 A.M.

74—The Teaching of Conservation in the Junior High School ....
*Room 301, Illman Building,
3944 Walnut Street*

Chairman: ROBERT MORAN, Co-ordinator of Science, Brookhaven Junior High School, Green Ridge, Chester

Speaker: KINGSLEY L. GREENE, Assistant Professor of Biology, Eastern Baptist College, St. Davids

75—Teaching of Affine Geometry .... *Alumni Hall,
Towne Building, 220 S. 33rd Street
(Enter from Smith Walk)*

Chairman: L. HOWARD FREEMAN, Head, Mathematics Department, Lansdowne-Aldan High School, Lansdowne

Speaker: ERNEST SNAPPER, Professor of Mathematics, Dartmouth College, Hanover, New Hampshire

76—The Elementary School Staff Considers the Need for the Development of Guidance Services .... *Auditorium,
Asbury Church, 33rd and Chestnut Streets*

Chairman: JOHN E. FREE, Director, Counseling Service, University of Pennsylvania

Discussants:
PATRICIA ELLIOT, Principal, Rydal Elementary School, Huntingdon Valley; ISABELLA BAYNE, First Grade Teacher, Demonstration School, West Chester State College; GEORGE W. DAVIS, Counselor, Pratt-Arnold Elementary School, Philadelphia; ANTHONY J. MANNINO, Director of Guidance and School Psychologist, Ridley Township School District

---

11:00 A.M.

77—Second General Session .... *Irvine Auditorium,
3401 Spruce Street*

Organ Prelude at 10:45 a.m. .... Muriel Draper
At the Curtis Memorial Organ

VALUES FOR A CHANGING AMERICA

Chairman: RICHARD S. HEISLER, Assistant to the Dean, Graduate School of Education, University of Pennsylvania

Greetings: MORRIS S. VITELES, Dean, Graduate School of Education, University of Pennsylvania

Introduction of the Speaker: DAVID R. GODDARD, Provost, University of Pennsylvania

Speaker: RALPH W. TYLER, Director, Center for Advanced Study in the Behavioral Sciences, Stanford, California

FRIDAY, OCTOBER 9, 2:00 P.M.

2:00 P.M.

78—Schoolmen's Week: Its Worth to the Elementary School Principal (In co-operation with the Department of Elementary School Principals, Southeastern Region) ....
(See Program #106)

(A Panel of Elementary School Principals discussing, reviewing, and evaluating five selected Schoolmen's Week sessions.)

79—Something Old, Something New, Something Borrowed, Something Blue (In co-operation with the Pennsylvania Learning Resources Association) .... *Auditorium, Asbury Church, 33rd and Chestnut Streets*

Chairman: CLARENCE A. LYNN, Chairman, Film Library Division, Pennsylvania Learning Resources Associaton

Speaker: RICHARD P. WEAGLEY, Chairman, Audio-Visual Department, West Chester State College, West Chester

80—An Industrial Arts Program for the Future ....
Sunday School Room, Asbury Church, 33rd and Chestnut Streets
Program to be announced

81—Study Skills in the Intermediate Grade Classroom .... *Auditorium, Christian Association, 3601 Locust Street*

Chairman: MARY CROCKER, Teacher, Bell Avenue Elementary School, Yeadon

Speaker: GEORGE BOND, Principal, The Campus School, State University College, New Paltz, New York

82—Evaluation in the Elementary School Social Studies Classroom ......
Auditorium, Drexel, 32nd and Chestnut Streets

Chairman: WALTER H. RHOADS, Teacher, Penn Valley Elementary School, Penn Valley

Speaker: J. WAYNE WRIGHTSTONE, Acting Associate Superintendent, Board of Education, New York City

83—Curriculum Change in the Post-Sputnik Era .... *Room 101 N, Student Activities Center, Drexel, Southwest Corner, 32nd and Chestnut Streets*

Chairman: JOSEPH D. MOORE, Director of Secondary Education, Paoli Area High School System

Speaker: NEIL ATKINS, Principal, Fox Lane and Middle Schools, Bedford, New York

Friday, October 9, 2:00 P.M.

84—New Directions in Foreign Language Instruction (In co-operation with the Modern Language Association of Philadelphia and Vicinity) .... *Auditorium, Houston Hall, 3417 Spruce Street*

Chairman: ARNOLD G. REICHENBERGER, Professor of Romance Languages, University of Pennsylvania

Part I

New Trends in the Teaching of Foreign Language
Speaker: RUTH CORNFIELD, Lecturer, University of Pennsylvania

Part II

Implications for the Intermediate Level (Panel discussion)

Panel:
JERRY A. CAPONIGRO, Head, Foreign Language Department, South Philadelphia High School—*Structural Study;* ELDRED R. MORRIS, Chairman, Language Department, Penncrest High School—*Reading for Comprehension;* MARIE M. GUILIANO, Teacher of Spanish, George Washington High School, Philadelphia—*Writing for Expression;* ERNESTO A. CANALES, Teacher of Spanish, Upper Darby High School—*Cultural Appreciation*

Part III

Teaching Demonstration

Demonstration Teacher: ARTHUR WATSON, Teacher of French, Swarthmore High School, Swarthmore

Demonstration Group: Students from Swarthmore High School

85—Current Trends in Juvenile Delinquency Research ....
Franklin Room, Houston Hall, 3417 Spruce Street

Chairman: JEAN S. STRAUB, Vice-Dean of Admissions, Graduate School of Education, University of Pennsylvania

Speaker: MARVIN E. WOLFGANG, Professor of Sociology, University of Pennsylvania

86—Lead-up Games and Conditioning Exercises Used in the Intermediate Grade Physical Education Program (A Demonstration) ......
Irvine Auditorium, 3401 Spruce Street

Chairman: EVELYN HALDEMAN, Supervisor of Elementary Physical Education, Abington Township School District

Directors:
LEONARD DEPUE, Teacher of Physical Education, Cheltenham Township Elementary Schools; EDWIN E. FERGUSON, Teacher of Physical Education, Cheltenham Township Elementary Schools

Demonstration Group: Students from Cheltenham Township Elementary Schools

FRIDAY, OCTOBER 9, 2:00 P.M.

87—Linguistics in the Secondary Schools: Promises and Problems ....
McClelland Hall Lounge, 37th and Spruce Streets

(The Lounge may be reached through the dormitory tower at 37th and Spruce Streets. Turn left within the dormitory area, pass through arch, and descend the stone steps. The Lounge is located under the arcade extending to the right)

Chairman: EDGAR H. SCHUSTER, Writer-Editor, McGraw-Hill Book Company, New York City

Speakers:
BARBARA ANN FOSTER, Chairman, English Department, Upper Merion Junior High School—*Structural Grammar: Earphones to Eyeglasses;* MARION STEET, Teacher of English, School District of Philadelphia—*Teacher Training in Linguistics;* ROBERT W. BOYNTON, Principal, Senior High Level, Germantown Friends School, Philadelphia—*Whose Grammar in the High School?*

88—Chemical Reactions: How? How Much? How Fast? How Far? (In cooperation with the American Chemical Society of Philadelphia —Part II of a Two-Part Sequence) .... **Medical Alumni Hall, Maloney Building, University of Pennsylvania Hospital, 36th and Spruce Streets**

Chairman: STEPHEN A. EDGERTON, Head, Science Department, William Penn Charter School, Philadelphia

Speaker: ARTHUR C. BREYER, Professor of Chemistry, Harvey Mudd College, Claremont, California

89—Books for Children .... **Auditorium, University Museum, 33rd and Spruce Streets**

Chairman: HELEN HUUS, Associate Professor of Education, University of Pennsylvania

Speakers:
BARBARA COONEY, Author and Illustrator, Pepperell, Massachusetts; ELIZABETH ENRIGHT, Author, New York City; MILLICENT SELSAM, Author, New York City

Panel:
MARIAN ANDERSON, Teacher, Junior High School #3, Trenton, New Jersey; ANITA R. GEBHART, Teacher, Wrightstown Elementary School, Wrightstown; GERALDINE M. KELSEY, Teacher, William Hunter School, Philadelphia

90—Off the Beaten Path in Spelling .... **Auditorium, Illman Building, 3944 Walnut Street**

Chairman: CLAIRE MORRIS, Assistant Professor of Education, Kutztown State College, Kutztown

Speaker: MARY ELISABETH COLEMAN, Associate Professor of Education, University of Pennsylvania

91—A Physician Looks at the Health of the Elementary School Child ....
C. I. V. Lounge, Commercial Museum, 34th and Convention Avenue

Friday, October 9, 2:00 P.M.

Chairman: Gladys Durboraw Snively, Teacher, Scenic Hills Elementary School, Springfield, Delaware County

Speaker: Charles D. Connor, Physician, Cheverly, Maryland

92—Major Concepts in History: Implications for the Secondary School Social Studies Program .... *Room 300, Convention Hall, 34th and Convention Avenue*

Chairman: G. Kenneth Merryman, Chairman, Social Studies Department, Keith Junior High School, Horsham

Speaker: Russell F. Weigley, Professor of History, Temple University, Philadelphia

93—Teacher Association-Board of Education Relations: Their Impact on the Improvement of Instruction (In co-operation with the Philadelphia Teachers Association) .... *Room 200, Convention Hall, 34th and Convention Avenue*

Chairman: Rosemary Mazzatenta, Elementary Consulting Teacher, District #3, School District of Philadelphia

Speaker: Walter J. O'Brien, Executive Secretary, Philadelphia Teachers Association

Interrogators:
Thomas C. Rosica, Administrative Assistant, Walton School, Philadelphia; Joyce Claybourne, Teacher of Science, Dobbins Technical High School, Philadelphia

94—Art Workshop .... *Room 301, Illman Building, 3944 Walnut Street* **(The same as Program 15)**

Chairman: Mary C. Renner, Director of Audio-Visual Instruction, Upper Darby Township Schools

Director: Jane Betsey Welling, Emeritus Professor of Education, Wayne State University, Detroit, Michigan

Assistant: Lucille W. Carlton, Teacher of Art, Beverly Hills Junior High School, Upper Darby

Note:
Only 40 persons can be accommodated at each session. Cards of admission may be obtained by writing to Schoolmen's Week, Attention: Art Workshop, Graduate School of Education, University of Pennsylvania, Philadelphia, Pa. 19104. Enclose a self-addressed, stamped envelope.

95—Teaching of Euclidean Geometry ...... *Alumni Hall, Towne Building, 220 S. 33rd Street (Enter from Smith Walk)*

Chairman: Martin F. Hubley, Chairman, Mathematics Department, Abington High School, Abington

Speaker: Ernest Snapper, Professor of Mathematics, Dartmouth College, Hanover, New Hampshire

Saturday, October 10

9:30 A.M.

96—The World Affairs Council of Philadelphia (In co-operation with the Philadelphia Board of Trade and Conventions) .. Ballroom, Commercial Museum, 34th and Convention Avenue
Education for Democracy in the New Africa

Moderator: RICHARD P. BROWN, JR., Board of Directors, World Affairs Council, Philadelphia

Speaker: HERBERT J. SPIRO, Associate Professor of Political Science, Amherst College, Amherst, Massachusetts

Participants:

Approximately 500 students representing public, private, and diocesan schools in the Delaware Valley area participate regularly in the series of Interscholastic Senior High School Forums, the first of which is scheduled as part of Schoolmen's Week.

Program Notes:

The purpose we hope to serve by means of the Forums was clearly expressed in the title of speech made by Secretary of State Rusk: "Education for Citizenship in the Modern World." The programs are planned by the students with the help of the staff of the Student Activities Department of the World Affairs Council and the faculty advisors in the schools. At a time when the rapid pace of events ". . . . brings world affairs into everyone's front parlor and everyone's back yard,"* the importance of stimulating interest in world affairs and of providing opportunities for students to become well-informed cannot be overemphasized. The program serves to illustrate the contribution of a community agency towards enriched educational experiences.

Seats are available for spectators; teachers of social studies will find this meeting particularly valuable.

*Address by the Honorable Adlai Stevenson, April 3, 1964.

Luncheon and Dinner Meetings

Wednesday, October 7

6:00 P.M.

97—Dinner Meeting: Guidance and Personnel Workers (In co-operation with the Personnel and Guidance Association of Greater Philadelphia) ...... Franklin Room, Houston Hall, 3417 Spruce Street

Chairman: ELEANORE S. ISARD, Director, University Counseling Center, Temple University, Philadelphia

Luncheon and Dinner Meetings

Revisiting an Old Topic: What Tests Can and Cannot Do for a Counselor

Speaker: HAROLD G. SEASHORE, Director, Test Division, The Psychological Corporation, New York City

Reservations with check should be sent not later than Friday, October 2, 1964, to E. Bruce Kirk, 2503 Lombard Street, Philadelphia 46, Pa. Price—$3.00

98—Dinner Meeting: Eastern Division Pennsylvania School Administrators Association .... Faculty Club, 3600 Walnut Street

Chairman: WILLIAM E. ARNOLD, Professor of Education, University of Pennsylvania

Legal Problems of Major Concern to School Administrators in Pennsylvania

Speaker: JOHN D. KILLIAN, III, Deputy Attorney General, Commonwealth of Pennsylvania, Harrisburg

Reservations should be sent to Raymond R. Baugher, Superintendent, Downingtown Joint Schools, Downingtown, Pa., by October 1, 1964. (Telephone 269-1170) Price—$3.50

Thursday, October 8

6:00 P.M.

99—The Seventy-five Club .... Pennsylvania Room, Sheraton Motor Inn, 39th and Chestnut Streets

Chairman: WILLARD R. HANCOCK, Superintendent, Yeadon School District

And You Think You Have Problems!

Speaker: WARREN A. KRAETZER, Manager of Educational TV Station WHYY, Channel 12, Philadelphia

Reservations are restricted to members and invited guests and should be made through Willard R. Hancock, Superintendent, Yeadon School District, Yeadon, Pa., by Thursday, October 1, 1964. Price—$5.50

100—Dinner Meeting: Pennsylvania Home Economics Association, Southeastern District .... Room 101 S, Student Activities Center, Drexel, Southwest Corner, 32nd and Chestnut Streets

Chairman: HELEN B. PARKER, Teacher, Home Economics Department, Henderson Senior High School, West Chester

Consumer Textile Problems Stimulate Research

Speaker: DOROTHY SIEGERT LYLE, Director of Consumer Relations, National Institute of Dry Cleaning, Silver Spring, Maryland

Reservations should be sent to Marion MacSkimming, Philadelphia Electric Company, 920 East Lincoln Highway, Coatesville, Pa., by October 5, 1964. Price—$4.00

Luncheon and Dinner Meetings

101—Dinner Meeting: School Librarians Association of Philadelphia and Vicinity .... *Rooms 34-35, Student Activities Building, Drexel, 32nd and Chestnut Streets*

This dinner follows Program #47 and is an opportunity to meet informally with the program participants. Send reservations and check to Inez Bieberman, Bok Technical High School, 8th and Mifflin Streets, Philadelphia 48, by October 5. Tickets will not be sent but reservations will be checked at the door. All friends and guests of Schoolmen's Week are invited to attend. Price—$3.25

6:15 P.M.

102—Phi Delta Kappa and Pi Lambda Theta Dinner Meeting .... *Faculty Club, 36th and Walnut Streets*

Chairman: VINCENT SAUERS, Principal, Marple-Newtown Junior High School, Newtown Square

A Golden Anniversary Salute to the School of Education at the University of Pennsylvania

Speaker: C. TAYLOR WHITTIER, Superintendent, School District of Philadelphia

Presentation of the fourth annual Phi Delta Kappa graduate award for outstanding scholarship to a candidate for the Ed. D. degree in the Graduate School of Education, University of Pennsylvania, during the Spring term of 1964.

Presentation of Philadelphia Alumnae Chapter, Pi Lambda Theta, Grant-in-Aid to a full-time graduate woman student in education.

Informal dinner for all Pi Lambda Thetans and Phi Delta Kappans, regardless of chapters, and guests. For reservations, write Phi Delta Kappa, 3812 Walnut Street, Philadelphia, Pa. 19104, by October 1, 1964. Price—$3.00

Friday, October 9

12:00 NOON

103—Education Alumni Association, University of Pennsylvania .... *Egyptian Room, University Museum, 33rd and Spruce Streets*

Chairman: MARY H. CARTER, Principal, Radnor Senior High School, Radnor

The Individual in a World of Revolution

Speaker: ALTHEA K. HOTTEL, Trustee, University of Pennsylvania, and Chairman, The Philadelphia Commission on Higher Education

Presentation of Education Alumni Association National Award of Distinction

Presentation of Education Alumni Association Award of Distinction to an Alumnus

Reservations, accompanied by check for $3.00 payable to the Education Alumni Association, should be sent by Monday, October 5, 1964, to Albert J. Snite, Treasurer, Education Alumni Association, 3812 Walnut Street, Philadelphia, Pa. 19104. (Phone 594-7344.) Indicate fish or meat. Tickets will not be mailed. Reservations will be checked at the door. Friends and guests of Schoolmen's Week are welcome to attend this luncheon.

Luncheon and Dinner Meetings

104—Luncheon Meeting: Pennsylvania Association of Women Deans and Counselors .... *Picture Gallery, Drexel, 32nd and Chestnut Streets*

Chairman: BARBARA OLIVER, Assistant to the Dean of Women, University of Pennsylvania

To Be Young Today

Speaker: HELEN C. BAILEY, Former Visiting Professor of Education, University of Pennsylvania

Please send reservations with check to Barbara Oliver, 117 Logan Hall, University of Pennsylvania, Philadelphia, Pa. 19104, by October 2, 1964. Price—$2.75

105—Luncheon Meeting: Industrial Arts and Vocational Education ...... *Christian Association, 3601 Locust Street*

Chairman: REX E. WRIGHT, Area Coordinator, Trade and Technical Education, University of Pennsylvania

The Area Technical School Program in Pennsylvania

Speaker: ROBERT JACOBY, Head State Supervisor, Technical and Industrial Education, Department of Public Instruction, Harrisburg

Send reservatons to Rex E. Wright, 3810 Walnut Street, Philadelphia, Pa. 19104 by October 1, 1964. Please specify fish or meat. Price—$2.25

1:00 P.M.

106—Luncheon Meeting: Department of Elementary School Principals, Southeastern Region

Meeting #78 will follow the luncheon

Place of luncheon and meeting to be announced. For details, contact Florence Shields, Principal, Lima Elementary School, Lima Pa. (Telephone LOwell 6-2679)

Index of Program Participants

Participant	Program
Abbott, Kathryn N.	35
Abdellah, Faye	50
Albright, Harold	19, 52
Althouse, John H.	19
Anderson, Marian	89
Andrews, Marie	35
Anliot, Richard B.	13
Arnold, William E.	58, 98
Ashhurst, Hazel M.	4
Atkins, Neil	83
Bailey, Helen C.	23, 104
Baker, Mary	51
Ballinger, Louise B.	70
Baugher, Raymond R.	98
Baum, Rosemere	38
Bayne, Isabella	76
Bean, William T.	37
Bieberman, Inez	101
Binzen, Peter	22
Bocchini, Richard R.	1
Bond, George	81
Bonelli, Jane D.	44
Bortner, Ross	27
Boynton, Robert W.	87
Bredahl-Petersen, Aase	33
Breyer, Arthur C.	62, 88
Brickman, William W.	2
Britsch, Wilhelmina	35
Bronstein, Judith F.	24
Brown, Richard P., Jr.	96
Bryn Mawr College Students	20
Buckley, Richard D.	31
Buikema, Kent A.	60
Campbell, Ruth Luty	21
Canales, Ernesto A.	84
Caponigro, Jerry A.	84
Carlton, Lucille W.	15, 94
Carter, Mary H.	103
Castaldi, Alfred	73
Castetter, William	22
Cheltenham Township Elementary School Students	86
Chern, Nona	55
Claybourne, Joyce	93
Coates, Robert H.	28
Coleman, Mary E.	90
Coleman, Ray	72
Connor, Charles D.	91
Cooke Junior High School Students	13
Cooney, Barbara	89

Participant	Program
Cooper, E. Virgil	21
Cornfield, Ruth	84
Crocker, Mary	81
Crook, Elizabeth	48
Cunningham, Sandra	41
Curtis, Arthur	32
Davis, George W.	76
DeAngelo, Rachael W.	47
Dengler, Clyde	48
Dengler, Clyde, Jr.	48
Dent, Frederick G.	59
DePue, Leonard	86
Dougherty, Rev. Francis D.	37
Doyle, Marjorie K.	56
Draper, Muriel	17, 77
Duckrey, Marjorie	7
Edgerton, Stephen A.	88
Edwards, Yvonne	47
Eifler, Anne	57
Elliott, Patricia	76
Encke, Ethel G.	60
Enright, Elizabeth	89
Enstrom, E. A.	24
Faust, Helen F.	7
Fay, Leo C.	9, 46
Fazzini, John	35
Fehr, Howard F.	43, 73
Ferguson, Edwin E.	86
Ferguson, Harold W.	62
Fink, Paul	48
Flury, Ablett H.	3
Foster, Barbara Ann	87
Frable, Dorothy	50
Frech, Andrew	48
Free, John E.	76
Freeman, L. Howard	75
French, William M.	2
Funk, Betty Anne	7
Gable, Martha A.	63
Garrison, Marian	51
Gaver, Mary	51
Gebhart, Anita R.	89
German, William Lee	49
Giammatteo, Michael	34
Giersch, Herman	48
Gladeck, Alberta A.	51
Glantz, Bernard	13
Gleeson, Cecilia G.	63
Gloster, Francis	48
Goddard, David R.	77
Gooden, O. Grant	56

Participant	Program
Gordon, Kenneth H.	50
Gordon, Oliver	28
Grace, James L., Jr.	2
Graham, Frank P.	49
Greene, Kingsley L.	74
Grimm, Robert L.	34
Gruber, Frederick C.	68
Guiliano, Marie M.	84
Gump, Larney	19
Haldeman, Evelyn	86
Hammer, Claire	56
Hammock, Robert C.	8
Hancock, Willard R.	26, 63, 99
Hand, Catherine F.	51
Hansen, Carl F.	59
Hanson, Lincoln	5
Hardy, Dorothy G.	29
Harnwell, Gaylord P.	17
Harris, Jane	25
Hearn, Philip B.	57
Heisler, Richard S.	77
Hess, B. Anton	3
Higgins, V. Louise	39, 66
Hooper, Jean	37
Hottel, Althea K.	103
Hu, C. T.	33
Hubley, Martin F.	95
Hutchinson, A. Elizabeth	56
Hutton, Harry K.	8
Huus, Helen	17, 89
Ifert, William	48
Irwin, Leonard B.	37
Isard, Eleanore S.	97
Jacoby, Robert	105
Jaffa, N. Neubert	58
Jensen, Robert H.	5
Johnson, Eric W.	40
Junkins, Laura	30
Kadyk, Folkert H.	16
Katz, Rhoda	63
Kelsey, Geraldine M.	89
Ketchum, E. Gillet	9
Killian, John D., III	98
Kirk, E. Bruce	97
Klinger, H. M.	52
Koopman, Philip U.	12
Kraetzer, Warren A.	63, 99
Kriebel, Gerald H.	35
Kubiak, Marion	71
Kushma, John J.	42

Index of Program Participants

Participant	Program
Larson, Arthur	17
Lawson, Warner	48
Lea School Students	47
LeCompte, Clair	41
Lee, Everett S.	71
Levin, Myrna	65
Lewis, Gerda	50
Link, Frances	36
Loane, Helen S.	30
Long, Mary	7
Loughrey, Rev. Thomas F.	39
Luke, Robert A.	28
Lukens, Byron	63
Lyle, Dorothy Siegert	100
Lynn, Clarence A.	79
MacDonald, Eugene	41
MacSkimming, Marion	100
Mannino, Anthony J.	76
Marks, Beatrice	7
Mason, Ann	20
Mason, Robert E.	68
Masterman School Students	23
Matthews, Kenneth D., Jr.	64
Mazurkiewicz, Albert J.	55
Mazzatenta, Rosemary	93
McAulay, John D.	31, 69
McKenna, John	51
Melson, Ruth V.	14
Merrill, Gilbert	64
Merryman, G. Kenneth	92
Miller, Abner A.	63
Minnich, J. Allen	37
Moon, Harold L.	5
Moore, Joseph D.	83
Moran, Robert	74
Morris, Claire	90
Morris, Eldred R.	84
Murphy, Helen A.	29, 65
Nagy, Mark C.	46
Nason, Leslie J.	45
Nassau, Dorothy P.	47
Navarra, John G.	25, 53
Neathery, Robert	64
Nichols, Roy F.	2
O'Brien, Walter J.	93
Oliver, Albert I.	37
Oliver, Barbara	104
Oster, Erwin I.	11
Parker, Helen B.	100
Parry, Stella	51

Participant	Program
Pillard, Matthew J.	12
Pira, Cathie	20
Quinn, James H. McK.	3
Raffel, Helen	42
Rehnig, Paul N.	51
Reichenberger, Arnold G.	84
Reinwald, Clio	38
Renner, Mary C.	15, 94
Rhoads, Walter H.	82
Robinson, Richard R.	32
Rochberg, George	16
Rogers, Katherine P.	51
Rohrback, Louise	21
Rosica, Thomas C.	93
Rowell, John A.	51
Rowland, Sydney V.	3
Rutter, T. Edward	63
Sack, Saul	2
Salantino, Joseph	48
Sanders, Minda	51
Santoro, Miriam	51
Sauers, Vincent	102
Scarangello, Aletha Pitts	54
Schaeffer, Edward J.	23
Schafer, Ronald K.	51
Schleifer, Benjamin	20
Schlosser, H. Curwen	51
Schmidt, Conrad J.	61
Scholz, Carol Krusen	50
Schuster, Edgar H.	66, 87
Scull, Mary Lou	44
Seashore, Harold G.	6, 97
Seip, Janet	35
Selsam, Millicent	89
Senesky, Therese	69
Serinsky, Eleanor	47
Shields, Florence	106
Shimberg, Benjamin	1
Singer, H. Halleck	67
Smith, Clem	48
Smith, Marie A.	6
Snapper, Ernest	75, 95
Snite, Albert J.	103
Snively, Gladys Durboraw	91
Snyder, Richard	11
Speece, Mary	13
Spiro, Herbert J.	96
Steet, Marion	87
Stehman, Ivan J.	72
Stewart, Homer N.	40
Stone, A. Harris	36
Straub, Jean S.	85

Participant	Program
Strickland, Ruth G.	27, 54
Sueltz, Ben A.	14
Swarthmore College Students	20
Swarthmore High School Students	84
Swingle, Frederick	48
Taiz, Malvena	20
Taylor, Frances M.	10
Teare, Ronald	48
Temple University Students	20
Terata, Alyn	20
Terezza, Mario	48
Thompson, Robert C.	53
Thomson, Frances	43
Tyler, Ralph W.	77
University of Pennsylvania Students	20
Upper Darby Senior High School Choir	48
Van Ryper, Enid	51
Vaughan, Robert	48
Viteles, Morris S.	77
Von Hilsheimer, George	10
Wakefield, Charles S.	18
Walter, Marguerite J.	4
Walton, John	2
Walton, Vivian	48
Warren, Dorothea C.	56
Watson, Arthur	84
Watts, Thomas M.	26
Weagley, Richard P.	79
Weakley, Emeline C.	21
Weber, Rosemary	51
Weigley, Russell F.	92
Weinmann, Harry	61
Welling, Jane Betsey	15, 94
Wentz, Louise	45
Whittier, C. Taylor	102
Wike, Harry R.	72
Wilson, Donna	56
Witt, Paul W. F.	47
Wolfgang, Marvin E.	85
Woodward, Grace E.	38
Wright, Rex E.	105
Wrightstone, J. Wayne	82
Young, Arthur R.	70
Young, Marechal-Neil E.	13
Zerr, Jesse	48

Index

ABCD program, of Boston, 93
Administrators, 74
Adventure Playgrounds, 63
Agriculture, 25
Agriculture, production, 25
Aladdin, M. P., 261
Alexander, Sir William, 280
American Home Economics Association, 214
Arbuthnot, May Hill, 121
Arnold, Matthew, 267
Art, children's, 256
Atteck, Sibyl C., 261
Attitude, in spelling, 114
Auctioneers, in Rome, 210
Augmented Roman Alphabet, 110
Aurelius, Marcus, 207
Automation, 186

Barrie, Sir James, 281
Bell, Vicars, 130
Biases, and values, 45
Binzen, Peter H., 76
Boord, Robert O., 125
Brauner, Charles J., 235
Britain, economic values, 21
Brown V Board of Education, 76
Building Materials, in Rome, 201
Burns, Arthur E., 17
Busing program, 83
"Butler Act," 268
Bryher, Winifred, 144

Camp David meeting, 22
Capitalism, 18
Carter, Barbara, 86
Charlton, Kenneth, 282
Chase, Mary Ellen, 121
Check lists, in evaluation, 159
Christensen, Francis, 140

Civil rights, issue, 171
Civil rights movement, 167
Civil War, the, 170
Clark, Kenneth B., 86, 87
Clarke, Sir Fred, 265
Class size, 71
Coleman, Mary Elisabeth, 113
College, early English, 264
College Entrance Examination Board, 147
Collier, Price, 266
Collins, John F., 84
Communication, 31
Communication Skills, 91
Communism, 14
Composition, 129
Conant, James B., 61, 86, 233
Concepts, about language, 124
Consonant blends, 115
Consumer demand, 189, 190
Council of Economic Advisors, 179
Crusoe, Robinson, 181
Cultural diversity, 35
Cultural Exchange programs, 255
Cummings, e. e., 144
Curriculum validity, of tests, 159
Curriculum, and values, 38
Curti, Merle, 77
Curtis, S. J., 267

Decision-making, 66
de la Mare, Walter, 121
Demers, Ella, 151
Democratic education, 66
"Demons," Spelling, 119
Densdale, Joseph, 145
Dent, H. C., 282
Depression, 194, 195
Description Grammar, 145
Desegregation, 84

Disadvantaged, 90
Distribution, in Roman economy, 208
D'Ortona, Paul, 83
Dry Cleaners, 224, 225
DuBois, W. E. B., 76

Early school idea, 85
Economic Opportunities Act, 85
Economics, course of study, 180
Economics, in high school, 177
Education, the Discipline of, 234
Elementary education, 70
Eliot, George, 140
Engineering, as a profession, 275
Evaluation, functions of, 154
Evaluation, in arithmetic, 153
Everett, Edward, 78

Fabric qualities, 228-230
Farjeon, Eleanor, 121
Fay, Leo C., 101
"Feather bedding," 196
Federal Trade Commission, 222
Fischer, John H., 88
Flexner, Abraham, 282
Ford, Henry, 21
Frank, Tenney, 207
Fries, Charles, 102
Fries, Charles C., 125
Frontier thesis, the, 172
Future Teachers of America, 97

Gage, Nathaniel, 251
Gaines, 204
Galbraith, J. K., 17
George Barden Act, 214
Gleason, H. A., Jr., 133
Goals, for the future, 26, 27
Goodman, Paul, 69
Gould, Sir Ronald, 280
Gowen, Franklin P., 169
Grace, James L., 241
Graduate Study, 246
Grammar, 133
Grants, for students, 272
Graphic patterns, of language, 124
Green, Martin, 282

Hall, Robert A., Jr., 116

Hanna, Jean S. & Paul R., 125
Hay, John, 176
Hazard, Paul, 128
Higgins, V. Louise, 133
Higher Education, in Britain, 263
Higher Horizons project, 92
History, and the Social Studies, 166
Holmes, Gerald, 75
Home Economics, programs, 217
Homonyms, in spelling, 120
Hopkins, Harry, 280
Homework centers, 98
Hutchinson, Michael, 282
Hutton, Harry K., 263

Ideology, of U. S., 15
Imports, to Rome, 198
Incentive principle, 22
India, economy, 17
Indiana University, 107
Individualized Reading, 110
Industry, in Rome, 202, 203
Ingham, George, 146
INSEA (International Society for Education through Art), 258
Installment buying, 20
Instruction, spelling, 114
International Education, 254
Irving, Washington, 166
Isolationism, 166
i/t/a project, 101
Jackson, Sidney L., 78
Jaffa, N. Neubert, 90
Jefferson, Thomas, 169, 170
Johnson, Albert E., 221
Jones, William J., 88
Juvenal, 210

Kelley, Ruby, 151
Khrushchev, Nikita, 22
Kindergarten, 85
Kjelgaard, Jim, 143
Kneller, George F., 282
Knowledge, in spelling, 114

Labels, in clothing, 221
Labor Unions, 17, 19
Lane, Homer, 61
Language, 122

Index

Larson, Arthur, 13
Lewis, A. H., 168
Lincoln, Abraham, 18, 21, 176
Linguistics, 122
Linguistic approach, 108
Linguistic Method, 102
Lippman, Walter, 15
Literature, 127
Little Commonwealth, the, 63
Lloyd, John W., 282
Loane, Helen J., 198
Lyle, Dorothy S., 221
Lysenko, T. D., 23

Maclure, Stewart, 271
Marshall, R. F., 275
Martial, 201, 204
Marx, Karl, 21, 24
Mason, Robert E., 45
Massachusetts Institute of Technology, 131
McParlan, James, 168
Mill, John Stewart, 21
Milovan, Djilas, 22
Moberly, Walter H., 282
Mollie Maguires, the, 168
Moral, dimension of education, 48, 49
Moral nurture, 57

NAACP, 82
National Commission on Teacher Education and Professional Standards, 243
National Council of Teachers of English, 147
National Institute of Dry cleaning, 221
Nebraska Project, 127
Neill, A. S., 59
Nero, 207, 209
New Single Sound alphabet, 110
Nicolay, John G., 176
Norms, test, 161
Norwood, Cyril, 266

Observation, as evaluation, 156
Olsen, Willard, 110
Operation Understanding, 97
Owen, Ralph D., 109

Page, David, 78
Palaemon, Q. Remmius, 211
Parker, John W., 80
Pasadena Program, 93
Pedagogy, defined, 243
  professor of, 243
Pedley, Robin, 281
Peer group, 40
Peltason, J. W., 81
Perceptual abilities, in Spelling, 114
Permissive philosophy, 67
Peterson, ADC., 282
Peterson, Merrill D., 169
Petronius, 201
Phonics Method, 102, 103
Plessy V. Ferguson, 78
Pliny, 199
Plurals, in spelling, 116
Pompeii, 203, 206
Population, 29, 190, 191
Postman, Neil, 134
Prefixes, and spelling, 118
Preschool education, 92
Prestolee, 74
Price, of a product, 188
Princeton Plan, 81
Production technique, 192
Productivity, 19, 24
Products, of Rome, 204, 206
Professional Studies, Professor of, 249
Professor of Education, preparation of, 233, 241
Project English, 127
Prosperity, 20
Public education, 60

Race problem, 76
Raffel, Helen, 177
Reading, 101
Ree, H. A., 279
Reinwald, Clio S., 212
Religion, 50, 51
Religious issue in education, 53-55
Religious nurture, 46
Research, in education, 235
Robbins Committee, 270
Roberts, Paul, 134, 135
Rome, economy of, 198

Roosevelt, Eleanor, 212
Roper, Elmo, 22
Rugg, Harold, 235

Sadler, Michael, 266
San Diego Reading Study Project, 109
School Interchange Program, 95
School Administration, the professor of, 248
Scott, Louise B., 103
Secular view, of education, 52
Self-diagnosis, pupil, 155
Seminars, Use of, 238
Semula, Vernon, 107
Sensory appeal, and spelling, 121
Sentence formation, 137
Settlement houses, 64
Smith, Adam, 17, 182
Smith-Hughes Act, 212
Smith, Mortimer, 103
Snow, C. P., 276
Social change, 77
Socialism, 18, 22
Social Security, 17
Sounds, in spelling, 115
Sound patterns, of language, 124
Spache, George, 109
Specialization, economic value of, 184-187
Spelling, 113
Spiritual dimension of education, 49, 50
Strabo, 199
Stratemeyer, Florence B., 247
Strickland, Ruth G., 122
Style, in composition, 139
Sueltz, Ben A., 153
Suetonius, 200
Suffixes, and Spelling, 117
Summerhill, 59
Summerlane School, 65
Supply and Demand, 187
Syntactic training, 142
Syntax, 125

Taba, Hilda, 213
Tacitus, 200
Tate, James, 83

Teacher Education, 232
Teacher role, 68
Teacher training, in Britain, 277
Teachers, of Home Economics, 218
Technical Schools, English, 268
Technological development, 29, 30
Test administration, 160
Tests, 156
Toynbee, Arnold, 16
Trinidad, 261
Turner, Frederick Jackson, 172
Tutorial programs, 97
Tyler, Ralph W., 28

Unemployment, 178
UNESCO, 256
Urbanization, 30, 31
U. S. Information Agency, 13

Vai Zey, John, 282
Values, individual, 28
Values, in education, 5
Values, listed, 32-34
Values, material, 36
Values, new, 34-35
Values, spiritual, 55
Van Horn, Rua, 214
Von Hilsheimer, George, 59

Walton, John, 233
Warren, Earl, 79
Washington's Farewell Address, 166, 167
Webster, Daniel, 77
Weigley, Russell F., 165
West Germany, 22
Westport program in descriptive grammar, 146
White, William A. P., 168
Whole-Word Method, 102, 103
Wilson, Percy, 280
Wine, in Rome, 200, 201
Women, in the work force, 215
Wood, Harold K., 82
Woodward, C. Van, 167
Workers, displaced, 193
World English Alphabet, 110
Writing, 72

Young, Arthur R., 255
Young, Christopher, 282